Modern Critical Views

Chinua Achebe
Henry Adams
Aeschylus
S. Y. Agnon
Edward Albee
Raphael Alberti
Louisa May Alcott
A. R. Ammons
Sherwood Anderson
Aristophanes
Matthew Arnold
Antonin Artaud
John Ashbery
Margaret Atwood
W. H. Auden
Jane Austen
Isaac Babel
Sir Francis Bacon
James Baldwin
Honoré de Balzac
John Barth
Donald Barthelme
Charles Baudelaire
Simone de Beauvoir
Samuel Beckett
Saul Bellow
Thomas Berger
John Berryman
The Bible
Elizabeth Bishop
William Blake
Giovanni Boccaccio
Heinrich Böll
Jorge Luis Borges
Elizabeth Bowen
Bertolt Brecht
The Brontës
Charles Brockden Brown
Sterling Brown
Robert Browning
Martin Buber
John Bunyan
Anthony Burgess
Kenneth Burke
Robert Burns
William Burroughs
George Gordon, Lord
  Byron
Pedro Calderón de la Barca
Italo Calvino
Albert Camus
Canadian Poetry: Modern
  and Contemporary
Canadian Poetry through
  E. J. Pratt
Thomas Carlyle
Alejo Carpentier
Lewis Carroll
Willa Cather
Louis-Ferdinand Céline
Miguel de Cervantes

Geoffrey Chaucer
John Cheever
Anton Chekhov
Kate Chopin
Chrétien de Troyes
Agatha Christie
Samuel Taylor Coleridge
Colette
William Congreve & the
  Restoration Dramatists
Joseph Conrad
Contemporary Poets
James Fenimore Cooper
Pierre Corneille
Julio Cortázar
Hart Crane
Stephen Crane
e. e. cummings
Dante
Robertson Davies
Daniel Defoe
Philip K. Dick
Charles Dickens
James Dickey
Emily Dickinson
Denis Diderot
Isak Dinesen
E. L. Doctorow
John Donne & the
  Seventeenth-Century
  Metaphysical Poets
John Dos Passos
Fyodor Dostoevsky
Frederick Douglass
Theodore Dreiser
John Dryden
W. E. B. Du Bois
Lawrence Durrell
George Eliot
T. S. Eliot
Elizabethan Dramatists
Ralph Ellison
Ralph Waldo Emerson
Euripides
William Faulkner
Henry Fielding
F. Scott Fitzgerald
Gustave Flaubert
E. M. Forster
John Fowles
Sigmund Freud
Robert Frost
Northrop Frye
Carlos Fuentes
William Gaddis
Federico García Lorca
Gabriel García Márquez
André Gide
W. S. Gilbert
Allen Ginsberg
J. W. von Goethe

Nikolai Gogol
William Golding
Oliver Goldsmith
Mary Gordon
Günther Grass
Robert Graves
Graham Greene
Thomas Hardy
Nathaniel Hawthorne
William Hazlitt
H. D.
Seamus Heaney
Lillian Hellman
Ernest Hemingway
Hermann Hesse
Geoffrey Hill
Friedrich Hölderlin
Homer
A. D. Hope
Gerard Manley Hopkins
Horace
A. E. Housman
William Dean Howells
Langston Hughes
Ted Hughes
Victor Hugo
Zora Neale Hurston
Aldous Huxley
Henrik Ibsen
Eugène Ionesco
Washington Irving
Henry James
Dr. Samuel Johnson and
  James Boswell
Ben Jonson
James Joyce
Carl Gustav Jung
Franz Kafka
Yasonari Kawabata
John Keats
Søren Kierkegaard
Rudyard Kipling
Melanie Klein
Heinrich von Kleist
Philip Larkin
D. H. Lawrence
John le Carré
Ursula K. Le Guin
Giacomo Leopardi
Doris Lessing
Sinclair Lewis
Jack London
Robert Lowell
Malcolm Lowry
Carson McCullers
Norman Mailer
Bernard Malamud
Stéphane Mallarmé
Sir Thomas Malory
André Malraux
Thomas Mann

Modern Critical Views

Katherine Mansfield
Christopher Marlowe
Andrew Marvell
Herman Melville
George Meredith
James Merrill
John Stuart Mill
Arthur Miller
Henry Miller
John Milton
Yukio Mishima
Molière
Michel de Montaigne
Eugenio Montale
Marianne Moore
Alberto Moravia
Toni Morrison
Alice Munro
Iris Murdoch
Robert Musil
Vladimir Nabokov
V. S. Naipaul
R. K. Narayan
Pablo Neruda
John Henry Newman
Friedrich Nietzsche
Frank Norris
Joyce Carol Oates
Sean O'Casey
Flannery O'Connor
Christopher Okigbo
Charles Olson
Eugene O'Neill
José Ortega y Gasset
Joe Orton
George Orwell
Ovid
Wilfred Owen
Amos Oz
Cynthia Ozick
Grace Paley
Blaise Pascal
Walter Pater
Octavio Paz
Walker Percy
Petrarch
Pindar
Harold Pinter
Luigi Pirandello
Sylvia Plath
Plato

Plautus
Edgar Allan Poe
Poets of Sensibility & the
  Sublime
Poets of the Nineties
Alexander Pope
Katherine Anne Porter
Ezra Pound
Anthony Powell
Pre-Raphaelite Poets
Marcel Proust
Manuel Puig
Alexander Pushkin
Thomas Pynchon
Francisco de Quevedo
François Rabelais
Jean Racine
Ishmael Reed
Adrienne Rich
Samuel Richardson
Mordecai Richler
Rainer Maria Rilke
Arthur Rimbaud
Edwin Arlington Robinson
Theodore Roethke
Philip Roth
Jean-Jacques Rousseau
John Ruskin
J. D. Salinger
Jean-Paul Sartre
Gershom Scholem
Sir Walter Scott
William Shakespeare
  Histories & Poems
  Comedies & Romances
  Tragedies
George Bernard Shaw
Mary Wollstonecraft
  Shelley
Percy Bysshe Shelley
Sam Shepard
Richard Brinsley Sheridan
Sir Philip Sidney
Isaac Bashevis Singer
Tobias Smollett
Alexander Solzhenitsyn
Sophocles
Wole Soyinka
Edmund Spenser
Gertrude Stein
John Steinbeck

Stendhal
Laurence Sterne
Wallace Stevens
Robert Louis Stevenson
Tom Stoppard
August Strindberg
Jonathan Swift
John Millington Synge
Alfred, Lord Tennyson
William Makepeace Thackeray
Dylan Thomas
Henry David Thoreau
James Thurber and S. J.
  Perelman
J. R. R. Tolkien
Leo Tolstoy
Jean Toomer
Lionel Trilling
Anthony Trollope
Ivan Turgenev
Mark Twain
Miguel de Unamuno
John Updike
Paul Valéry
Cesar Vallejo
Lope de Vega
Gore Vidal
Virgil
Voltaire
Kurt Vonnegut
Derek Walcott
Alice Walker
Robert Penn Warren
Evelyn Waugh
H. G. Wells
Eudora Welty
Nathanael West
Edith Wharton
Patrick White
Walt Whitman
Oscar Wilde
Tennessee Williams
William Carlos Williams
Thomas Wolfe
Virginia Woolf
William Wordsworth
Jay Wright
Richard Wright
William Butler Yeats
A. B. Yehoshua
Emile Zola

Modern Critical Views

MARY SHELLEY

Modern Critical Views

MARY SHELLEY

Edited with an introduction by
Harold Bloom
Sterling Professor of the Humanities
Yale University

CHELSEA HOUSE PUBLISHERS
New York

THE COVER:
Mary Wollstonecraft Shelley emerges in the matrix of a Promethean scene of creation, akin to that in which Dr. Victor Frankenstein brings into being his tragic daemon.—H.B.

PROJECT EDITORS: Emily Bestler, James Uebbing
EDITORIAL COORDINATOR: Karyn Gullen Browne
EDITORIAL STAFF: Linda Grossman, Peter Childers, Laura Ludwig, Julia Myer
DESIGN: Susan Lusk

Cover illustration by Michael Garland

Printed and bound in the United States of America

10   9   8   7

Library of Congress Cataloging in Publication Data

Mary Shelley.
    (Modern critical views)
    Bibliography: p. 197
    Includes index.
    1. Shelley, Mary Wollstonecraft, 1797–1851—Criticism
and interpretation—Addresses, essays, lectures.
I. Bloom, Harold.   II. Series.
PR5398.M25   1985   823'.7   85-6608
ISBN 0–87754–619–3

Contents

Editor's Note

This volume gathers together chronologically a representative selection of the best critical essays devoted to the fiction of Mary Shelley during the last third of this century, from 1951 until the present. Though most of the emphasis is upon *Frankenstein*, there are also discussions of the autobiographical *Mathilda* and of the apocalyptic *The Last Man*. The critics reprinted here tend to concur in seeing *Frankenstein* both as a Promethean fiction, linked to the High Romanticism of Byron and of Shelley, and as a precursor of much modern and contemporary science fiction and films.

The editor's "Introduction," first published in 1965 as an "Afterword" to a popular edition of the novel, attempts to give a general account of Mary Shelley's relation to the Romantic mythology of the self, with its central image of the double. This image is developed in Muriel Spark's observations of 1951, influential upon the editor's "Introduction," and curiously central in many of her own novels.

Lowry Nelson's witty "Night Thoughts on the Gothic Novel" domesticates *Frankenstein* in that genre. The essay by James Rieger traces a Gnostic patterning that the critic sees *Frankenstein* as sharing with Shelley's poetry. William Walling's parallel emphasis upon Victor Frankenstein's duality, and Robert Kiely's contextualization of the book in the tradition of the Romantic novel, are more literary placements of Mary Shelley's thematic concerns.

A very different tradition, that of realistic fiction, is invoked by George Levine, who sees the book as mediating between romance and reality. With the essay by Peter Brooks, a Freudian perspective is introduced which is supplemented by the feminist reading ventured by Sandra Gilbert and Susan Gubar in their pioneering study, *The Madwoman in the Attic*.

The three most recent essays are both advanced criticisms of Mary Shelley's other fiction and applications of contemporary critical modes to *Frankenstein*. Paul Sherwin's investigation of catastrophe creation, Jay Macpherson's analysis of narcissism and romance conventions in *Mathilda* and *Frankenstein*, and Giovanna Franci's reading of *The Last Man* together provide a final conspectus upon the troubled legacy bequeathed to Mary Shelley, and so memorably transmitted to us by her.

Introduction

The motion-picture viewer who carries his obscure but still authentic taste for the sublime to the neighborhood theater, there to see the latest in an unending series of *Frankensteins*, becomes a sharer in a romantic terror now nearly one hundred and fifty years old. Mary Shelley, barely nineteen years of age when she wrote the original *Frankenstein*, was the daughter of two great intellectual rebels, William Godwin and Mary Wollstonecraft, and the second wife of Percy Bysshe Shelley, another great rebel and an unmatched lyrical poet. Had she written nothing, Mary Shelley would be remembered today. She is remembered in her own right as the author of a novel valuable in itself but also prophetic of an intellectual world to come, a novel depicting a Prometheanism that is with us still.

"Frankenstein," to most of us, is the name of a monster rather than of a monster's creator, for the common reader and the common viewer have worked together, in their apparent confusion, to create a myth soundly based on a central duality in Mrs. Shelley's novel. A critical discussion of *Frankenstein* needs to begin from an insight first recorded by Richard Church and Muriel Spark: the monster and his creator are the antithetical halves of a single being. Miss Spark states the antithesis too cleanly; for her Victor Frankenstein represents the feelings, and his nameless creature the intellect. In her view the monster has no emotion, and "what passes for emotion . . . are really intellectual passions arrived at through rational channels." Miss Spark carries this argument far enough to insist that the monster is asexual and that he demands a bride from Frankenstein only for companionship, a conclusion evidently at variance with the novel's text.

The antithesis between the scientist and his creature in *Frankenstein* is a very complex one and can be described more fully in the larger context of Romantic literature and its characteristic mythology. The shadow or double of the self is a constant conceptual image in Blake and Shelley and a frequent image, more random and descriptive, in the other major Romantics, especially in Byron. In *Frankenstein* it is the dominant and recurrent image and accounts for much of the latent power the novel possesses.

Mary Shelley's husband was a divided being, as man and as poet, just as his friend Byron was, though in Shelley the split was more radical. *Frankenstein: or, The Modern Prometheus* is the full title of Mrs. Shelley's novel, and while Victor Frankenstein is *not* Shelley (Clerval is rather more like the poet), the Modern Prometheus is a very apt term for Shelley or for Byron. Prometheus is the mythic figure who best suits the uses of Romantic poetry, for no other traditional being has in him the full range of Romantic moral sensibility and the full Romantic capacity for creation and destruction.

No Romantic writer employed the Prometheus archetype without a full awareness of its equivocal potentialities. The Prometheus of the ancients had been for the most part a spiritually reprehensible figure, though frequently a sympathetic one, in terms both of his dramatic situation and in his close alliance with mankind against the gods. But this alliance had been ruinous for man in most versions of the myth, and the Titan's benevolence toward humanity was hardly sufficient recompense for the alienation of man from heaven that he had brought about. Both sides of Titanism are evident in earlier Christian references to the story. The same Prometheus who is taken as an analogue of the crucified Christ is regarded also as a type of Lucifer, a son of light justly cast out by an offended heaven.

In the Romantic readings of Milton's *Paradise Lost* (and *Frankenstein* is implicitly one such reading) this double identity of Prometheus is a vital element. Blake, whose mythic revolutionary named Orc is another version of Prometheus, saw Milton's Satan as a Prometheus gone wrong, as desire restrained until it became only the shadow of desire, a diminished double of

creative energy. Shelley went further in judging Milton's Satan as a n
imperfect Prometheus, inadequate because his mixture of heroic and base
qualities engendered in the reader's mind a "pernicious casuistry" inimical
to the spirit of art.

Blake, more systematic a poet than Shelley, worked out an antithesis
between symbolic figures he named Spectre and Emanation, the shadow of
desire and the total form of desire, respectively. A reader of *Frankenstein*,
recalling the novel's extraordinary conclusion, with its scenes of obsessional
pursuit through the Arctic wastes, can recognize the same imagery applied
to a similar symbolic situation in Blake's lyric on the strife of Spectre and
Emanation:

> My Spectre around me night and day
> Like a Wild beast guards my way.
> My Emanation far wit..in
> Weeps incessantly for my Sin.

> A Fathomless and boundless deep,
> There we wander, there we weep;
> On the hungry craving wind
> My Spectre follows thee behind.

> He scents thy footsteps in the snow,
> Wheresoever thou dost go
> Thro' the wintry hail and rain. . . .

Frankenstein's monster, tempting his revengeful creator on through a
world of ice, is another Emanation pursued by a Spectre, with the enormous
difference that he is an Emanation flawed, a nightmare of actuality, rather
than dream of desire. Though abhorred rather than loved, the monster is
the total form of Frankenstein's creative power and is *more imaginative* than
his creator. The monster is at once more intellectual and more emotional
than his maker; indeed he excels Frankenstein as much (and in the same
ways) as Milton's Adam excels Milton's God in *Paradise Lost*. The greatest
paradox and most astonishing achievement of Mary Shelley's novel is that
the monster is *more human* than his creator. This nameless being, as much a
Modern Adam as his creator is a Modern Prometheus, is more lovable than
his creator and more hateful, more to be pitied and more to be feared, and
above all more able to give the attentive reader that shock of added
consciousness in which aesthetic recognition compels a heightened realization of the self. For like Blake's Spectre and Emanation or Shelley's Alastor
and Epipsyche, Frankenstein and his monster are the solipsistic and
generous halves of the one self. Frankenstein is the mind and emotions

turned in upon themselves, and his creature is the mind and emotions turned imaginatively outward, seeking a greater humanization through a confrontation of other selves.

I am suggesting that what makes *Frankenstein* an important book, though it is only a strong, flawed novel with frequent clumsiness in its narrative and characterization, is that it contains one of the most vivid versions we have of the Romantic mythology of the self, one that resembles Blake's *Book of Urizen*, Shelley's *Prometheus Unbound*, and Byron's *Manfred*, among other works. Because it lacks the sophistication and imaginative complexity of such works, *Frankenstein* affords a unique introduction to the archetypal world of the Romantics.

William Godwin, though a tendentious novelist, was a powerful one, and the prehistory of his daughter's novel begins with his best work of fiction, *Caleb Williams* (1794). Godwin summarized the climactic (and harrowing) final third of his novel as a pattern of flight and pursuit, "the fugitive in perpetual apprehension of being overwhelmed with the worst calamities, and the pursuer, by his ingenuity and resources, keeping his victim in a state of the most fearful alarm." Mary Shelley brilliantly reverses this pattern in the final sequence of her novel, and she takes from *Caleb Williams* also her destructive theme of the monster's war against "the whole machinery of human society," to quote the words of Caleb Williams while in prison. Muriel Spark argues that *Frankenstein* can be read as a reaction "against the rational-humanism of Godwin and Shelley," and she points to the equivocal preface that Shelley wrote to his wife's novel, in order to support this view. Certainly Shelley was worried lest the novel be taken as a warning against the inevitable moral consequences of an unchecked experimental Prometheanism and scientific materialism. The preface insists that:

> The opinions which naturally spring from the character and situation of the hero are by no means to be conceived as existing always in my own conviction; nor is any inference justly to be drawn from the following pages as prejudicing any philosophical doctrine of whatever kind.

Shelley had, throughout his own work, a constant reaction against Godwin's rational humanism, but his reaction was systematically and consciously one of heart against head. In the same summer in the Swiss Alps that saw the conception of *Frankenstein*, Shelley composed two poems that lift the thematic conflict of the novel to the level of the true sublime. In the *Hymn to Intellectual Beauty* the poet's heart interprets an inconstant grace and loveliness, always just beyond the range of the human senses, as being the only beneficent force in life, and he prays to this force to be more constant in its attendance upon him and all mankind. In a greater sister-hymn, *Mont Blanc*, an awesome meditation upon a frightening natural scene, the poet's head issues an allied but essentially contrary report. The force, or power, is there, behind or within the mountain, but its external workings upon us are either indifferent or malevolent, and this power is not to be prayed to. It can teach us, but what it teaches us is our own dangerous freedom from nature, the necessity for our will to become a significant part of materialistic necessity. Though *Mont Blanc* works its way to an almost heroic conclusion, it is also a poem of horror and reminds us that Frankenstein first confronts his conscious monster in the brooding presence of Mont Blanc, and to the restless music of one of Shelley's lyrics of Mutability.

In *Prometheus Unbound* the split between head and heart is not healed, but the heart is allowed dominance. The hero, Prometheus, like Franken-stein, has made a monster, but this monster is Jupiter, the God of all institutional and historical religions, including organized Christianity. Salvation from this conceptual error comes through love alone; but love in this poem, as elsewhere in Shelley, is always closely shadowed by ruin. Indeed, what choice spirits in Shelley perpetually encounter is ruin mas-querading as love, pain presenting itself as pleasure. The tentative way out of this situation in Shelley's poetry is through the quest for a feeling mind and an understanding heart, which is symbolized by the sexual reunion of Prometheus and his Emanation, Asia. Frederick A. Pottle sums up *Pro-metheus Unbound* by observing its meaning to be that "the head must sincerely forgive, must willingly eschew hatred on purely experimental grounds," while "the affections must exorcize the demons of infancy, whether personal or of the race." In the light cast by these profound and precise summations, the reader can better understand both Shelley's lyrical drama and his wife's narrative of the Modern Prometheus.

There are two paradoxes at the center of Mrs. Shelley's novel, and each illuminates a dilemma of the Promethean imagination. The first is that Frankenstein *was* successful, in that he did create Natural Man, not as he was, but as the meliorists saw such a man; indeed, Frankenstein did better than this, since his creature was, as we have seen, more imaginative than himself. Frankenstein's tragedy stems not from his Promethean excess but from his own moral error, his failure to love; he *abhorred his creature*, became terrified, and fled his responsibilities.

The second paradox is the more ironic. This either would not have happened or would not have mattered anyway, if Frankenstein had been an aesthetically successful maker; a beautiful "monster," or even a passable one, would not have been a monster. As the creature bitterly observes in Chapter 17:

> Shall I respect man when he contemns me? Let him live with me in the interchange of kindness, and instead of injury I would bestow every benefit upon him with tears of gratitude at his acceptance. But that cannot be; the

human senses are insurmountable barriers to our union.

As the hideousness of his creature was no part of Victor Frankenstein's intention, it is worth noticing how this disastrous matter came to be.

It would not be unjust to characterize Victor Frankenstein, in his act
of creation, as being momentarily a moral idiot, like so many who have done
his work after him. There is an indeliberate humor in the contrast between
the enormity of the scientist's discovery and the mundane emotions of the
discoverer. Finding that "the minuteness of the parts" slows him down, he
resolves to make his creature "about eight feet in height and proportionably
large." As he works on, he allows himself to dream that "a new species would
bless me as its creator and source; many happy and excellent natures would
owe their being to me." Yet he knows his is a "workshop of filthy creation,"
and he fails the fundamental test of his own creativity. When the "dull
yellow eye" of his creature opens, this creator falls from the autonomy of a
supreme artificer to the terror of a child of earth: "breathless horror and
disgust filled my heart." He flees his responsibility and sets in motion the
events that will lead to his own Arctic immolation, a fit end for a being who
has never achieved a full sense of another's existence.

Haunting Mary Shelley's novel is the demonic figure of the Ancient
Mariner, Coleridge's major venture into Romantic mythology of the purgatorial self trapped in the isolation of a heightened self-consciousness.
Walton, in Letter 2 introducing the novel, compares himself "to that
production of the most imaginative of modern poets." As a seeker-out of an
unknown passage, Walton is himself a Promethean quester, like Frankenstein, toward whom he is so compellingly drawn. Coleridge's Mariner is of
the line of Cain, and the irony of Frankenstein's fate is that he too is a Cain,
involuntarily murdering all his loved ones through the agency of his
creature. The Ancient Mariner is punished by living under the curse of his
consciousness of guilt, while the excruciating torment of Frankenstein is
never to be able to forget his guilt in creating a lonely consciousness driven
to crime by the rage of unwilling solitude.

It is part of Mary Shelley's insight into her mythological theme that
all the monster's victims are innocents. The monster not only refuses
actively to slay his guilty creator, he *mourns* for him, though with the
equivocal tribute of terming the scientist a "generous and self-devoted
being." Frankenstein, the Modern Prometheus who has violated nature,
receives his epitaph from the ruined second nature he has made, the God-
abandoned, who consciously echoes the ruined Satan of *Paradise Lost* and
proclaims, "Evil thenceforth became my good." It is imaginatively fitting
that the greater and more interesting consciousness of the creature should
survive his creator, for he alone in Mrs. Shelley's novel possesses character.

Frankenstein, like Coleridge's Mariner, has no character in his own right; both figures win a claim to our attention only by their primordial crimes against original nature.

The monster is of course Mary Shelley's finest invention, and his narrative (Chapters 11 through 16) forms the highest achievement of the novel, more absorbing even than the magnificent and almost surrealistic pursuit of the climax. In an age so given to remarkable depictions of the dignity of natural man, an age including the shepherds and beggars of Wordsworth and what W. J. Bate has termed Keats' "polar ideal of disinterestedness"—even in such a literary time Frankenstein's hapless creature stands out as a sublime embodiment of heroic pathos. Though Frankenstein lacks the moral imagination to understand him, the daemon's appeal is to what is most compassionate in us:

> Oh, Frankenstein, be not equitable to every other, and trample upon me alone, to whom thy justice, and even thy clemency and affection, is most due. Remember that I am thy creature; *I ought to be thy Adam, but I am rather the fallen angel, whom thou drivest from joy for no misdeed.* Everywhere I see bliss, from which I alone am irrevocably excluded. I was benevolent and good; misery made me a fiend. Make me happy, and I shall again be virtuous.

The passage I have italicized is the imaginative kernel of the novel and is meant to remind the reader of the novel's epigraph:

> Did I request thee, Maker, from my clay
> To mold me man? Did I solicit thee
> From darkness to promote me?

That desperate plangency of the fallen Adam becomes the characteristic accent of the daemon's lamentations, with the influence of Milton cunningly built into the novel's narrative by the happy device of Frankenstein's creature receiving his education through reading *Paradise Lost* "as a true history." Already doomed because his standards are human, which makes him an outcast even to himself, his Miltonic education completes his fatal growth in self-consciousness. His story, as told to his maker, follows a familiar Romantic pattern "of the progress of my intellect," as he puts it. His first pleasure after the dawn of consciousness comes through his wonder at seeing the moon rise. Caliban-like, he responds wonderfully to music, both natural and human, and his sensitivity to the natural world has the responsiveness of an incipient poet. His awakening to a first love for other beings, the inmates of the cottage he haunts, awakens him also to the great desolation of love rejected when he attempts to reveal himself. His own duality of situation and character, caught between the states of Adam and Satan, Natural Man and his thwarted desire, is related by him directly to his reading of Milton's epic:

> It moved every feeling of wonder and awe that the picture of an omnipo-
> tent God warring with his creatures was capable of exciting. I often
> referred the several situations, as their similarity struck me, to my own.
> Like Adam, I was apparently united by no link to any other being in
> existence, but his state was far different from mine in every other respect.
> He had come forth from the hands of God a perfect creature, happy and
> prosperous, guarded by the especial care of his Creator; he was allowed to
> converse with and acquire knowledge from beings of a superior nature; but
> I was wretched, helpless, and alone. Many times I considered Satan as the
> fitter emblem of my condition, for often, like him, when I viewed the bliss
> of my protectors, the bitter gall of envy rose within me.

From a despair this profound, no release is possible. Driven forth into
an existence upon which "the cold stars shone in mockery," the daemon
declares "everlasting war against the species" and enters upon a fallen
existence more terrible than the expelled Adam's. Echoing Milton, he asks
the ironic question "And now, with the world before me, whither should I
bend my steps?" to which the only possible answer is, toward his wretched
Promethean creator.

If we stand back from Mary Shelley's novel in order better to view its
archetypal shape, we see it as the quest of a solitary and ravaged consciousness first for consolation, then for revenge, and finally for a self-destruction
that will be apocalyptic, that will bring down the creator with his creature.
Though Mary Shelley may not have intended it, her novel's prime theme is a
necessary counterpoise to Prometheanism, for Prometheanism exalts the
increase in consciousness despite all cost. Frankenstein breaks through the
barrier that separates man from God and gives apparent life, but in doing so
he gives only death-in-life. The profound dejection endemic in Mary
Shelley's novel is fundamental to the Romantic mythology of the self, for all
Romantic horrors are diseases of excessive consciousness, of the self unable
to bear the self. Kierkegaard remarks that Satan's despair is absolute
because Satan, as pure spirit, is pure consciousness, and for Satan (and all
men in his predicament) every increase in consciousness is an increase in
despair. Frankenstein's desperate creature attains the state of pure spirit
through his extraordinary situation and is racked by a consciousness in
which every thought is a fresh disease.

A Romantic poet fought against self-consciousness through the
strength of what he called imagination, a more than rational energy by
which thought could seek to heal itself. But Frankenstein's daemon, though
he is in the archetypal situation of the Romantic Wanderer or Solitary, who
sometimes was a poet, can win no release from his own story by telling it.
His desperate desire for a mate is clearly an attempt to find a Shelleyan

Epipsyche or Blakean Emanation for himself, a self within the self. But as he is the nightmare actualization of Frankenstein's desire, he is himself an emanation of Promethean yearnings, and his only double is his creator and denier.

When Coleridge's Ancient Mariner progressed from the purgatory of consciousness to his very minimal control of imagination, he failed to save himself, since he remained in a cycle of remorse, but he at least became a salutary warning to others and made of the Wedding Guest a wiser and a better man. Frankenstein's creature can help neither himself nor others, for he has no natural ground to which he can return. Romantic poets liked to return to the imagery of the ocean of life and immortality, for in the eddying to and fro of the healing waters they could picture a hoped-for process of restoration, of a survival of consciousness despite all its agonies. Mary Shelley, with marvelous appropriateness, brings her Romantic novel to a demonic conclusion in a world of ice. The frozen sea is the inevitable emblem for both the wretched daemon and his obsessed creator, but the daemon is allowed a final image of reversed Prometheanism. There is a heroism fully earned in the being who cries farewell in a claim of sad triumph: "I shall ascend my funeral pile triumphantly and exult in the agony of the torturing flames." Mary Shelley could not have known how dark a prophecy this consummation of consciousness would prove to be for the two great Promethean poets who were at her side during the summer of 1816, when her novel was conceived. Byron, writing his own epitaph at Missolonghi in 1824, and perhaps thinking back to having stood at Shelley's funeral pile two years before, found an image similar to the daemon's to sum up an exhausted existence:

> The fire that on my bosom preys
> Is lone as some volcanic isle;
> No torch is kindled at its blaze—
> A funeral pile.

The fire of increased consciousness stolen from heaven ends as an isolated volcano cut off from other selves by an estranging sea. "The light of that conflagration will fade away; my ashes will be swept into the sea by the winds" is the exultant cry of Frankenstein's creature. A blaze at which no torch is kindled is Byron's self-image, but he ends his death poem on another note, the hope for a soldier's grave, which he found. There is no Promethean release, but release is perhaps not the burden of the literature of Romantic aspiration. There is something both Godwinian and Shelleyan about the final utterance of Victor Frankenstein, which is properly made to Walton, the failed Promethean whose ship has just turned back. Though chastened, the Modern Prometheus ends with a last word true, not to his accomplishment, but to his desire:

> Farewell, Walton! Seek happiness in tranquillity and avoid ambition, even if it be only the apparently innocent one of distinguishing yourself in science and discoveries. Yet why do I say this? I have myself been blasted in these hopes, yet another may succeed.

Shelley's Prometheus, crucified on his icy precipice, found his ultimate torment in a Fury's taunt: "And all best things are thus confused to ill." It seems a fitting summation for all the work done by Modern Prometheanism and might have served as an alternate epigraph for Mary Shelley's disturbing novel.

MURIEL SPARK

"Frankenstein"

Othello, Don Juan, Micawber, Becky Sharpe—such characters have become popular terms; but out of that vampire-laden fog of gruesomeness known as the English Gothic Romance, only the forbidding acrid name *Frankenstein*, remains in general usage.

To call *Frankenstein* a Gothic novel, is, of course, a loose definition, and one which would defeat the claim I hope to establish, that this novel was the first of a new and hybrid fictional species. But if we remember for the moment, that the wayward plethora of Mrs. Radcliffe's thrillers had already captured the reading public's imagination before Mary Shelley was born, and that Shelley's delight in the weird, the horrific and the awful was enough to intensify Mary's own interest in such themes, we must recognise the primary Gothic influence on *Frankenstein*. But we can see this novel both as the apex and the last of Gothic fiction—for though many other works of the Radcliffe school were to follow, their death-stroke was delivered, their mysteries solved, by *Frankenstein's* rational inquisition.

In the year 1818, the work created a wonderful and *nouveau frisson*. The limits of the horror-novel had been reached, and old props of haunted castles, hanged babes and moonlit dagger scenes, were beginning to raise a shrug rather than a shudder. Much earlier, the young though perceptive Coleridge had foreseen the crumbling of Gothic literature when he said, in reviewing *The Mysteries of Udolpho*, "... in the search of what is new, an author is apt to forget what is natural; and in rejecting the more obvious conclusions, to take those which are less satisfactory."

This was, of course, an eighteenth century opinion, and what was

---

"natural" was expected to be the rational protraction of an idea.

Frankenstein, then, was a best-seller; it occurred at the propitious moment when it was necessary for works of fiction to produce, not only repellant if vicarious sensations in the pit of the stomach, but speculation in the mind: The *Edinburgh Magazine's* comment on the book—"There never was a wilder story imagined; yet, like most fictions of this age, it has an air of reality attached to it by being connected with the favourite projects and passions of the times"—was one of many that arrived in a blundering sort of way at this conclusion.

"Methinks" wrote Byron to John Murray, "it is a wonderful work for a girl of nineteen—*not* nineteen, indeed, at that time." But perhaps the wonder of it exists, not despite Mary's youth but because of it. *Frankenstein* is Mary Shelley's best novel, because at that early age she was not yet well acquainted with her own mind. As her self-insight grew—and she was exceptionally introspective—so did her work suffer from causes the very opposite of her intention; and what very often mars her later writing is its extreme explicitness. Mary came to understand every sentence she wrote, and to write nothing which she did not understand. In *Frankenstein*, however, it is the implicit utterance which gives the theme its power.

It was not until 1831, when Mary revised *Frankenstein*, that she wrote her Introduction to it. (The book had previously appeared with a Preface by Shelley purporting to come from the author's hand.) By this time Mary had reached a higher degree of consciousness, but even she, now, seemed aghast at the audacity of the work—her "hideous progeny" as she called it; the question she asked herself, "How I, then a young girl, came to think of, and to dilate upon, so very hideous an idea?" was one which many people had asked, and which she attempted to answer by giving an account of the circumstances of *Frankenstein's* inception, naming the place, the people and the books which had influenced her. She took this task very seriously, and succeeded as far as (probably further than) any artist will, who tries to get at the root of his own work. The Introduction is too long to reproduce here, but the most revealing passages may be profitably examined.

In the summer of 1816, we visited Switzerland, and became the neighbours of Lord Byron....But it proved a wet, ungenial summer, and incessant rain often confined us for days to the house. Some volumes of ghost stories, translated from the German into French, fell into our hands. There was the *History of the Inconstant Lover*, who, when he thought to clasp the bride to whom he had pledged his vows, found himself in the arms of the pale ghost of her whom he had deserted. There was the tale of the sinful founder of his race, whose miserable doom it was to bestow the kiss of death on all the younger sons of his fated house just when they reached the age of promise. His gigantic, shadowy form, clothed like the ghost in *Hamlet*, in complete armour, but with the beaver up, was seen at midnight, by the moon's fitful beams, to advance slowly along the gloomy avenue. The shape was lost beneath the shadow of the castle walls; but soon a gate swung back, a step was heard, the door of the chamber opened, and he advanced to the couch of the blooming youths, cradled in healthy sleep. Eternal sorrow sat upon his face as he bent down and kissed the forehead of the boys, who from that hour withered like flowers snapped upon the stalk. I have not seen these stories since then; but their incidents are as fresh in my mind as if I had read them yesterday.

"We will each write a ghost story," said Lord Byron; and his proposition was acceded to. There were four of us. . . .

I busied myself *to think of a story*—a story to rival those which had excited us to this task. One which would speak to the mysterious fears of our nature, and awaken thrilling horror—one to make the reader dread to look round, to curdle the blood, and quicken the beatings of the heart. If I did not accomplish these things, my ghost story would be unworthy of its name. I thought and pondered—vainly. I felt that blank incapability of invention which is the greatest misery of authorship, when dull Nothing replies to our anxious invocations. *Have you thought of a story?* I was asked each morning, and each morning I was forced to reply with a mortifying negative.

This, then, was the atmospheric environment of *Frankenstein's* origin. The volumes of ghost stories, the Swiss mountains rearing through the rain, and the supernatural themes of their nightly conversations—all were enough to infuse the Gothic element into her proposed story. But not enough to give it substance. "Every thing must have a beginning" are her next words as she goes on to speak of these circumstances that revealed, among her nebulous imaginings, a single embodied idea.

Invention consists in the capacity of seizing on the capabilities of a subject, and in the power of moulding and fashioning ideas suggested to it.

Many and long were the conversations between Lord Byron and Shelley, to which I was a devout but nearly silent listener. During one of these, various philosophical doctrines were discussed, and among others the nature of the principle of life, and whether there was any probability of its ever being discovered and communicated. They talked of the experiments of Dr. Darwin (I speak not of what the Doctor really did, or said that he did, but, as more to my purpose, of what was then spoken of as having been done by him), who preserved a piece of vermicelli in a glass case, till by some extraordinary means it began to move with voluntary motion. Not thus, after all, would life be given. Perhaps a corpse would be re-animated; galvanism had given token of such things; perhaps the component parts of a creature might be manufactured, brought together, and endued with vital warmth.

. . . When I placed my head on my pillow, I did not sleep, nor could I be said to think. My imagination, unbidden, possessed and guided me, gifting the successive images that arose in my mind with a vividness far beyond the usual bounds of reverie. I saw—with shut eyes, but acute mental vision—I saw the the pale student of unhallowed arts kneeling beside the thing he had put together. I saw the hideous phantasm of a man stretched out, and then, on the working of some powerful engine, show signs of life, and stir with an uneasy, half vital motion. Frightful must it be; for supremely frightful would be the effect of any human endeavour to mock the stupendous mechanism of the Creator of the world. His success would terrify the artist; he would rush away from his odious handywork, horror-stricken. He would hope that, left to itself, the slight spark of life which he had communicated would fade; that this thing, which had received such imperfect animation, would subside into dead matter; and he might sleep in the belief that the silence of the grave would quench for ever the transient existence of the hideous corpse which he had looked upon as the cradle of life. He sleeps; but he is awakened; he opens his eyes; behold the horrid thing stands at his bedside, opening his curtains, and looking on him with yellow, watery, but speculative eyes.

I opened mine in terror. The idea so possessed my mind, that a thrill of fear ran through me, and I wished to exchange the ghastly image of my fancy for the realities around....

Swift as light and as cheering was the idea that broke in upon me. "I have found it! What terrified me will terrify others; and I need only describe the spectre which had haunted my midnight pillow." On the morrow I announced that I had *thought of a story.*

So, among the raw materials of *Frankenstein* were two forces that ultimately combined—firstly and generally that of the supernatural and harrowing; secondly and specifically, the scientific proposition: "Perhaps a corpse would be re-animated; galvanism had given token of such things: perhaps the component parts of a creature might be manufactured, brought together, and enbued with vital warmth."

It is not surprising that Mary should be excited by a scientific and rational theme; throughout *Frankenstein,* her father, Godwin's voice is never far off:

"I heard," says the Monster, "of the division of property, of immense wealth and squalid poverty; of rank, descent, and noble blood.

...I learned that the possessions most esteemed by your fellow-creatures were high and unsullied descent united with riches. A man might be respected with only one of these advantages; but without either, he was considered, except in very rare instances, as a vagabond and a slave doomed to waste his powers for the profits of the chosen few."

This was the lesson Mary knew by rote. But it had not gone for nothing that she had heard, while still a child, a rendering of *The Ancient Mariner* from the poet's own lips; and she was never released from her enthralment by the poem. Her character, Walton, who is introduced merely for the purpose of recounting Frankenstein's story, but whose vocation makes him none the less a sort of shadow-Frankenstein, informs his sister:

> I am going to unexplored regions, to "the land of mist and snow"; but I
> shall kill no albatross, therefore do not be alarmed for my safety, or if I
> should come back to you as worn and woeful as the 'Ancient Mariner?' You
> will smile at my allusion; but I will disclose a secret. I have often attributed
> my attachment to, my passionate enthusiasm for, the dangerous mysteries
> of ocean, to that production of the most imaginative of modern poets.
> There is something at work in my soul which I do not understand. . . .

And Frankenstein himself, in his first flight from his Monster, feels
himself to be

> Like one who, on a lonely road,
>   Doth walk in fear and dread,
> And, having once turned round, walks on,
>   And turns no more his head;
> Because he knows a frightful fiend
>   Doth close behind him tread.

And indeed, the many conversations between Coleridge and
Godwin, which Mary had listened to, were not lost on her. The influential
currents of these two minds—Godwin representing the scientific empiricism
of the previous century, and Coleridge, the nineteenth century's imaginative reaction, met in Mary's first novel. And this imaginative reaction in
Frankenstein is a violent one, which places her work in the category of the
"horror" novel as distinct from that of "terror"—the former comprehending
disgust as well as dismay (Mary repeatedly stresses the loathsomeness and
filth of Frankenstein's task, no less than of the Monster himself) and the
latter, merely panic and alarm.

This fusion of the ways of thought of two epochs occurred, then, in
Frankenstein, and gave rise to the first of that fictional genre which was later
endorsed by H. G. Wells and M. P. Shiel; and of which there are numerous
examples in present-day literature.

And comparatively recent literature can probably best illustrate
where *Frankenstein* and the Gothic novel parted company, for the latter was
destined to lose its status as a literary *genre,* to be revived merely in its
capacity as an influence on the surrealist movement, for which it became a
focus of curiosity; and we may say that where the "Wellsian" scientific
romance differs from surrealist literature, *Frankenstein* differs from the works
of Horace Walpole and Mrs. Radcliffe. We can say that, although these two
main arteries have moved apart, there are definite affinities between the
modern scientific romance and surrealism, which point to a closer affilia-
tion nearer their source. When Mr. Richard Church writes of *Frankenstein*
"It has in it a touch of the genius of Edgar Allan Poe" he pinpoints a phase

in this affinity, despite the renunciation of Poe by the later surrealists. *Frankenstein* is not, indeed, without its moments of surrealistic effect—when, for example, Frankenstein traverses the Alps through darkness and storm, thinking of his murdered child-brother:

> ...I perceived in the gloom a figure which stole from behind a clump of trees near me: I stood fixed, gazing intently. I could not be mistaken. A flash of lightning illuminated the object, and discovered its shape plainly to me; its gigantic stature, and the deformity of its aspect, more hideous than belongs to humanity, instantly informed me that it was the wretch, the filthy demon, to whom I had given life. What did he there? Could he be (I shuddered at the conception) the murderer of my brother? No sooner did that idea cross my imagination than I became convinced of its truth; my teeth chattered, and I was forced to lean against a tree for support. The figure passed me quickly, and I lost it in the gloom. Nothing in human shape could have destroyed that fair child. *He* was the murderer! I could not doubt it. The mere presence of the idea was an irresistible proof of the fact. I thought of pursuing the devil; but it would have been in vain, for another flash discovered him to me hanging among the rocks of the nearly perpendicular ascent of Mont Salêve....

That statement of an intuitive process in the words, "No sooner did that idea cross my imagination, than I became convinced of its truth"; the final image of the fiend "hanging among the rocks of the nearly perpendicular ascent"—indeed, the entire passage, impregnated with surmise, with the larger-than-life quality of a dream—contains the general flavour and specific Gothic elements of surrealism. So far as I know, the early surrealists did not seize on *Frankenstein* for their own purposes, and I wonder they did not.

II

Perhaps because *Frankenstein* was born of ideas, not fully realised by its author but through the dream-like vision she has described, there are several ways in which it can be considered; this variety of interpretative levels being part of its artistic validity.

There are two central figures—or rather two in one, for Frankenstein and his significantly unnamed Monster are bound together by the nature of their relationship. Frankenstein's plight resides in the Monster, and the Monster's in Frankenstein. That this fact has received wide, if unwitting, recognition, is apparent from the common mistake of naming the Monster "Frankenstein" and emanates from the first principle of the story, that Frankenstein is perpetuated in the Monster. The several implicit themes I propose to examine, show these characters both as complementary beings and as antithetical ones.

The most obvious theme is that suggested by the title, *Frankenstein—Or, The Modern Prometheus*. (That casual, alternative *Or* is worth noting, for though at first Frankenstein is himself the Prometheus, the vital fire-endowing protagonist, the Monster, as soon as he is created, takes on the role. His solitary plight—"... but am I not alone, miserably alone?" he cries—and more especially his revolt against his creator, establish his Promethean features. So, the title implies, the Monster is an alternative Frankenstein.)

The humanist symbol of Prometheus was one that occupied Shelley in many forms beside that of his *Prometheus Unbound*, and Shelley's influence on Mary had gained time to give figurative shape to Godwin's view of mankind's situation. It is curious that Shelley should have written in his Preface to *Frankenstein*:

> The opinions which naturally spring from the character and situation of the hero are by no means to be conceived as existing always in my [that is, Mary's] own conviction; nor is any inference justly to be drawn from the following pages as prejudicing any philosophical doctrine of whatever kind.

Curious, because one cannot help inferring a philosophical attitude; but not so curious when we remember Shelley's refusal to admit the didactic element in his own poetry.

Less curious, however, is the epigraph to the book (unfortunately omitted in the *Everyman* edition of *Frankenstein*):

> Did I request thee, Maker, from my clay
> To mould me man? Did I solicit thee
> From darkness to promote me?
> *(Paradise Lost)*

The *motif* of revolt against divine oppression, and indeed, against the concept of a benevolent deity, which is prominent in much of Shelley's thought, underlines the "Modern Prometheus" theme of *Frankenstein*. "You accuse me of murder" the Monster reproaches his maker, "and yet you would, with a satisfied conscience, destroy your own creature"—not the least of *Frankenstein's* echoes from Shelley.

The Prometheus myth is one of action but not of movement; that is, the main activity of the original story is located around the tortured Prometheus himself, chained to one spot. A novel, however, demands a certain range of activity, and in *Frankenstein* the action is released from its original compression by a secondary theme—that of pursuit, influenced most probably by Godwin's *Caleb Williams*. It is this theme that endows the novel, not only with movement, but with a pattern, easily discernible because it is a simple one.

It begins at Chapter V with the creation of the Monster who

becomes, within the first two pages, Frankenstein's pursuer. He is removed for a time from the vicinity of his quarry, but continues to stalk the regions of Frankenstein's imagination, until it is discovered that he has been actually prosecuting his role through the murder of Frankenstein's young brother, William. Frankenstein is then hounded from his homeland to the remote reaches of the Orkney islands where he is to propitiate his tormentor by creating a Monster-bride for him.

If we can visualise this pattern of pursuit as a sort of figure-of-eight *macabaresque*, executed by two partners moving with the virtuosity of skilled ice-skaters—we may see how the pattern takes shape in a movement of advance and retreat. Both partners are moving in opposite directions, yet one follows the other. At the crossing of the figure-eight they all-but collide. Such a crossing occurs when Frankenstein faces his Monster alone in the mountains, and another, when Frankenstein makes his critical decision to destroy his nearly completed female Monster. Once these crises are passed, however, we find Frankenstein and the Monster moving apparently away from each other, but still prosecuting the course of their pattern. It is not until Frankenstein, on his bridal night, finds his wife murdered by the Monster, that the roles are reversed. Frankenstein (to keep to our image) increases his speed of execution, and the Monster slows down; now, at Chapter XXIV, Frankenstein becomes the pursuer, the Monster, the pursued.

Thenceforward, this theme becomes the central focus of the story. Motives have already been established, and we are induced to forget them, since hunter and hunted alike find a mounting exhilaration in the chase across frozen Arctic wastes, until it becomes the sole raison d'être of both. Frankenstein is urged in his pursuit, and in fact sustained, by the Monster:

> Sometimes, indeed, he left marks in writing on the barks of the trees, or cut in stone, that guided me and instigated my fury. . . . You will find near this place, if you follow not too tardily, a dead hare; eat and be refreshed. Come on, my enemy. . . .

And one of the most memorable passages in the book occurs where the Monster again instructs his creator:

> . . . wrap yourself in furs and provide food; for we shall soon enter upon a journey where your sufferings will satisfy my everlasting hatred.

I find that "wrap yourself in furs" very satisfying; as I do Frankenstein's rationalisation of his own fanatical relish in the chase; he swears

> . . . to pursue the demon who caused this misery until he or I shall perish in mortal conflict. For this purpose will I preserve my life. . . .

until he comes to conceive himself divinely appointed to the task, his purpose "assigned . . . by Heaven."

The whole ironic turn of events is, I think, a stroke of genius. Mary's treatment of this theme alone elevates her book above *Caleb Williams* and other novels which deal with the straightforward hunter-and-hunted theme. By these means, if we recall the ice-skating analogy, the figures retain their poise to the very end. No collision occurs, and the pattern is completed only by Frankenstein's natural death and the representation of the Monster hanging over him in grief. They merge one into the other, entwined in final submission.

What I have called the pattern of pursuit is the framework of the novel, a theme in itself which encloses a further theme; there, Frankenstein's relationship to the Monster expresses itself in the paradox of identity and conflict—an anticipation of the Jekyll-and-Hyde theme—from which certain symbolic situations emerge.

Frankenstein himself states:

> I considered the being whom I had cast among mankind . . . nearly in the light of my own vampire, my own spirit let loose from the grave, and forced to destroy all that was dear to me.

We may visualise Frankenstein's doppelganger or Monster firstly as representing reason in isolation, since he is the creature of an obsessional rational effort. (Mr. Richard Church has, in fact, discovered an autobiographical significance in this aspect of the Monster. "That creature" writes Mr. Church, "was a symbol of Mary's overstrained intellectual conscience. The child of her mother, wilful, impetuous, and generous to all-comers, she had been taught by her father to distrust these intuitions and impulses.")

The manifest change in Frankenstein's nature after the creation of the Monster, can be explained by the part-separation of his intellect from his other integral properties. He becomes a sort of Hamlet figure, indecisive and remorseful too late. He decides to destroy the Monster, but is persuaded to pity him—he decides to make a female Monster, but fails at the last moment—he receives the Monster's threat of revenge and does nothing: "Why had I not followed him, and closed with him in mortal strife? But I had suffered him to depart. . . ." Frankenstein muses bitterly when the damage has been done. And he admits,

> . . . through the whole period during which I was the slave of my creature, I allowed myself to be governed by the impulses of the moment.

After the Monster's "birth," then, Frankenstein is a disintegrated being—an embodiment of emotion and also of imagination minus intellect. When, in his final reflections, Frankenstein realises that it was not always so, and exclaims,

> My imagination was vivid, yet my powers of analysis and application were intense; by the union of these qualities I conceived the idea and executed the creation of a man.

he reminds us of those eighteenth century geniuses (the story of Franken-stein is set in that century) whose too-perfect balance of imaginative and rational faculties, did in fact so often disintegrate and ultimately destroy them.

Generally speaking, therefore, it is the emotional and the intellectual that conflict in the form of Frankenstein and his Monster. The culminating emotional frustration by the intellect is reached in the murder of Franken-stein's bride by the Monster. Thereafter, Frankenstein's hysterical pursuit of his fleeting reason completes the story of his madness—a condition per-ceived in the tale only by the Genevan magistrate, who, when Frankenstein demands of him the Monster's arrest, "endeavoured" says Frankenstein, "to soothe me as a nurse does a child."

Mr. Church, once more, has recognised a parallel in Mary Shelley's life, when he discusses the murder of Frankenstein's brother, William. "At the time that she was writing this book," Mr. Church remarks, "the baby William was in the tenderest and most intimate stage of dependent infancy. ... It is almost inconceivable that Mary could allow herself to introduce a baby boy into her book; deliberately call him William, describe him in terms identical with those in which she portrays her own child in one of her letters—and then let Frankenstein's monster waylay this innocent in a woodland dell and murder him by strangling."

It *is* almost inconceivable; and Mr. Church describes Mary's motives as a "miserable delight in self-torture." But I would prefer to revert to Mr. Church's previous statement for a clue to this coincidence. The creature who murdered William "was a symbol of Mary's overstrained intellectual conscience." The conflict between the emotional and the intellectual Fran-kenstein, was Mary Shelley's also. Her baby, William, we know was the child Mary loved more than any; and when she began to feel her intellect grow under her new task, she automatically identified the child with her threat-ened emotions.

But the symbolic ramifications of the Jekyll-and-Hyde theme reach further than Mary's own life. For in so far as she, like others of her time, was beginning to work out her own salvation, her *Frankenstein* expresses the prevalent frustrate situation and reaction to it; the dichotomous elements in the novel are those which were tormenting the ethos. As Frankenstein clashed with his Monster, so did fixed religious beliefs with science; so did imaginative and emotional substitutes for religion, with scientific rational-ism; so did the intuitive and lush passions of the new era, with the dialectical, material and succinct passions of the eighteenth century.

And *Frankenstein* represents, also, that unresolvable aspect of the Romantic temperament which was very soon to be expressed in the quasi-cult of Doubt. Shelley, it is true, had approached these issues with a more emphatic voice, a more perfect heart, as it were; his ideas were beliefs, not doubts, and Mary adapted many of them to her novel. But *Frankenstein*, I think, bears the signature of a less positive way of thought which nevertheless held sway in a large number of intelligent minds. Shelley, for example, would see Frankenstein, in his role of creator, as the perpetrator of human misery and therefore an object of hatred. And, Mary added, he is the sufferer from human misery and therefore an object of pity. But, she also added, he is an amoral product of nature, on whom no responsibility can be attached, towards whom no passion can logically be entertained. It was probably with some insight into the deadlock at which such propositions arrived, that Shelley wrote his equivocal Preface to *Frankenstein*.

Although these questions, typical of the Romantic outlook, form the moral spirit of her novel, Mary Shelley does not allow them to end in deadlock, but resolves them by introducing a process of psychological compensation, which also has a counterpart in history. Her intellectual image, the Monster, comes to ultimate repentance. But his repentance has not the rational flavour of Calvinism; for his resolve to perish by fire has all the ecstatic feeling of Revivalism:

> I shall ascend my funeral pyre triumphantly, and exult in the agony of the torturing flames.

The more rigid the logic, therefore, the more fervent the imaginative reaction.

III

"I wish you would strike your pen into some more genial subject (more obviously so than your last)" Leigh Hunt wrote to Mary after reading *Frankenstein*, "and bring up a fountain of gentle tears for us. That exquisite passage about the cottagers shows what you could do." The passage about the cottagers shows, in fact, what Mary Shelley could do at her worst. Hunt was a bit of a humbug at times, especially as regards women, and really did more harm to Mary's conscience by disapproving of this and that, than did a more or less open hater like Hogg.

But the reviews of *Frankenstein* were nothing like so lame. The "Author of Frankenstein" was generally taken to be a man; and the notice in *Blackwood's*, written by Sir Walter Scott, was the most favourable one of any importance:

...the author seems to us to disclose uncommon powers of poetic imagination. The feeling with which we perused the unexpected and fearful, yet, allowing the possibility of the event, very natural conclusion of Frankenstein's experiment, shook a little even our firm nerves....It is no slight merit in our eyes, that the tale, though wild in incident, is written in plain and forcible English, without exhibiting that mixture of hyperbolical Germanisms with which tales of wonder are usually told....

Upon the whole, the work impresses us with a high idea of the author's original genius and happy power of expression. We shall be delighted to hear that he had aspired to the *paullo majora*; and in the meantime, congratulate our readers upon a novel which excites new reflections and untried sources of emotion.

Of course *Frankenstein* received the usual blasting reserved for works of originality, from the *Quarterly Review,* which bore the book a further grudge on account of its dedication to the deadly "Mr. Godwin." Though the *Quarterly* decided:

Our taste and our judgment alike revolt at this kind of writing, and the greater the ability with which it may be executed the worse it is—it inculcates no lesson of conduct, manners or morality; it cannot mend, and will not even amuse its readers, unless their taste have been deploreably vitiated....

it adds a grudging allowance that

The author has powers, both of conception and language, which employed in a happier direction might, perhaps (we speak dubiously), give him a name among those whose writings amuse or amend their fellow-creatures.

As *Blackwood's* pointed out, Mary Shelley's prose style, compared with other writers of horror-fiction, was very restrained. As a prose writer she never developed any idiosyncrasy which pronounced her writings to be peculiarly her own; and as she became a more conscious writer, her efforts to fetch the deepest layers of her thought up to the surface had a devitalising effect on her style. But in *Frankenstein*, her quite unremarkable, and often tedious language, is rescued by its concentration throughout on direct effect rather than elaboration. She achieved some notably lurid effects by concentrating every word on the merciless exploration of her grim subject.

Who shall conceive the horrors of my secret toil, as I dabbled among the unhallowed damps of the grave, or tortured the living animals to animate the lifeless clay?

I collected bones from charnel-houses; and disturbed, with profane fingers, the tremendous secrets of the human frame. In a solitary chamber, or rather cell, at the top of the house, and separated from all other apartments by a gallery and staircase, I kept my workshop of filthy creation.

The effect only, is of the Gothic, but the language is that of realism. If we compare this, for example, with a passage from a Gothic "classic":

"What!" exclaimed she; "must I lose then my tower! my mutes! my negresses! my mummies! and, worse than all, the laboratory in which I have spent so many a night!...No! I will not be the dupe! Immediately will I speed to support Morakanabad. By my formidable arts the clouds shall sleet hail-stones in the faces of the assailants, and shafts of red-hot iron on their heads. I will spring mines of serpents and torpedoes from beneath them...."

(from *Vathek* by William Beckford; 1784)

we find that by contrast, Mary Shelley's narrative style reads like a scientific treatise; yet her effect is far more horrifying than anything in *Vathek*.

There is, also, a directness of description, a sort of eye-witness convincingness about the portrayal of her principal characters, as when Frankenstein describes his newly-created Monster,

...His limbs were in proportion, and I had selected his features as beautiful. Beautiful!—Great God! His yellow skin scarcely covered the work of muscles and arteries beneath; his hair was of a lustrous black, and flowing; his teeth of a pearly whiteness; but these luxuriances only formed a more horrid contrast with his watery eyes, that seemed almost of the same colour as the dun white sockets in which they were set, his shrivelled complexion and straight black lips.

The minute particularisation of hair, teeth, eyes, sockets, lips, shows, of course, exactly what the man who pieced the creature together would have noticed, and this effect is achieved merely by wasting no words on "effects," as may be more fully realised when the passage is contrasted with a similar piece from a later Gothic novel which enjoyed considerable fame in its time,

Her skin was yellow as the body of a toad; corrugated as its back. She might have been steeped in saffron from her finger tips, the nails of which were of the same hue, to such proportions of her neck as were visible, and which was puckered up like the throat of a turtle. To look at her, one might have thought the embalmer had experimented her art upon herself. So dead, so bloodless, so blackened seemed the flesh, where flesh remained, leather could scarce be tougher than her skin. She seemed like an animated mummy.

(from *Rookwood* by William Harrison Ainsworth; 1834)

This is good writing, and so far as imagery and phraseology go, it is superior to Mary's. But it fails, where Mary's account succeeds, in the effect of immediate and realistic reportage; for it commits the fault of talking round itself—the fault that an extreme-romantic theme will not stand up to, and the fault which *Frankenstein* as a whole, escapes. Even that supreme worker-up of atmosphere, Mrs. Radcliffe, does not seem to achieve the clean stabs of ghastliness that we find in *Frankenstein*. Mary's descriptive passage, once more, may be compared with Mrs. Radcliffe's portrait of a monk:

> His figure was striking, but not so from grace; it was tall, and, though extremely thin, his limbs were large and uncouth and as he stalked along, wrapped in the black garments of his order, there was something terrible in his air; something almost superhuman. His cowl, too, as it threw a shade over the livid paleness of his face, increased its severe character, and gave an effect to his large melancholy eye which approached to horror.... There was something in his phisiognomy extremely singular and that cannot easily be defined.

Those last words "cannot easily be defined" seem an irritating confession of ineptitude from one whose purpose it is to define. I have quoted a typical passage of Mrs. Radcliffe's, and that vague "something terrible in his air," or the "something almost superhuman" occur throughout her voluminous volumes and volumes. Mary Shelley, however, by bearing a definite image of her character in mind, succeeded in conveying it in a style which, if we examine it carefully, is denuded of melodramatic elaboration—the incidents, alone, are melodramatic. What is probably the most melodramatic incident in the novel, will furnish an example—where Frankenstein discovers his murdered bride:

> She was there, lifeless and inanimate, thrown across the bed, her head hanging down, and her pale and distorted features half covered by her hair. Everywhere I turn I see the same figure—her bloodless arms and relaxed form flung by the murderer on its bridal bier.

The point I wish to establish is, not that Mary Shelley excelled as a prose writer—I believe otherwise—but that where her comparatively utilitarian style is combined with an elaborate theme, her writing is distinctive. In the case of *Frankenstein* this combination was a strong contributive factor to its novelty and success as a fictional *genre*. The horror produced by Gothicism was dissipated in vapour, but *Frankenstein's* sharp outlines intensified the horror element to a most sinister degree.

Frankenstein is beset by many faults—mainly those of technique. The story could have been better constructed; the chain which links important events together is weakened by improbable situations. More important is the poverty of characterisation, and by this I do not mean that the principal characters, Frankenstein and the Monster, are defectively portrayed, but that all other characters are weak.

Concerning the construction of *Frankenstein*, Mr. Church finds the book "marred very seriously by a certain haste, an indolence, a vagueness ..." suggested by such incidents as that where "the ardent young chemist, who after only *two years* of study has achieved his purpose, is allowed to lose sight of his monstrous creature until nearly half-way through the book." I believe this impression of haste, indolence and vagueness in construction to be due partly to Mary's inexperience as a writer, and partly to an over-deliberate striving to create suspense.

The calculated slyness in Frankenstein's patient and prolonged account of his early life, which closes with his remark to Walton:

> But I forget that I am moralising in the most interesting part of my tale; and your looks remind me to proceed.

is too excessive a preparation for the story Frankenstein straightaway plunges into, the creation of the Monster. And between the excellent and highly-charged scene in the Orkneys,

> ... looking up, I saw, by the light of the moon, the demon at the casement. A ghastly grin wrinkled his lips as he gazed on me, where I sat fulfilling the task which he had allotted to me. Yes, he had followed me in my travels; he had loitered in forests, hid himself in caves, or taken refuge in wide and desert heaths; and he now came to mark my progress, and claim the fulfilment of my promise.
>
> As I looked on him, his countenance expressed the utmost extent of malice and treachery. I thought with a sensation of madness on my promise of creating another like to him, and trembling with passion, tore to pieces the thing on which I was engaged.

between this, and the fulfilment of the climax it is working towards—the Monster's reprisal by the murder of Elizabeth—Frankenstein wastes too long in being wrongfully arrested for the murder of his friend Clerval, and in being ineffectually released, before returning to marry Elizabeth. The real fault of construction in *Frankenstein* is in the timing of important events. Impatience is evoked where suspense was intended.

Very often, however, Mary's efforts are effectively justified. It is true that the Monster's absence from the scene of action between Chapters V and X is noticeable; but very swiftly after his reappearance the impact Mary intended him to make is made. Having recently learned that the Monster is the murderer of William and the cause of Justine's being hanged, the reader's sympathy is transported, in Chapter XI, to the Monster, as he unfolds the story of his struggles and development. Murderer and fiend as he is, it is his most casual words that seem to arouse the deepest pity; had he appeared earlier in the narrative, the reader would by now have become inured to his plight. For example, he tells how he discovered a fire left in a wood by someone, and having found the elementary advantages of it, was forced by circumstances to leave the spot:

> In this emigration, I exceedingly lamented the loss of the fire which I

had obtained through accident, and knew not how to reproduce it. I gave several hours to the serious consideration of this difficulty.

The essence of such a passage as this, resident in the last sentence "I gave several hours..." with all its primitive implications of mankind's patient attempts to grapple with nature, gives pathetic force to the Monster's narrative, which would not have been so apparent, had we not till now been occupied with Frankenstein's fate, the murder of his brother and the hanging of Justine—had we not, in fact, first conceived the Monster as a villain.

This alternating play upon the sympathy of the reader is Frankenstein's highest claim so far as the structural technique of the work is concerned, and compensates for the minor faults of improbable incident, which should have been avoided. I consider they are minor faults, since the story as a whole, induces a basic "suspension of disbelief." It is true, the epistular convention of the first few pages has a clumsy lack of conviction (though it is skilfully handled in the last pages where the opening situation is picked up, and suspense held very nicely). And it is unlikely that the nurse Justine should be hanged on so slight evidence; that the Monster should so conveniently find a cloak beneath a tree; that he should discover a hide-out so secure as that adjacent to the cottager's dwelling; or that a foreign visitor should so obligingly receive linguistic instruction which the Monster is in a position to overhear and benefit by. But the Monster himself is so incredible, and yet, we are persuaded, so real a being, that we can accept these artificial aids to his development and history.

As I have suggested, I think that Frankenstein's main failing resides not in its construction, but in general characterisation. But also I believe its greatest power to occur in the specific development and depiction of the two protagonists, Frankenstein and the Monster. These are characters, however, so essentially complementary to each other, so engrossed one with the other, and in so many ways facets of the same personality, that they defeat powerful characterisation, which demands a positive interplay of different temperaments. Beside these two half-beings, another, or several other, forceful personalities were needed, but these are not present.

But within these limitations, and concentrating intently upon her two main figures, Mary Shelley performed a feat of individual portraiture which she was never again to repeat. Though the preliminary five chapters postpone the real substance of the tale, they are not wasted, for they methodically build up an interest in Frankenstein. He is established as an exceptional personality, and seems incidentally, in his adolescent stage to reflect the person of Shelley—a role which he discards when the Monster is created, and which is then adopted by Frankenstein's friend, Clerval.

Frankenstein's temperamental category is settled in a brief, clear passage:

> I confess that neither the structure of languages, nor the code of govern-
> ments, nor the politics of various states, possessed attraction for me. It was
> the secrets of the heaven and earth that I desired to learn; and whether it
> was the outward substance of things, or the inner spirit of nature and the
> mysterious soul of man that occupied me, still my inquiries were directed
> to the metaphysical, or, in its highest sense, the physical secrets of the
> world.

Then, with commendable insight into adolescent behaviour, the
reaction of child against parent, and its consequences are demonstrated:

> ...I chanced to find a volume of the works of Cornelius Agrippa. I opened
> it with apathy; the theory which he attempts to demonstrate, and the
> wonderful facts which he relates, soon changed this feeling into enthusi-
> asm. A new light seemed to dawn upon my mind; and, bounding with joy,
> I communicated my discovery to my father. My father looked carelessly at
> the title page of my book, and said, "Ah! Cornelius Agrippa! My dear
> Victor, do not waste your time upon this; it is sad trash."
>
> If, instead of this remark, my father had taken the pains to explain
> to me that the principles of Agrippa had been entirely exploded, and that
> a modern system of science had been introduced, which possessed much
> greater powers than the ancient, because the powers of the latter were
> chimerical, while those of the former were real and practical; under such
> circumstances, I should certainly have thrown Agrippa aside, and have
> contented my imagination, warmed as it was, by returning with greater
> ardour to my former studies. It is even possible that the train of my ideas
> would never have received the fatal impulse that led to my ruin.

Mary also understood, young though she was herself, how profoundly
the youthful mind is influenced by the appearance and personality rather
than the intelligence and wisdom of an older person. This question of
Cornelius Agrippa, moreover, seems to have formed in Frankenstein an
instinctive nerve-centre. When he arrives at college, M. Krempe, the first
professor whom he encounters, unwittingly strikes at this point of sensitivity; which makes Frankenstein the more acutely aware of the older man's
unfavourable exterior:

> He was an uncouth man, but deeply embued in the secrets of his science.
> He asked me several questions concerning my progress in the different
> branches of science appertaining to natural philosophy. I replied carelessly;
> and, partly in contempt, mentioned the names of my alchymists as the
> principal authors I had studied. The professor stared: "Have you," he said,
> "really spent your time in studying such nonsense?"
>
> M. Krempe was a little squat man, with a gruff voice and a repulsive
> countenance; the teacher, therefore, did not prepossess me in favour of his
> pursuits.

It is another teacher, M. Waldman, tolerant, benevolent and attractive, who becomes the presiding genius of Frankenstein's career. His lecture on chemistry is the turning point:

> "The ancient teachers of this science," said he, "promised impossibilities, and performed nothing. The modern masters promise very little; they know that metals cannot be transmuted, and that the elixir of life is a chimera. But these philosophers, whose hands seem only made to dabble in dirt, and their eyes to pose over the microscope or crucible, have indeed performed miracles. They penetrate into the recesses of nature, and show how she works in her hiding places. They have acquired new and almost unlimited powers; they can command the thunders of heaven, mimic the earthquake, and even mock the invisible world with its own shadows."

Thus Frankenstein was seduced—not by a denunciation of his first and deepest enthusiasms, but by a transformation of them; the ancient wizards gave way to modern scientists who were wizards, nevertheless. M. Waldman's personality was, however, the vital stimulus (his voice, Frankenstein said, was the sweetest he had ever heard), but it is only in retrospect that Frankenstein recognises this fact:

> Such were the professor's words—rather let me say the words of fate, enounced to destroy me. As he went on, I felt as if my soul were grappling with a palpable enemy. One by one the various keys were touched which formed the mechanism of my being: chord after chord was sounded, and soon my mind was filled with one thought, one occupation, one purpose.

After the creation of the Monster, since Frankenstein loses to him an integral portion of his being, his character is a study, and a well-executed one, in the mounting obsession of a lost soul to find itself.

But the Monster's development is a larger proposition than Frankenstein's. He does not, like Frankenstein, inherit a civilized way of thought—he inherits nothing but life itself, and the whole gamut of mankind's journey from savage to modern times is played throughout the years of his life.

> It is with considerable difficulty [the Monster tells Frankenstein] that I remember the original era of my being: all the events of that period appear confused and indistinct. A strange multiplicity of sensations seized me, and I saw, felt, heard, and smelt, at the same time. . . .

From among these elementary sensations, he distinguishes first hunger, thirst, and cold. He eats, drinks, and covers himself; and his next instinct is revealed in primitive moon-worship:

> No distinct ideas occupied my mind; all was confused. I felt light, and hunger, and thirst, and darkness; innumerable sounds rung in my ears, and on all sides various scents saluted me: the only object that I could

distinguish was the bright moon, and I fixed my eyes on that with pleasure.

His faculties of discrimination develop, and he begins to acquire, even, an aesthetic sense:

> I distinguished the insect from the herb, and, by degrees, one herb from another. I found that the sparrow uttered none but harsh notes, whilst those of the blackbird and thrush were sweet and enticing.

By imitation, trial and error, the Monster learns the rudiments of survival; the domestic manners of cottagers whom he observes from the peep-hole in his hut, awaken his communal instincts; while the books he (miraculously) comes by, *Plutarch's Lives, Sorrows of Werther* and *Paradise Lost* are carefully selected by the author to stimulate the mental process which his learning of language has initiated.

Once more, Mary Shelley emphasises the influence of outward appearance on human relationships. The Monster has evolved into an intelligent though simple man, "Who am I? What was I? Whence did I come? What was my destination?" the Monster was then able to ask himself; and he has acquired a moral sense:

> I felt the greatest ardour for virtue rise within me, and abhorrence for vice, as far as I understood the significance of those terms, relative as they were, as I applied them, to pleasure and pain alone.

Yet, he discovers, all human creatures with whom he meets, flee before his hideous approach. A canker of resentment eats into him, and it is Frankenstein, his creator, whom he accuses for his miserable solitude. When he seizes a young child, in the desperate hope of educating him as a friend, this hope is forgotten when the Monster learns that the child is Frankenstein's relative:

> He struggled violently. Let me go, he cried; monster! ugly wretch! you wish to eat me, and tear me to pieces—You are an ogre—Let me go, or I will tell my papa.
> "Boy, you will never see your father again; you must come with me."
> "Hideous monster! let me go. My papa is a Syndic—he is M. Frankenstein—he will punish you. You dare not keep me."
> "Frankenstein! you belong then to my enemy—to him towards whom I have sworn eternal revenge; you shall be my first victim."
> The child still struggled, and loaded me with epithets which carried despair to my heart; I grasped his throat to silence him, and in a moment he lay dead at my feet.

The development of the Monster's character does not cease here, although his first murder gives it a new direction. It is only after his almost-completed female counterpart is destroyed by Frankenstein that he is depicted as an all-out perpetrator of evil. One important factor in the unfolding of his character, is his lack of emotion. What passes for emotion—his need for companionship, his feelings of revenge towards Frankenstein—are really intellectual passions arrived at through rational channels. He is asexual, and demands his bride as a companion, never as a lover or even merely a mate; since his emotions reside in the heart of Frankenstein, as does Frankenstein's intellect in him.

Neither of these characters, therefore, are brought to full maturity. It is impossible that they should be, for, if they were, *Frankenstein* would be a different story. It is not without relevance to this point, however, that the novel was the product of a girl in her teens, herself an immature character. Still, we cannot but admire the patient, analytical and perceptive record of the Monster's evolution, and Frankenstein's arrival at adulthood.

Frankenstein has entertained, delighted and harrowed generations of readers to this day; its fate, however, has not depended upon literary criticism, for it has been most singularly ignored, both in specific reference, and in general works on the English novel. What appreciative criticism exists on *Frankenstein* has waned, in the present century, in conformance with current whims and cults. (The "rediscovery" of Jane Austen, for example, was one which could scarcely have coincided with an enthusiasm for Mary Shelley's work.)

Mr. Church's judgment (pronounced at a time when *Frankenstein* would probably have been condemned, if considered at all, as "escapist") that *Frankenstein* "must be considered as a permanent addition to the world's literature of the macabre" must have sounded almost ostentatious in 1928.

Ten years later, Miss Glynn Grylls recorded her directly opposite opinion that "*Frankenstein* remains a 'period piece,' of not very good date; historically interesting, but not one of the living novels of the world." I do not know if, by the phrase "the living novels of the world" Miss Glynn Grylls had in mind such criteria as Dostoievsky, Conrad, Tolstoy or even Dickens; if so, of course, she is correct. But a novel need not be mighty in order to be vital; it need not be a product of genius to survive as a classic; and if such a medley as *Northanger Abbey, Jane Eyre, The Antiquarian* and *Vanity Fair* are living novels, then *Frankenstein* is one.

LOWRY NELSON, JR.

Night Thoughts on the Gothic Novel

Horror fiction has only a recent history. In the ancient past tyrants like Phalaris and Nero provided fabulists and historians with lurid events unmitigated by the distance of guiltily pleasurable fiction. Such early monsters of the mind as Scylla and Charybdis, Polyphemus, Cerberus, and Procrustes existed only as prisoners of places which could be braved or avoided according to need and daring. At least they could be counted upon not to stalk about at random. The ancients, however much they felt themselves exposed to the delinquent passions of the gods, seem not to have imagined fiendish supermen who at any moment might come to terrorize or kill. Even the two famous haunted houses in antiquity, the one reported in a letter of Pliny the Younger and the entirely specious one in Plautus's *Mostellaria*, were easily exorcised.

In the later eighteenth century a complicated and irregular pullulation began. It would be satisfying to ascribe the rise of the gothic novel to the growing ranks of graveyard enthusiasts and to the relatively new passion for the awesome in secular nature, the "sublime" as distinct from the "beautiful." That may well be too simple, though it is tempting to suppose that once God had been secularized out of the graveyard and the terrifying manifestations of nature, what remained was the primeval horror of demonic violence and bodily decay. When the ancient gods took on human or animal form they generally did no more than rape. At most they punished for some palpable reason. They were not a nameless and unpredictable

From *The Yale Review* 2, vol. 52 (Winter 1963). Copyright © 1963 by *The Yale Review*.

terror to the general populace: indeed, they were far more ingeniously malicious toward each other. It might seem that once the totemic animal loses its godhead it can become an unpropitiable terror and that degeneration of the fabric of mythology and religion is conducive to gothic terrors, just as, conversely, mythology is often thought to be the safe-making systematizing of the otherwise uncontrollable terrors known as natural phenomena. Whatever the explanation, it remains a fact that on the threshold of the romantic revolution a vigorous new genre got under way, principally in northern countries where Grendels and trolls and werewolves had long stalked through the marshes of folklore.

One might ascribe the origins of the gothic novel to the several revivals in the later eighteenth century: interest in folklore, in the mythified Middle Ages, in the eccentric asocial individual, and in the mysterious Mediterranean world. A cruder ascription would be to the heightened imagination of youth and inexperience. Matthew Lewis and Mary Shelley, though precociously experienced, were hardly twenty when they composed their horror tales; Ann Radcliffe and Emily Brontë were quite limited in their knowledge of the outside world. Charles Maturin, author of *Melmoth the Wanderer*, is perhaps an exception, but he comes toward the end of the efflorescence of pure gothic and can hardly be called a founder though he was one of the best, if not the most original, of the practitioners. But it is hazardous in literature to assign simple causes to complex phenomena. A more secure office would be to define, describe, and judge what we have.

The gothic novel owes much to the popularity of exotic themes and to the emancipation of the novel from overt moral commitment. Perhaps it derives most from the enormous interest around the turn of the century in the solitary eccentric, the misfit, the social outcast, or, to use the handy phrase, the guilt-haunted wanderer. In the romantic transvaluation of values Cain becomes a sympathetic figure, unjustly cursed by a vengeful God and incapable of ever purging his guilt. He looks in vain for human trust and friendship; his "benevolent" impulses are thwarted; at worst he is twisted by circumstances into a monster of inhumanity—a tortured image of his tormentors. We see the rudiments in Byron's play called *Cain: a Mystery*. The hero is a malcontent who blames his parents for their expulsion from Eden and also blames the tyrannical deity who will not readmit them. Even his beloved wife and sister Adah (incest is handily unavoidable) cannot give him the sympathy he craves. Only Lucifer, the voice of independence and illumination, can open to him a vision of proud freedom and fulfilment. After Cain in a frenzy kills Abel at the altar, it is Eve who pronounces the curse of alienation on her son. His faithful Adah insists on accompanying him. At the very end of the play Cain laments his brother's death; but Adah exclaims, "Peace be with him!" while Cain can only query and lament, "But with *me!*—." What might happen later—the wandering and the pangs of nameless guilt—is of course the favorite subject, boasting its Alastors, its Manfreds, its Childe Harolds, and its more natively gothic heroes.

Curiously enough, the fascination for the bizarre, the individual peculiarity, the monstrous seems to have led more significantly to a fictional discovery of the true depths of human nature than to a mere exploitation of the sensational and the perverse. By its insistence on singularity and exotic setting, the gothic novel seems to have freed the minds of readers from direct involvement of their superegos and allowed them to pursue daydreams and wish fulfilment in regions where inhibitions and guilt could be suspended. Those regions became thereby available to great writers who eventually demonstrated that sadism, indefinite guiltiness, mingled pleasure and pain (Maturin's "delicious agony"), and love-hate, were also deeply rooted in the minds of the supposedly normal.

Still, if we look to the earlier gothicists for psychological profundity we are bound to be disappointed. Horace Walpole's *Castle of Otranto* (1765) is most impressive for its early date. The plot is mechanical and the characterization primitive. That the mysterious helmet is larger than life and made of stone seems the main reason for calling it the prime ancestor of the gothic novel. In other respects the exoticism of the setting and the "naked" passions in it are surely outdone by such a work as *The Duchess of Malfi*. Ann Radcliffe's various novels, notably the *Romance of the Forest* (1791) and *The Mysteries of Udolpho* (1794), now seem more like childish fantasies than evocations of primal horror. Their dungeons, swarthy Italians, and rattling chains were properly and neatly satirized by Jane Austen in *Northanger Abbey*. That Catherine finds the mysterious documents to be only a roll of laundry lists seems a fitting rebuke to the pretensions of Mrs. Radcliffe and her school. Jane Austen thus enrolls herself among those who since Cervantes were to make their Juliens and Emmas victims of "bad literature."

William Beckford's *Vathek* (1786) is a somewhat more serious matter. It shows the trend of the time in the genre of the oriental tale. But, at least on the surface, nothing could be further removed from the moral atmosphere of Dr. Johnson's costume novel *Rasselas*. Though *Vathek* is almost as much an Englishman's fantasy *travestie*, it fully exploits, as Johnson of course does not, the potential licentiousness of a furtive reader's imagination encouraged to attribute exotic vice and magic diabolism to a safely alien milieu. Yet even though he is absorbed by his sadistic and homoerotic fantasies, Beckford occasionally informs the reader that nothing must be taken entirely seriously. At one point Vathek's diabolic mother Carathis amuses herself by inviting "the fairest and most delicate ladies of the city" to her gay parties and then letting loose vipers and scorpions. In his jaunty manner, Beckford writes that "they all bit to a wonder, and Carathis would have left her friends to die, were it not that, to fill up the time, she now and then amused herself in curing their wounds, with an excellent anodyne of her own invention: for this good Princess abhorred being indolent." When Vathek, in league with a boy-eating devil, makes the delicate virgin Nouronihar into a teen-age sex-pot and enters a pseudo-Mohammedan hell, Beckford cannot forbear to draw a silly moral against bad conduct. Though the habit of easy moralizing comes back like a tic, the full weight of the book rests on its self-indulgent pornography.

With Matthew Gregory Lewis's *The Monk* (1796) and Mary Shelley's *Frankenstein* (1818) we are in a different fictional world. The urbane smile may well freeze on our faces and the titillating fantasies probe more deeply than we wish.

In narrow summary *The Monk* might seem trite: the saintliest man in Madrid revealed as the grossest sinner. It could superficially be dismissed as a Protestant's cautionary tale of Roman Catholic hypocrisy. Though the charges of triteness and naïveté cannot wholly be avoided, there are good reasons for seeing the book as an importantly symptomatic novel. The monk Ambrosio is not a monster of vice to begin with. By his own ambition and the adulation of the faithful, he is elevated to an impossible pinnacle of perfection. When the devil's temptations surround him he finds himself drawn into contradictory behavior: since he falls short of his ideal he must be damned; since he is led into debauchery he must be unredeemable; since he has sinned he must continue to be wicked to insure his damnation. His downfall is the handsome little novice who devotedly follows him about the monastery and soon reveals that he is really the lovestricken Matilda. By arousing Ambrosio's pity and thereby his senses, she seduces him and he becomes a slave to passion. "Ambrosio again raged with desire: the die was thrown: his vows were already broken: he had already committed the crime, and why should he refrain from enjoying its reward? . . . Ambrosio rioted in delights till then unknown to him . . . his only fear was lest death should rob him of enjoyments, for which his long fast had only given a keener edge to his appetite." Yet in a week's time he exhausts the variety of Matilda's literal charms and casts about for another partner in vice. How had he, the saintly monk, come to such a pass? His great natural virtues and force of character, we are told half-heartedly, were perverted by the monks who brought him up. They thwarted his innate generosity, compassion, and benevolence, and fostered his pride, ambition, and disdain. "Still in spite of the pains taken to pervert them, his natural good qualities would occasionally break through the gloom cast over them so carefully." Ambrosio's inclinations swing extravagantly from "natural" virtue to "natural" vice. While capable of the greatest good, he gives himself over to the greatest evil. In fact, his character and circumstances are such that his good impulses become, when frustrated, entirely evil.

In the fullness of his newly aroused sensuality which Matilda can no longer satisfy, he is approached by a tender innocent maiden, Antonia, who beseeches him to visit her mother, Elvira, who is gravely ill. It is part of his complexity that "he felt not the provocation of lust.... On the contrary, what he now felt was a mingled sentiment of tenderness, admiration, and respect. A soft and delicious melancholy infused itself into his soul, and he would not have exchanged it for the most lively transports of joy." Gradually, however, on repeated visits he conceives such a passion for Antonia that he undertakes the formidable task of corrupting her innocence. It proves impossible without the help of sorcery: through Matilda's complaisant agency the devil appears as a beautiful naked youth with a "mysterious melancholy impressed upon his features, betraying the fallen angel." The means are provided for Ambrosio to enjoy the sleeping body of Antonia, but in the act he is discovered by her mother. His inner thoughts on being discovered continue to show his ambiguous good and evil nature. "It was now his turn to suffer, and he could not but acknowledge that his punishment was just." Yet when exposure becomes imminent he desperately and savagely kills the mother. While still in the throes of contrition he nevertheless schemes with Matilda to drug the orphaned Antonia and remove her to an underground vault where he might use her *ad libidinem*. In the gothic gloom of the sepulchre he brutally rapes her. But immediately afterward, to continue the heightened ambivalence of his character, he feels only "aversion and rage." Finally, about to be discovered in the tomb, and urged on by Matilda, he wildly plunges a dagger into the "bosom" of the screaming Antonia.

Now in the dungeons of the Inquisition, Ambrosio gives himself over to despair. "If he read the books of morality which were put into his hands, he saw in them nothing but the enormity of his offenses. If he attempted to pray, he recollected that he deserved not Heaven's protection, and believed his crimes so monstrous as to exceed even God's infinite goodness." Tortured beyond endurance, he succumbs to the final temptation and signs a compact with the devil for his escape. The final ironies are rapid and crude: Matilda was a demon in disguise; Antonia was his sister and Elvira his mother; the guards he heard coming to take him to his death, so he thought, were actually bringing his pardon. In this last scene the devil, a severe moralizer, flings all of Ambrosio's weakness and evil in his face, then carries him aloft and drops the despairing monk onto the jagged rocks below.

The final paragraph is the local masterpiece of gothic novel writing. In it are described the terrible six days of suffering Ambrosio underwent before he died and the rain-swollen river carried away his corpse. In an obverse way it is quite as violent and yet rhetorically finished as Pushkin's poem "The Prophet," which it strangely resembles. Somehow it manages to be more than a final condemnation of monasticism. For once we encounter in the gothic novel a seemingly preposterous character whose motivation is carefully, if awkwardly, delineated. To create successfully such a violently self-contradictory character was perhaps impossible in Lewis's day. That he half-succeeded would seem to portend the later success of Dostoevsky. Ambrosio is not simply evil masquerading as good; he is not the stock hypocrite. In one sense it would be proper to characterize him as an instance of what may happen when normal impulses are unnaturally thwarted. In another, historically more important, sense, it would be proper to see in him a heightened model of the universal good-bad conflict in human nature. By implication, whoever is capable of great good is also capable of great evil. The archetype, of course, would be Lucifer himself. In ordinary people good and evil seem to dilute each other with their small quantities. In unusual people, either extreme continuously dominates the other or the two violently alternate in ascendancy. Such would be the superficial view, and the psychology of *The Monk* often stays on the surface. It is surprising, though, how close Ambrosio's outward struggles can come to a presentation of the subconscious drama of the mind. Not that *The Monk* is significantly pre-Freud or that Freud is significantly post-Lewis. But it is important to note that *The Monk*, with other novels of the school, presented under the license of sensationalism significant and basic traits of human nature that elsewhere, in "polite" fiction, went unexpressed. Lewis takes his characterization of Ambrosio seriously enough not to intrude a pat moral at the end. He leaves us with the impression that it may be once again possible to create a character like Edmund or like Claudius or like Macbeth.

Though he minimizes it, Lewis does not dispense with the supernatural claptrap of the gothic mode: there is the fortune-teller's prophecy, the magic mirror in which the lusting Ambrosio is made to see Antonia undressing, and the actual appearance of Lucifer and Matilda, the devil's handmaiden. In Mrs. Shelley's *Frankenstein* things are quite different. Once we are induced to believe that it is possible to infuse life into a composite corpse, we need no longer worry about sudden supernatural intervention. Rather than a tale of the noumenous supernatural, her book is more nearly an example of science fiction *avant la lettre*. Again, the main theme of the book is the good-bad nature of man. Again, heavy stress is laid on the influence of environment. But, wittingly or not, her most striking achievement is the creation of universal symbolic significance in a narrative that on the surface lays claim to utter oddity and uniqueness.

By excellent documentary instinct, Mrs. Shelley begins her novel with a series of letters written by a certain Robert Walton to his sister Mrs. Saville: in fact, the whole narrative, including the recitals of Frankenstein and the "monster," is communicated to Mrs. Saville with all the defensive incredulity of an eyewitness. At once the reader's good will to believe is enlisted: he must work with Walton to convince the stay-at-homes. Walton, we learn, is a young man determined to sail from St. Petersburg to the North Pole in a passionate effort to discover the secret of the magnet and simply to see what had never been seen before. In effect, his Faustian impulse will take him back to the heart of Europe and even to the heart of man. At the very beginning one of the main themes of the novel is sounded, as Walton laments: "I have no friend, Margaret: when I am glowing with the enthusiasm of success, there will be none to participate in my joy. I desire the company of a man who could sympathize with me.... You may deem it romantic, my dear sister, but I bitterly feel the want of a friend." In the characteristic vocabulary of the time Mrs. Shelley's narrator expresses what we might call the desire to be loved. More significantly, he expresses both the depth of his own feelings and the seeming impossibility of communicating them to someone who cares. Very quickly, then, the major theme of "sympathy" is established, as is the documentary and "sincere" mode which helps to domesticate the strange events.

In the midst of Arctic ice floes Walton and his crew catch sight of an extraordinary figure racing along in a dog sled. Not only is it incredible that something human should be seen in those wastes, but that that something should be so huge. Soon afterward appears a "normal" figure of a man, utterly exhausted, with only a single dog left alive, though still passionate to pursue the giant. It is Victor Frankenstein, citizen of Geneva, whose account of his misfortunes provides the substance of the book and justifies its subtitle "The Modern Prometheus." As a student of chemistry in Ingolstadt he had managed feverishly to combine the arcane medieval and modern "secrets of science" to produce an elixir of life. He then tested it on a body which he had put together out of bits and pieces from graves and charnel houses. All the while his energies and emotions had been utterly subordinated to his one great passion: he became oblivious to familial duties, to affections, and to "nature." In an orgy of narcissism, and as a sort of horrible retribution, he had succeeded in creating his own Doppelgänger, his alter ego, his objectified id: a hideous humanoid figure of more than human proportions. Exhausted by his years of effort, he falls into a troubled sleep. In his dreams he sees his beloved die as he kisses her for the first time; he sees himself embracing the worm-infested corpse of his mother. At that point the "monster" he has created awakens him: "He held up the curtain of the bed; and his eyes, if eyes they may be called, were fixed on me. His jaws opened, and he muttered some inarticulate sounds, while a grin wrinkled his cheeks. He might have spoken, but I did not hear; one hand was stretched out, seemingly to detain me, but I escaped, and rushed down stairs." The point here is not horror for its own sake, but rather the effects of rejection, even on a monster of one's own guilty creation.

For a while the nameless monster is lost sight of. Frankenstein, seriously ill, is nursed and consoled by his great friend Clerval. To keep his mind off other things he follows his friend's bent and takes up the study of Persian, Arabic, and Sanscrit, without, as he says, attempting "a critical knowledge of their dialects." Suddenly news comes from Geneva of the murder of his younger brother. Frankenstein hurries homeward, but on the way encounters a storm during which a flash of lightning illumines the dread shape of his unshapely creature: *"He* was the murderer! I could not doubt it," exclaims Frankenstein. But someone else, unjustly accused, dies for the deed. The two dead innocents are, says Frankenstein, "the first hapless victims of my unhallowed arts."

Yet there is no way of revealing his "guilt," since no one would believe him. For solace he seeks out the lonely grandeurs of Mont Blanc: "solitude was my only consolation—deep, dark, deathlike solitude"—again, a retreat from his whole self and into desolate nature. As he approached it, "Mont Blanc, the supreme and magnificent Mont Blanc, raised itself from the surrounding *aiguilles*, and its tremendous *dôme* overlooked the valley." From a distance such scenes of nature are for him "mighty friends," yet they are solitary and potentially dangerous: avalanches threaten and the surface of glaciers rise "like the waves of a troubled sea." In this setting of awesome "sublimity," in which beauty and terror mingle, the monster reappears. Frankenstein hurls execrations at him. In reply we hear the monster, who has not, so far as known, been educated, acquit himself with a certain rhetorical finesse. In effect, he asks for love from his creator, and at the same time threatens that if he is rejected again he will "glut the maw of death." As the monster rightly says to Frankenstein, "I ought to be thy Adam; but I am rather the fallen angel, whom thou drivest from joy for no misdeed." At the highest pitch of programmatic articulation the monster exclaims: "Everywhere I see bliss, from which I alone am irrevocably excluded. I was benevolent and good; misery made me a fiend. Make me happy, and I shall again be virtuous." Like Robert Walton, the monster wants a friend, more particularly a female friend and that can only issue from the plasmatic hands of Frankenstein. By horrible threat he persuades his creator to suspend his abhorrence and listen to his tale.

As neorealists we may be frozen by the rhetoric which the monster displays as he begins his narrative: "It is with considerable difficulty," he declares, "that I remember the original era of my being." We are not, however, reading a novel of gothic terrors so much as a treatise on benevolence and its opposite, on the education or perversion of primal innocence. The monster's account of his awakening consciousness and his education is Mrs. Shelley's version of her father William Godwin's notions derived from Rousseau. Not that it is not accomplished with unexpectedly imaginative skill. We are taken plausibly through a rapid evolution of native ability: from inarticulate feelings and tabula rasa to conceptualized emotions and education. It is not easy to educate a monster expelled from all human society. Mrs. Shelley manages resourcefully in having him take refuge in a lean-to "hovel" beside a house whose interior is visible to him through a chink. The inhabitants are simple but articulate practitioners of virtue. It might have been impossible for the monster to learn their language if by fortunate pedagogic chance a beautiful Turkish girl had not happened along much in need of learning the local tongue. In the course of his education the monster reveals himself an *anima naturaliter moralis*, though fully aware of the curse of his appearance and his loneliness. His primer was Volney's *Ruins of Empires*; his outside reading, *Paradise Lost*, a volume of Plutarch's *Lives*, and the *Sorrows of Werther*.

Naturally he was particularly impressed by *Paradise Lost*: though he seemed like Adam in having no forebears, he many times considered Satan as the "fitter emblem" of his condition. He curses his creator, as he narrates his past: "God, in pity, made man beautiful and alluring, after his own image; but my form is a filthy type of yours, more horrid even from the very resemblance. Satan had his companions, fellow-devils, to admire and encourage him; but I am solitary and abhorred." After a year of virtuous instruction through the chink, the monster, full of love and admiration for the cottagers, decides to present himself first to the blind old father and then, after all explanations, to the others. His plan goes awry as the others return unexpectedly and, horrified, beat him away. He could have destroyed them, but with a "bitter sickness" in him he refrained. "I, like the archfiend, bore a hell within me; and, finding myself unsympathized with, wished to tear up trees, spread havoc and destruction around me, and then to have sat down and enjoyed the ruin." The family in horror flee the house forever, and the monster burns it in a wild fury. He has undeservedly fallen from grace and he himself destroys his former Eden. It is with literate irony that he then asks, "And now, with the world before me, whither should I bend my steps?" He, like Adam, is very much his own Satan and his own vengeful God. Life is inexorably against him and he can only turn from love and "benevolence" to hate and revenge for the imperfect gift of life from his imperfect creator. Eventually he will destroy all those who are dear to Frankenstein. But in mid-career he appeals to his creator to perform the one act that will assuage his loneliness and rancor. "I am alone, and miserable; man will not associate with me; but one as deformed and horrible as myself would not deny herself to me. My companion must be of the same species, and have the same defects. This you must create." He must have an Eve. But Frankenstein cannot bring himself to perform such a second horror of creation. The monster takes his course.

Already it should be clear, without tracing the plot further, that Mrs. Shelley's text is rich enough in historical implication to deserve some close attention to weighted words like "romantic," "benevolence," "sympathy," and that prime sufferer of linguistic devaluation, "interest." What I should like to stress especially is that *Frankenstein* is not a mere tale of horror, but rather a significant fictional model of the mind. For the first time in gothic fiction characters take on the full symbolic resonance of inner psychological reality. To say flatly that the monster is Frankenstein's id on the rampage and that he subconsciously desires his family's extermination would be pretentious and anachronistic. Or to say that the monster uses murder as an attention-getting device would be foolishly reductive. It is quite different to argue that Frankenstein and his monster have much in common, that they are objectified parts of a single sensibility, and that they represent the intimate good and bad struggle in the human personality. Evil is within; in one's own works and creations. Good impulses are thwarted and evil ones encouraged by some inner perversity. The source of that perversity is perhaps a desire to be loved alone or an urge toward narcissism. Yet there is also the strong fascination with the gratuitous pursuit of one's evil nature. Frankenstein pursuing his monster is searching for his whole self. Human nature being what it is, total benevolence seems to create the spectre of monsters haunting the outskirts of Elysium: some sort of compromise must be made between the good and evil instincts of human nature in order to survive, since human nature deeply drives toward both good and evil; or at least some sort of modus vivendi must be found, most hopefully through full self-knowledge and self-discipline. While Ambrosio's unconscious incest was a form of unself-critical narcissism, Frankenstein's rejection of his created monster was a denial of his nether forces for which he should have accepted a fully aware responsibility.

Such mythifying interpretations of gothic novels may seem obvious and unnecessary, a case of misplaced solemnity. Still, it may not be excessive to hazard a generalization. In its earlier and cruder forms the gothic novel made irresponsible use of such claptrap as chains and dungeons and prodigies of weather. With *The Monk* and especially with *Frankenstein* we find that the claptrap has begun to take on symbolic resonance. Ambrosio's descent into the tombs is a descent into evil. His rape of Antonia in those surroundings prompts him to say, "This sepulchre seems to me Love's bower," thus reviving the old mythic and Shakespearean theme of the sepulchral marriage bed. But in Mrs. Shelley's novel much wider echoes resound. The cottage where the monster received his "upbringing" is an Eden in which he is the unwilling serpent or the reluctant Cain: his uncomprehended desire to be loved has destroyed the tranquillity of the uncomprehending others. The icy reaches in which Walton first descries the monster and his creator, and the brooding, glistening presence of Mont Blanc are ambiguous symbols of nature's innocence and also her indifference or cruelty: we are well on the way to the whiteness of the whale. Then, too, the moods of Frankenstein and his creature are often at variance with those of nature; instead of a one-to-one correspondence, often the sinister and the unnatural in men are heightened by nature's own innocent or indifferent serenity. Nature in Mrs. Shelley's novel is not the benevolently sympathetic or chastening nature of Byron and Wordsworth. In social terms we witness in *Frankenstein* a failure of "benevolence"; in personal terms, a mind incomplete without its "other" mind. There is even the implication that in the idyllic family life the "monster" must be or at least should be faced and laid and caged, not avoided and left to roam the wilderness of marsh or mind.

The gothic hero easily shades into what is commonly called the romantic hero; or, perhaps to put it better, both are members of the same genus. Both share an essential loneliness and feeling of incommunicability; both are generally scapegoats or guilt-haunted wanderers. Without attempting a perhaps futile contrast between the two, we may provisionally confine ourselves to describing the gothic cousin. Characteristically he harbors a nameless guilt. He is haunted by an acute feeling of the discrepancy between good and evil. Indeed, both qualities are present in him in heightened form. He possesses some extraordinary virtue (scientific genius, strength, sanctity) which is transformed somehow into an extraordinary vice. Finally, he is in touch with nether forces, originally demonic but later inside the mind. Mrs. Radcliffe and her like presented a rather crude mixture of sensibility and sensationalism in which virtue laboriously triumphed over evil. Lewis, though he makes his survivors happy at the end of his novel, rejected the simplistic notion that virtue is always rewarded or, indeed, that anyone has a monopoly on virtue. Ambrosio is close to becoming a true villain-hero. Mrs. Shelley had the unusual courage to create a chaotic world in which virtue is rewarded perhaps in heaven but not necessarily on earth, and in which evil is rampant still and in this life may be inexorable.

In the course of development of the gothic hero and his setting one also notices an evolution away from dependence for effect upon the rigged supernatural and toward a recognition of what we might call, for the sake of contrast, the "subnatural," that is, the irrational, the impulse to evil, the uncontrollable unconscious. It is tempting to say that that improbable mixture of sensibility and sensationalism, freed of the supernatural and concentrated in the mind, led eventually to the American and French versions of symbolism and to a recognition or rediscovery of myth as an expression of the psychic drama of the whole mind. To cast more widely, but perhaps more securely, it could be claimed that the development of the gothic novel foreshadows the future interest, both in art and science, in hidden workings, contradictory impulses, irrational and gratuitous evil, the intimacy of love and hate, whose effects are so diversely seen (whether expressed or suppressed) in Balzac, Dickens, Browning, Baudelaire, Dostoevsky and their heirs.

Is this a triumph of irrationalism in an age of rationalism? We may well have a sense that everything was happening in the nineteenth century, and all at once: symbolism and realism, rationalism and irrationalism, civilizing progress and utopian primitivism. If there is any convenient common denominator it might be a renewed sense of the profound, perhaps unfathomable, discrepancy between appearance and reality. The rejection of the supernatural and the descent into the mind may seem to reveal at the same time the "realities" of life and the irrational symbolism, quite impractical or unrealistic, of the unconscious. The plunge into the depths of the mind, so fateful for the age, seems to have revealed both a yearning for the utopian, simplistic solution and an indulging of irrational impulses. The reductio ad absurdum occurred early in the stereotype of the villain with a heart of gold. It continues in mediocre literature today, where uncontrollable social forces have not taken over as prime movers. Such sentimental villain-heroes find some sort of salvation or justification in society. But the gothic hero and his immediate successors show an almost solipsistic struggle within themselves. In their struggle with society they do not become either victims or conformists; they are relatively free agents. Their trouble is both more cosmic and more personal.

It would be too simple to say that the "mystery tale" or the gothic novel arose in reaction to rationalism or empiricism or "science." In fact, it could be urged that it could arise only under their influence, since they create the right atmosphere for willing though temporary suspension of disbelief. The Castle of Otranto and Vathek are mainly titillations of sensuality, whether simple shudder or sadomasochism. They seem, strangely enough, still within the imaginative and moral scope of Voltaire and Dr. Johnson. With The Monk and with Frankenstein we enter upon new possibilities. The Monk is transitional, in that some attempt is made, despite the mere sensationalism, to delineate the complex psychological reactions to abnormal situations. But it is in Frankenstein that the mythic possibilities of the genre begin to emerge. Instead of a parade of horrors and marvels, the gothic novel has begun to suggest a mythology of the mind. Fantasy and exoticism, employed before as mere claptrap, become elemental and symbolic; decorative oddity becomes new myth. If these seem claims too large to be sustained so narrowly, the examples given may be urged as symptomatic of larger changes. We must at least allow that "realism" in the nineteenth century was "realistic" in plumbing mythic or symbolic depths, that such writers as Dickens and Browning were caught betwixt and between (between, for instance, merry old England and the gloomy old jungles of the mind), and that the continuity from *The Scarlet Letter* to *The Rose Tattoo* is fairly obvious.

The gothic hero's most successful immediate heirs are Heathcliff and Ahab. If one were to rehearse briefly the similarities between *Wuthering Heights* and *Moby Dick* one might catalogue the following: they are both set in remote or isolated surroundings; both novels are narrated by quite ordinary people; good impulses in the heroes have been thwarted or affronted and both are bent on massive and calculating revenge; both heroes bear marks of difference (Heathcliff's darkness suggesting the cursed race of Ham, and Ahab's scar the mark of Cain); the origins of both heroes are relatively vague; both are guilt-haunted wanderers whose skills for good (their omnicompetence in practical matters) are diverted to the service of "evil." Besides, both novels are quite unchristian, perhaps for the time daringly so: the pagan Queequeg comes off much better than the Quakers and the "grand, ungodly, godlike" Ahab pursues his quest under a ceremonial covenant with the crew of his own diabolistic invention; in *Wuthering Heights* religion is almost savagely parodied in the figure of the bigoted Joseph and supernatural reality in the novel is quite unsanctioned by conventional Christianity.

Emily Brontë follows Mrs. Shelley in the momentously significant technique of having extraordinary or even incredible events narrated by a quite ordinary and credible observer. There are here, in fact, two such narrators: Mr. Lockwood, a trivial urbanite who moves to what he supposes to be the tranquillity of the country, and Nelly Dean, a servant-companion of self-righteous and self-serving character. Through them the transcendent and even supernatural relation between Heathcliff and Cathy is conveyed to a reader who, if properly responsive, knows much more from what the narrators tell than they do themselves. We learn that Heathcliff's origins are obscure, that he was simply found by Mr. Earnshaw in the streets of Liverpool. In the novel, cities, or the urban world, represent sinister mystery and the unknown, and so it is a powerful paradox that Heathcliff comes from the city and yet is in touch with elemental nature in the country which only he and Cathy really know. When old Mr. Earnshaw, Cathy's father, uncovers his find he exclaims: "See here, wife! I was never so beaten with anything in my life: but you must e'en take it as a gift of God; though it's as dark almost as if it came from the devil."

Already we are presented with the tension between potential extremes of good and evil. The love that united Cathy and Heathcliff was utter devotion, quite beyond the conventional sentimental attachment or even the fast bond of romantic love: the two, by common feeling, were immutably committed to each other despite any impediment, even marriage to someone else. Their relationship, as we can clearly surmise through the commonplace narrators, was for them beyond time and place and, significantly, beyond good and evil. Heathcliff becomes evil and vindictive when his love for Cathy is thwarted. He is not significantly a victim of social injustice: the forces for good or evil are within himself and within his relation to Cathy. Since his great good on earth is thwarted he pitilessly commits great evil. His supreme goal, like that of Frankenstein's monster and like Ahab's, is ruthlessly and singlemindedly pursued. That schism of the mind—Heathcliff and Cathy, Frankenstein and his monster, Ahab and the whale—that mingled impulse of great good and great evil, begins to generate a latter-day model of the warring human mind. As in *Frankenstein*, nature in *Wuthering Heights* is elemental and unpersonified, neither beneficent nor purposive, but rather inexorable and often, in relation to human beings, ironically indifferent. Heathcliff is at one with that version of nature. As Cathy describes him, he is "an unreclaimed creature, without refinement, without cultivation: an arid wilderness of furze and whinstone . . . he's a fierce, pitiless, wolfish man." It would be entirely wrong to sentimentalize him and make him into another Childe Harold or Manfred: his complexity is much greater than that of the Byronic heroes and it derives in large measure, we may suppose, from the gothic novel.

Ahab too is a distant cousin of Werther, the Ancient Mariner, and the Byronic figures. His neo-Faustian or neo-Promethean traits are clear enough. He belongs also in the company of guilt-haunted wanderers or reluctant scapegoats, bent on revenge or escape or expiation or simply knowledge. But he is neither reconciled, like Faust, nor confined by God, like Prometheus. The universe of *Moby Dick*, like that of *Wuthering Heights* and *Frankenstein*, is almost frighteningly without either God or devil; the God of conventional fiction, even a tyrant God, has effectually disappeared, just as the devil of earlier gothic diabolism has disappeared as the archfiend. In a universe without the presence of divine justice or retribution, notions of good and evil lose their simple polarity and generate shadowy and unexpected complexities. William Blake, to put it starkly, had called conventional good evil and conventional (in his sense of energetic, inventive, liberating) evil good. Again starkly, *Moby Dick* seems to ask what is good and what is evil, and to assert that the struggle is not between any external forces but rather within the turbulence of the mind. The solipsism or even narcissism of Ahab is quite evident: his wife and children receive only passing or even careless mention; he masterfully preserves his solitude though he is, to begin with, relatively isolated on the open seas; his monomaniacal interest is to pursue his savage and mysterious alter ego which, in costing him his leg, has consumed a part of him. Ocean, isolation, pursuit, monster: no wonder *Moby Dick* seems open to infinite exegesis.

It is at least arguable that the basic traits that make the novel so symbolically suggestive are those deriving eventually from the gothic novel: its simple unsocial setting, its omnicompetent hero, its embodiment of nether forces of the mind, and its "confusion" of conventional good and evil. Even of the claptrap of gothic fiction we discern significant though somewhat reinterpreted remnants. Ahab's single name seems to suggest, like Heathcliff's or Ambrosio's or, for that matter, like Frankenstein's monster's namelessness, a lonely and perhaps sinister independence from social ties. Ahab too is emblematically "stricken" and "blasted" in the scar described as "a slender rod-like mark, lividly white," which may well be the birthmark of a son of Cain. His gaze is withering and imperious, like Vathek's and Melmoth's, when he first confronts his crew. "And not only that, but moody stricken Ahab stood before them with a crucifixion in his face; in all the nameless regal overbearing dignity of some mighty woe." When his black entourage mysteriously appear from below deck, they seem mute supers from an old gothic drama, indeed, from *Vathek*. His mysterious communion with Fedallah, their leader, is a strangely tantalizing version of overt communion with the devil. But since the forces of good and evil must remain complexly intertwined for the success of Melville's sophisticated design, any silly diabolism would destroy the balance. In preserving such balance as he does, Melville interiorizes the struggle and makes it personal, not theological or social. Further gothic traits, such as the prophecies of "the old squaw Tistig" and "Elijah," add minor and less successful touches of the eerie.

Most important is Ahab's pursuit of the whale. It is both a search for significant evil and for his own identity. Only by knowing and conquering the whale can Ahab find peace with himself. It is supremely ironic and instructive that Ahab should perish at the moment of knowledge or, better, self-knowledge. That knowledge, as in the garden of Eden, was the knowledge of evil and good, since not to know evil is, in this world, not to know good. At the very end Ahab seems to pour forth his essence. He urges the billows to carry him on to Moby Dick, and cries out: "Towards thee I roll, thou all-destroying but unconquering whale." He commands Tashtego to nail his banner higher as the ship sinks. Ishmael, the only survivor, sees a "red arm and a hammer" above the waves in their hopeless office. At that moment a sky-hawk plummets down and is caught between the hammer and the spar: "so the bird of heaven, with archangelic shrieks, and his imperial beak thrust upwards, and his whole captive form folded in the flag of Ahab, went down with his ship, which, like Satan, would not sink to hell till she had dragged a living part of heaven with her, and helmeted herself with it." Though the resonances are almost too deafening, we may remember that Ahab's Biblical prototype was indeed regal or imperial Ahab of cursed memory. We also realize that the emblematic bird is an image of falling Lucifer which, in being bound up in the flag of the Pequod, is also richly symbolic of Ahab. Another great hero of defiance, beyond good and evil, has challenged supreme mystery to the death. But is the whale evil and God or Ahab good? That dilemma for exegetes is a heritage of the gothic novel.

In *Frankenstein, Moby Dick,* and *Wuthering Heights* there occurs a final moment of intimate confrontation. After Frankenstein lingeringly dies on Walton's ship, the mysteriously clairvoyant monster appears for the last time in a kind of anguish to know the end of his despairing hope. Walton enters the cabin where his dead friend lies. "Over him hung a form which I cannot find words to describe; gigantic in stature, yet uncouth and distorted in appearance.... When he heard the sound of my approach he ceased to utter exclamations of grief and horror and sprung towards the window." "That is also my victim!" the monster exclaims. "In his murder my crimes are consummated; the miserable series of my being is wound to its close! Oh, Frankenstein! generous and self-devoted [i.e., self-doomed] being! what does it avail that I now ask thee to pardon me? I, who irretrievably destroyed thee by destroying all thou lovedst. Alas! he is cold, he cannot answer me." As in the other two novels, the conclusion is a complex tangle of identities and motives of love and hate, of good and evil. In the last moments of *Moby Dick* Ahab is forcibly caught up by the line that suddenly coils round his neck, rips him from the boat, and binds him forever to the harpoon-studded whale. Whether Moby Dick is fatally "stricken" or simply struck remains an ambiguity of Melville's archaizing diction. At the end of *Wuthering Heights* we see, through the eyes of Lockwood, the final "union" of Cathy and Heathcliff: on his last visit Lockwood lingered around their graves "and wondered how anyone could ever imagine unquiet slumbers, for the sleepers in that quiet earth." But we know enough about the protagonists and their interpreter to take Emily Brontë's masterful conclusion at its fullest ironic ambiguity. The struggle is inconclusive and the suggestion that, despite Lockwood, it continues beyond the grave invokes the timelessness and the implacability of its mental model in the subconscious where there is no time or respite. In all three novels good and evil become in the end emblematically inseparable: there is great good and great evil, but which is really which?

To try to prove any direct influence of this or that gothic novel on the work of Emily Brontë and Herman Melville, one would have to begin with little fact and continue with much conjecture. It may well seem significant that Melville's London publisher made him a present, in late December of 1849 as he was planning *Moby Dick*, of a whole collection of circumstantial evidence: *Vathek*, *The Castle of Otranto*, Zschokke's *The Bravo of Venice* (translated by "Monk" Lewis), William Godwin's *Caleb Williams*, Thomas Hope's *Anastasius*, and *Frankenstein*. Whether he then read or had already read the books is mostly a matter of conjecture. Just how much of the gothic novel Emily Brontë read is still more conjectural. But it is improbable that they knew nothing of the genre and perfectly probable, indeed unmistakable, that they were both significantly influenced by it. Surely no one would dispute that so widely popular a genre could easily and quickly penetrate to the wilderness of Yorkshire or Massachusetts.

One could construct some grandiose theory of the gothic mode and at the same time trace the whole course of its trajectory. In the Renaissance good and evil are distinct opposites, and good, with some exceptions, wins out in the end; in the Baroque good and evil are allowed a more intimate dialogue in which one seems to generate the other and the outcome becomes confusedly profound; in Neoclassicism the result is a mature, worldly-wise accommodation and compromise in which evil is acknowledged and harnessed to good; but in Romanticism good and evil reappear in starkly theatrical and dialectical form, attitudinizing and polemicizing, though strongly suggestive of unexpected new departures, such as that "evil" is really "good." Wicked old archetypes, like Don Juan and Faust, are "reconstructed" as ultimately good. While with Blake conventional "good" is evil and generative "evil" is good, his successors, like Baudelaire, Swinburne, and Lautréamont, attempted at times a kind of protesting diabolism or espousal of the devil as Promethean figure. That Milton's Satan was hailed as a prime ancestor is less reprehensible as an interpretation of seventeenth-century attitudes than it is revealing as a manifestation of nineteenth-century sensibility. Nowadays such diabolism is out of fashion. In fashion are a kind of social determinism (they are that way because society made them so) and a kind of universal sentimentality (they may be rough but they are rough diamonds). Both notions are optimistic, since the implication of even "existential" literature is that once everybody takes the proper view all will be well or at least as well as it will ever be.

To remain so on the surface is both exhilarating and risky. It may seem to the philosopher and theologian either frivolous or irreverent to discourse schematically and summarily on limitlessly profound matters like good and evil. Nevertheless, when notions of good and evil are represented in literature they are at once translated to the esthetic realm and thus exposed to the vicissitudes of convention and taste. Since for gothic novels, and for the novels that followed, the representation of good and evil was momentously important, it is surely a proper topic for literary and historical discussion. Surprisingly perhaps, we may well be convinced that the gothicists for all their outlandish oddities were in effect among the most fruitful literary explorers of the psyche. As citizens of the romantic revolution they plotted their diversionary intrigues and, scarcely aware, found themselves in the vanguard of literary history. Even if we may be inclined to disparage the gothic novel we must still grant that it boldly and often garishly presented fictionally fertile dilemmas of characterization and situation which slipped into the mainstream of Western literature and, along with many other things, helped bring about what we have now.

JAMES RIEGER

"Frankenstein; or, the Modern Prometheus"

. . . only bones abide
There, in the nowhere, where their boats were tossed
Sky-high, where mariners had fabled news
Of IS, the whited monster.

—ROBERT LOWELL

The virgin's wedding dress, the judge's ermine, and the priest's alb are no whiter than the duck jacket, the badge of a crippling and specious innocence, which nearly became Herman Melville's shroud when he fell from the yardarm into the sea. He reminds us in *Moby-Dick* that for all its holy associations, white is the color of the polar bear, the tropical shark, and the albatross; of the revenant and the pale horse of the Apocalypse; of cowardice and the most dread, because invisible, of ocean squalls; of the albino and the leper. Is it for such reasons, he asks, "that there is such a dumb blankness, full of meaning, in a wide landscape of snows—a colorless, all-color of atheism from which we shrink?"

The sky-god of *Prometheus Unbound* perches on a glacier, from which his curses, "Like snow on herbless peaks, fall flake by flake"; under his "wrath's night" humanity "climbs the crags of life, step after step,/ Which wound it, as ice wounds unsandalled feet" (III, i, 12–15). He fails to see that his throne will become a toboggan to perdition as man's mind begins to discharge its collected lightning and Promethean defiance melts into love. "Hark!" Asia cries,

> ... the rushing snow!
> The sun-awakened avalanche! whose mass,
> Thrice sifted by the storm, had gathered there
> Flake after flake, in heaven-defying minds
> As thought by thought is piled, till some great truth
> Is loosened, and the nations echo round,
> Shaken to their roots, as do the mountains now.
>   (II, iii, 36–42)

Jupiter's chthonic counterpart in "Mont Blanc" is "the old Earthquake-daemon," who may have "taught her young/ Ruin" among these "frozen floods" (72–73, 64). Her realm snowblinds the bodily eye, one may say, and allows the poet to imagine the Power beyond her, the "secret Strength of things" which "inhabits" the world of mere appearance and cancels its significance (139, 141). The whiteness reflected by Mont Blanc's congealed coldness opposes that which radiates from *Adonais'* living waters, from the "burning fountain" of Eternity.

The Shelleys visited the Chamouni area from the twenty-first to the twenty-seventh of July, 1816. At noon on the twenty-fifth they reached the top of Montanvert: "We ... behold *le Mer de Glace*. This is the most desolate place in the world; iced mountains surround it." Taking the wife first, let us try to illuminate the practice of each by comparing the metaphoric uses to which the Shelleys put the Sea of Ice. For both it symbolizes those spiritual "desert places" whose "blanker whiteness of benighted snow" scared Robert Frost—who knew too that however one might prefer holocaust,

> ... for destruction ice
> Is also great
> And would suffice.

"FRANKENSTEIN; OR, THE MODERN PROMETHEUS" (1818)

"Mr. Godwin," Hazlitt wrote of *Political Justice* in 1825, "has rendered an essential service to moral science, by attempting (in vain) to pass the Arctic Circle and Frozen Regions, where the understanding is no longer warmed by the affections, nor fanned by the breeze of fancy!" Whether or not Hazlitt nods here towards his old friend's daughter's novel makes little difference. The metaphor is just, as the narrative frame of Robert Walton's voyage to discover the secret of the magnet is the absolutely right emblem of Victor Frankenstein's researches into the *elixir vitae*:

"I try in vain," Walton writes to his sister in England,

to be persuaded that the pole is the seat of frost and desolation; it ever presents itself to my imagination as the region of beauty and delight. There, Margaret, the sun is for ever visible; its broad disk just skirting the horizon, and diffusing a perpetual splendour.... there snow and frost are banished; and, sailing over a calm sea, we may be wafted to a land surpassing in wonders and in beauty every region hitherto discovered on the habitable globe.... What may not be expected in a country of eternal light? I may there discover the wondrous power which attracts the needle.

But from that sun no heat. The connection between brilliant light and freezing cold reverses Milton's dark flames and signifies a direct ratio of increase between the knowledge and the loneliness of all northward discoverers. The metaphor is second in importance only to that of the sea-voyage itself. "I desire," says Walton, "the company of a man who could sympathise with me; whose eyes would reply to mine. You may deem me romantic, my dear sister, but I bitterly feel the want of a friend." This cordial lack is felt too by Frankenstein, whom Walton is quick to clasp, shortly after their meeting, as "the brother of my heart." But Frankenstein sees this sympathy for what it really is: "'Unhappy man! Do you share my madness?'"

The absurdity of Walton's belief in eternal light at the pole is an obvious but necessary feature of Mary Shelley's metaphoric irony. The expedition sets sail from Archangel shortly after the vernal equinox and is given up in September, when the ship is locked fast in ice, and night begins again to assert her ancient prerogative. The allegorical meaning is plain: absolute isolation is reached before absolute enlightenment. The arctic frost of the soul is revealed as the only ignorance, and when the novel ends, seasonal darkness is about to bury all.

Mrs. Shelley's use of the sea-voyage to signify the self-destructive pride of an adventurous soul clearly reflects her husband's influence. Even Henry Clerval's removal to the university at Ingolstadt is described as "'a voyage of discovery to the land of knowledge.'" The image is also Coleridgean. "I am going," Walton announces, "to unexplored regions, to 'the land of mist and snow'; but I shall kill no albatross." The major application of the metaphor is reserved for Frankenstein; as Walton puts it, "Strange and harrowing must be his story; frightful the storm which embraced the gallant vessel on its course, and wrecked it—thus!" The scientist's moment of greatest moral confusion is that preceding his nervous breakdown, when he has reneged on his bargain to create a mate for the monster. Having fallen asleep in the skiff he has taken out to drown the remains of his experiment, he wakes to find himself compassless on the ocean, with "the sun ... of little benefit to me." Where is either the true or the magnetic North? With prophetic irony—for a harsher doom is reserved—"I looked upon the sea, it was to be my grave."

The crime of the "modern Prometheus" is partly the conventional overreacher's wish to "explore unknown powers, and unfold to the world the deepest mysteries of creation. "The words of fate, enounced to destroy me," are contained in Professor Waldman's introductory lecture on the modern chemists, who "'penetrate into the recesses of nature. . . . ascend into the heavens. . . . command the thunders of heaven, mimic the earthquake, and even mock the invisible world with its own shadows.'" Equally important is Frankenstein's lifelong exaltation of the technological understanding (Godwin's and Shelley's "reason") at the expense of sensibility and imagination. Unlike Clerval, who reminds one of Godwin's Falkland as he forms his childhood values out of "books of chivalry and romance," Frankenstein's leading passion is a "thirst for knowledge. . . . The world was to me a secret which I desired to divine. Curiosity, earnest research to learn the hidden laws of nature . . . are among the earliest sensations I can remember." Is his curiosity any less damnable than Caleb Williams' old-womanish nosiness because its object is not human? The answer depends on whether the source of life is material or divine. Mary Shelley seems content to wonder. But Frankenstein himself has little doubt regarding "the metaphysical, or, in its highest sense, the physical secrets of the world."

Muriel Spark asks the reader of the later chapters of *Frankenstein* to "visualise this pattern of pursuit as a sort of figure-of-eight *macabaresque*, executed by two partners moving with the virtuosity of skilled ice-skaters." The compass-directions followed are significant at all times. As Walton voyages towards the pole, Frankenstein goes north to study at Ingolstadt and later removes from Geneva to the Orkneys to set up the laboratory in which he has promised to create a female monster. So long as he considers himself primarily an intellectual, he is the slave of the magnet and of his artifact, although the monster does not address him as such—"'You are my creator, but I am your master'"—until, having fruitlessly tracked him to his northern workshop, it has no further use for him.

Frankenstein then reverses his moral and geographical direction, flying southward to restore his frozen heart. He marries Elizabeth Lavenza in Geneva, and they plan to honeymoon even further south at Como. Their destination lies precisely east southeast, but the great *massif* of the Alps bars their way. The new husband decides "to commence our journey by water, sleeping that night at Evian"; he makes the characteristic and fatal error of trying to reach the south by setting out in a northerly direction. They sail towards Elizabeth's strangulation, for the mateless monster has resolved to execute the *lex talionis*. Forgetfully (as we shall see), Frankenstein thinks of Mont Blanc as "beautiful," and with even greater irony Elizabeth finds the play of clouds above it "'interesting.'" At other times, "coasting the opposite banks, we saw the mighty Jura"—the antithesis of overreaching, an emblem of domestic humanity—"opposing its dark side to the ambition that would quit its native country."

When Frankenstein's love was frustrated by death, "I awakened to reason, at the same time awakened to revenge." *Eros*, thwarted, yields *thanatos*. The destructive urge becomes "'the devouring and only passion of my soul'" as scientific curiosity had been earlier. Reason and revenge are sides of a coin. Fire and ice, Promethean desire and polar hate, are both opposed to love, and both drive fanatics north. Between these intemperate extremes lies the warmth by which men live.

Invoking "'thee, O Night, and the spirits that preside over thee'" to his aid, Frankenstein begins the chase to the sunlit, frozen Arctic, where the monster will be in his own element, the reverse of Lucifer's dark flames. "'I seek,'" he tells his maker, "'the everlasting ices of the north, where you will feel the misery of cold and frost to which I am impassive.'" This is the kingdom of uncircumscribed intellect, where the moral needle vacillates ever more wildly as the voyager nears his goal. As in *Caleb Williams*, what appears to be a one-sided blood-hunt is actually a campaign of mutual harassment, a game of catch-me-if-you-can. Neither antagonist is free to break out of the charmed figure-eight danced upon the frozen sea, an antipastoral setting as jail-like as Caleb's England. For the monster, like the rationalist, is "'filled ... with an insatiable thirst for vengeance'" and is "'the slave, not the master, of an impulse which I detested, yet could not disobey.'"

The monster had earlier seized the Arve glacier for his domain, as Milton's Devil embraced his horrors and profoundest hell: "'the caves of ice, which I only do not fear, are a dwelling to me. ... These bleak skies I hail.'" Mont Blanc is the southern prototype of the frozen ocean. Frankenstein's first conversation with his creature takes place here, amid summits which Mrs. Shelley described in her *Journal* as "higher one would think than the safety of God would permit, since it is well known that the Tower of Babel did not nearly equal them in immensity." The glacier fills Frankenstein "with a sublime ecstasy that gave wings to the soul, and allowed it to soar from the obscure world to light and joy." The three aesthetic categories of Burke and Uvedale Price are used several times and with precision in this scene. Mary Shelley meant the mountain to be literally terrible in its beauty, just as Babel's sublime tower, the proudest artifact of the overweening, geometrical understanding, was awful in its temerity.

The twofold metaphor of ice and sunlight, emblematic of the unlawful quest, recurs here from Walton's opening reverie and anticipates the climactic encounter at the pole: "The sea, or rather the vast river of ice, wound among its dependent mountains, whose aerial summits hung over its recesses. Their icy and glittering peaks shone in the sunlight over the clouds." When Frankenstein first approaches Mont Blanc through the Arve ravine, it seems to him that the precipices speak of "a power mighty as Omnipotence." The "white and shining pyramids and domes" appear, in the chill sunlight, "as belonging to another earth, the habitations of another race of beings." The summits are "the faces of those mighty friends." But when he stands on the Mer de Glace and invokes their help ("'Wandering spirits, if indeed ye wander, and do not rest in your narrow beds'"), he conjures up only the monster, who comes bounding towards him over the crevasses "with superhuman speed."

A higher power does govern man in the material universe, but Frankenstein is cruelly deluded every time he thinks of it as benevolent. The diction and sentiments of what he rejects as superstition are closer to actuality: "the evil influence, the Angel of Destruction . . . asserted omnipotent sway over me from the moment I turned my reluctant steps from my father's door." He cannot make up his mind. At the end of the book, when he knows he must die unsatisfied, he persists in thinking that "the ministers of vengeance" are on his side and will conduct the monster into Walton's hands.

Mary Shelley's irony is too obvious when Frankenstein, pursuing the blood-trail northward, insists that "a spirit of good followed and directed my steps; and, when I most murmured, would suddenly extricate me from seemingly insurmountable difficulties. Sometimes, when nature, overcome by hunger, sunk under exhaustion, a repast was prepared for me in the desert that restored and inspirited me." On the next page more manna—this time a dead hare—is left for him by the monster with a note explaining that the scientist must be kept alive until they wrestle to the death at the pole. Even in these last hours of his madness, Frankenstein has half-glimpses of the source of his vindictive efficiency: "I pursued my path towards the destruction of the daemon more as a task enjoined by heaven, as the mechanical impulse of some power of which I was unconscious, than as the ardent desire of my soul."

The world does in fact wag on its poles by a mechanical impulse. Godwin's materialistic Necessity is felt through his daughter's whole creation as magnetism, animal and mineral. It draws the desiring needle, shudders through the scientist's "soul" as the fixed idea, and awakens the constituent clay of his laboratory Adam. Frankenstein never realizes that his self-destructive vengeance is predicated on his murderous curiosity. The perfect incarnation of this power, its Logos and filius dilectus, is the prosy monster. Its court of judgment is the arctic ice-cap, and its thrones the pole and Mont Blanc. Mary Shelley keeps the Fates who drive her antagonists morally neutral. The magnetic chemist has not so much defied them as he has interloped in a game which only they know how to play and win. They permit him, in accordance with the rules, to get himself into trouble, but as croupiers everywhere with any amateur, they refuse to get him out again. Shelley's "Strength... Which governs thought" is neither malevolent nor insane in his wife's book. It is mindless.

Frost and fire join once more in the suicide that ends the novel. "'I shall quit your vessel,'" the monster tells Walton, "'on the ice-raft which brought me thither, and shall seek the most northern extremity of the globe; I shall collect my funeral pile and consume to ashes this miserable frame, that its remains may afford no light to any curious and unhallowed wretch who would create such another as I have been.'" The monster is more than a sentimental *Urmensch*, corrupted from original benevolence into a principle of daemonic, insouciant, self-propelled violence by the frustration of love, which should have been his birthright. He is a botched and dangerous experiment which, in destroying itself, discredits the scientific understanding in whose name and image it was made. Hazlitt's words on the final historical import of Godwinian reason may be applied to the monster:

> if it is admitted that Reason alone is not the sole and self-sufficient ground of morals, it is to Mr. Godwin that we are indebted for having settled the point. No one denied or distrusted this principle (before his time) as the absolute judge and interpreter in all questions of difficulty; and if this is no longer the case, it is because he has taken this principle, and followed it into its remotest consequences with more keenness of eye and steadiness of hand than any other expounder of ethics. His grand work is (at least) an *experimentum crucis* to show the weak sides and imperfections of human reason as the sole law of human action.

The flames to which the crucial experiment consigns himself redeem nothing and mean nothing. They are not purgatorial, nor are they pentecostal tongues, like those Eliot thinks of at Little Gidding on a midwinter afternoon, when, "with frost and fire,/ The brief sun flames the ice, on pond and ditches,/ In windless cold that is the heart's heat." Intellectual fire, Yeats says, consumes everything that is not God. But when the creator is a flesh-and-blood intellectualist and his Adam literally the reason's naked self, then the Promethean element, eating up itself, leaves only the obscure night of the Arctic winter and of the atheist's spiritual negation.

What, meanwhile, of the Rationalist himself? As he lies dying on a ship locked in the ice, Frankenstein reproves Walton's mutinous sailors in words that recall yet another voyager:

> Are you then so easily turned from your design? Did you not call this a glorious expedition? And wherefore was it glorious? Not because the way was smooth and placid as a southern sea, but because it was full of dangers and terror; because at every new incident your fortitude was to be called forth and your courage exhibited; because danger and death surrounded it, and these you were to brave and overcome. For this was it a glorious, for

this was it an honourable undertaking. You were hereafter to be hailed as
the benefactors of your species.... Oh! be men, or be more than men. Be
steady to your purposes and firm as a rock. This ice is not made of such
stuff as your hearts may be; it is mutable and cannot withstand you if you
say that it shall not.

Or, as it has been better put,

> Considerate la vostra semenza:
> Fatti non foste a viver come bruti,
> Ma per seguir virtute e canoscenza.
>
> (*Inf.*, XXVI, 118–120)

Ulysses, the smooth-tongued, speaks from the flames reserved in the
eighth Malebolgia for evil counselors. At one edge of the known world lies
Caucasus, with its writhing Titan; in the southern hemisphere, beyond
Hercules' pillars, "Acciò che l'uom più oltre non si metta," Purgatory rises
from the sea. And at the pole, as Walton's ship swings southward in fright,
another beacon, the pyre of the self-immolated monster, blazes out its
warning against the proud, the curious, the obsessed and solitary.

It is hard to remember one's origins at the pole, and how one was
meant to live. In such utter isolation, one's private moral compass seems the
least untrustworthy guide, together with that "private opinion" which,
according to Hobbes, sometimes renders the Greek *hairesis*. The accumulated wisdom of men and the claims of the affections are too distant to bear
thinking of, even if the cold would permit it.

A generation later, Melville's questing Pierre disregards this lesson in
moral geography. The magnet draws him on ever faster and faster until it
holds him paralyzed against the frozen iron:

> In those Hyperborean regions, to which enthusiastic Truth, and Earnest-
> ness, and Independence, will invariably lead a mind fitted by nature for
> profound and fearless thought, all objects are seen in a dubious, uncertain,
> and refracting light. Viewed through that rarefied atmosphere the most
> immemorially admitted maxims of men begin to slide and fluctuate, and
> finally become wholly inverted....
>
> But the example of many minds forever lost, like undiscoverable
> Arctic explorers, amid those treacherous regions, warns us entirely away
> from them; and we learn that it is not for man to follow the trail of truth
> too far, since by so doing he entirely loses the directing compass of his
> mind; for arrived at the Pole, to whose barrenness only it points, there, the
> needle indifferently respects all points of the horizon alike.

WILLIAM A. WALLING

Victor Frankenstein's Dual Role

The implications of *Frankenstein* can be seen to cut much more deeply than would a mere expatiation upon the wisdom of Pope's couplet of a century earlier: "*Know thy own point: This kind, this due degree/Of blindness, weakness, Heaven bestows on thee.*" (Essay on Man, I, 283–84). Indeed, it is quite clear that *Frankenstein*, like Shelley's *Alastor* (1816), reflects a most ambiguous attitude toward the conflict between the individual desire for fulfillment and the persistent social demand for the compromise of individuality necessary in human relationships.

Thus in Shelley's poem, both subtitle (*The Spirit of Solitude*) and preface seem to promise the reader a reassuring poetic homily—in the best eighteenth-century tradition—on the sturdy superiority of social virtues. "The picture [given in the poem of the central figure's disappointment and death] is not barren of instruction to actual men," Shelley writes in the preface. "The Poet's self-centred seclusion was avenged by the furies [the avenging spirit of solitude] of an irresistible passion pursuing him to speedy ruin. . . . Among those who attempt to exist without human sympathy, the pure and tender-hearted perish through the intensity and passion of their search after its communities, when the vacancy of their spirit suddenly makes itself felt." Yet, in the poem itself, the reassuring social moral dissolves under the glorification of the dead Poet who rejected all but his own, personal dream:

> Art and eloquence,
> And all the shows o' the world are frail and vain

From *Mary Shelley*. Copyright © 1972 by Twayne Publishers, division of G. K. Hall & Co., Boston.

> To weep a loss that turns their lights to shade.
> It is a woe "too deep for tears," when all
> Is reft at once, when some surpassing Spirit,
> Whose light adorned the world around it, leaves
> Those who remain behind, not sobs or groans,
> The passionate tumult of a clinging hope;
> But pale despair and cold tranquillity.
>
> (Alastor, 710–18)

And so it is in *Frankenstein*, where the ostensible didactic surface is undercut by quite contradictory implications. For, if we can argue that the over-all effect of Frankenstein's "tale" upon Walton is to cause the would-be explorer, however reluctantly, to view his earlier dreams of glory as "mad," it is equally certain that in the heart of Frankenstein, even as he dies, burns an unrepentant flame of hope: "Farewell, Walton! Seek happiness in tranquillity and avoid ambition, even if it be only the apparently innocent one of distinguishing yourself in science and discoveries. Yet why do I say this? I have myself been blasted in these hopes, yet another may succeed." And the persistence of this dream, even in the face of the most painful disillusionment, suggests a secondary, subversive theme: that in the very nature of man, under the present conditions of spiritual and social oppression, a radical split resides, condemning him to a perpetual sense of nonfulfillment.

When we recognize this aspect of the novel, the uneasiness of the first reviewers becomes more understandable. The review article in the *Edinburgh Review*, for example, spoke of "views . . . bordering too closely on impiety," and then complained that, although a sound moral (that is, one congenial to the conservative spirit of Pope's couplet) might be found in *Frankenstein*, the author had gone much too far in the audacity of his imagination: "Some of our highest and most reverential feelings receive a shock from the conception on which [the book] turns, so as to produce a painful and bewildered state of mind while we peruse it. . . . It might, indeed, be the author's view to shew that the powers of man have been wisely limited, and that misery would follow their extension,—but still the expression, 'Creator', applied to a mere human being, gives us [a sensation] of shock."

Nor, of course, was this sensation of "shock" anything but an intended effect on Mary's part. The subtitle to *Frankenstein* is *The Modern Prometheus*; and the novel's epigraph is taken from *Paradise Lost* (X. 743–45): "*Did I request thee, Maker, from my clay,/To mould me Man, did I solicit thee/ From darkness to promote me?*" That is, the unmistakable implication of both together is to cast Victor Frankenstein in a dual role. On the one hand, he is that Promethean figure striving against human limitations to bring more light and benefit to mankind—a sort of prose Shelley, as it were, at least in the early stages of his career. On the other hand, as the novel proceeds and Frankenstein carries out the traditional achievement of Prometheus by forming and giving life to man, he clearly transcends his merely Promethean aspect and becomes, in the texture of the novel, a version of the "Creator"— of God Himself. And in this second role—especially in the relationship between Frankenstein and his creature—we find a pervasive criticism of orthodox piety.

"All men hate the wretched," the monster declares to Frankenstein; "how, then, must I be hated, who am miserable beyond all living things! Yet you, my creator, detest and spurn me, thy creature" (Chapter 10). Still later, as the monster recalls the anguish he has endured because the life given him has fallen so short of his innate desires, he cries bitterly to Frankenstein: "Cursed, cursed creator! Why did I live? Why... did I not extinguish the spark of existence which you had so wantonly bestowed?" (Chapter 16). In other words, what Mary Shelley is clearly doing, through the monster, is asserting one fundamental ground for denying the concept of a benevolent deity. Since man is so undeniably limited under the present order of things—so frequently oppressed by his sense of incompleteness—then his existence, at least as the orthodox conceive it, must be regarded more as a curse than as a blessing.

And this suggestion that the present ruling power of the world falls short of benevolence is expanded into an implication of actual tyranny through the fusion in the monster of the two central Christian symbols of the loss of divine favor—Satan and Adam. "Oh, Frankenstein," the monster pleads, "be not equitable to every other and trample upon me alone, to whom thy justice, and even thy clemency and affection, is most due. Remember that I am thy creature; I ought to be thy Adam, but I am rather the fallen angel, whom thou drivest from joy for no misdeed" (Chapter 10). Again, in his account of the effect the reading of *Paradise Lost* has had upon him, the monster, by his ignorance of the true condition of fallen Adam, suggests once more the theme of divine oppression:

> But *Paradise Lost* excited different and far deeper emotions. I read it, as I had read the other volumes which had fallen into my hands, as a true history. It moved every feeling of wonder and awe that the picture of an omnipotent God warring with his creatures was capable of exciting. I often referred the several situations, as their similarity struck me, to my own. Like Adam, I was apparently united by no link to any other being in existence; but his state was far different from mine in every other respect. He had come forth from the hands of God a perfect creature, happy and prosperous, guarded by the especial care of his Creator; he was allowed to converse with and acquire knowledge from beings of a superior nature, but I was wretched, helpless, and alone. Many times I considered Satan as the

fitter emblem of my condition, for often, like him, when I viewed the bliss of my protectors [the family he is living near], the bitter gall of envy rose within me.

(Chapter 15)

For, if the monster looks upon Adam's condition as preferable to Satan's, Victor Frankenstein is himself corrective to that illusion. As a composite of "Modern Prometheus," fallen Adam, and enchained Satan, Frankenstein asserts an identity among all three, as well as pointing to the disintegrative sense of incompleteness that is man's fate under the orthodox deity. "Sweet and beloved Elizabeth!" Frankenstein says to Walton, likening himself to Adam as he recalls the period leading to his marriage. "I read and reread her letter, and some softened feelings stole into my heart and dared to whisper paradisiacal dreams of love and joy; but the apple was already eaten, and the angel's arm bared to drive me from all hope" (Chapter 22). And later, as Frankenstein draws near to death, he points to the similarity between his destiny and that of Prometheus and Satan:

> My feelings are profound, but I possessed a coolness of judgment that fitted me for illustrious achievements. This sentiment of the worth of my nature supported me while others would have been oppressed, for I deemed it criminal to throw away in useless grief those talents that might be useful to my fellow creatures. When I reflected on the work I had completed, no less a one than the creation of a sensitive and rational animal, I could not rank myself with the herd of common projectors. But this thought, which supported me in the commencement of my career, now serves only to plunge me lower in the dust. All my speculations and hopes are as nothing, and like the archangel who aspired to omnipotence, I am chained in an eternal hell.

In this respect, then, in the novel's presentation of Victor Frankenstein as a "Modern Prometheus" condemned to suffer guilt and isolation for the grandeur of his aspirations, *Frankenstein* comes remarkably close to the theme of Byron's own "Prometheus," written in the summer of 1816 while Mary was working on the earlier stages of her book. "Titan!" Byron apostrophizes,

> ... to thee the strife was given
>   Between the suffering and the will,
>   Which torture where they cannot kill:
> And the inexorable Heaven,
> And the deaf tyranny of Fate,
> The ruling principle of Hate,
> Which for its pleasure doth create
> The things it may annihilate.
>
> Like thee, man is in part divine,

A troubled stream from a pure source;
And man in portions can foresee
His own funereal destiny;
His wretchedness and his resistance,
And his sad unallied existence.

And this similarity between poem and novel takes on unusual significance when we realize how much light it sheds on a relatively neglected question: the interrelationship and interinfluence among three people that summer—Shelley, Byron, and Mary. For Byron, as we know, produced his "Prometheus" as the direct result of Shelley's translation of Aeschylus' drama; Shelley, in his turn, if we are to believe the Byron scholars, drew from this contact with Byron the original impetus for what was to culminate in his masterpiece, *Prometheus Unbound* (1818–19). But what no one seems to have recognized, at least so far as I have been able to discover, is that Mary's novel provides in many places a transitional point between the Byronic view of Prometheus (as evidenced in his short poem) and the Shelleyan transformation of the Titan in *Prometheus Unbound*.

Thus, Harold Bloom is quite right when he points to Mary's enrichment of the Promethean theme by her concentration on the "equivocal potentialities" inherent in the Titan's symbolic nature. But we might add that in Byron's short poem these "equivocal potentialities" are largely ignored while Mary has chosen to employ in her treatment of the Promethean theme a more genuinely intellectual and philosophical interest than Byron (characteristically) cared to do. For no matter how well intentioned the bringer of knowledge may be, he inevitably also brings to mankind the painful consequence of increased consciousness: an exacerbated capacity to comprehend man's alienation from the oneness of the truly divine. And so in her novel Mary links Frankenstein's achievement to the imagery of Eden and to the sense of loss which followed the Fall. "You seek for knowledge and wisdom, as I once did," Frankenstein tells Walton; "and I ardently hope that the gratification of your wishes may not be a serpent to sting you, as mine has been." And the monster echoes this paradoxical sense of loss-through-gain, complaining to his creator in a cry that we have come increasingly to recognize as the anguish of the modern sensibility: "Increase of knowledge only discovered to me more clearly what a wretched outcast I was" (Chapter 15).

Furthermore, although a sound argument could easily be made to view Frankenstein's continuing aspiration (even though defeated and dying) as a Byronic defiance of "inexorable Heaven," we would be unfair to the richness of Mary's dual conception not to see also that Frankenstein's other role—as "Creator"—suggests a most Shelleyan attitude toward the composite tyranny of the world.

Clearest of all, of course, is the indication that Frankenstein is far from omnipotent. Like "the erroneous and degrading idea which men have conceived of a Supreme Being" (preface to *The Revolt of Islam*) and like the presentation of Jupiter in *Prometheus Unbound*, the figure of Frankenstein is shown to depart from his dream of becoming godlike in direct proportion to his failure to love. Indeed, it is clear that the motive for the creation itself—the desire in Frankenstein to bring forth "a new species" that "would bless me as its creator and source" (Chapter 4)—springs from a spirit within him that wishes to assert its own selfhood over others. And so, as Frankenstein continues his enumeration of the advantages of becoming a creator, he declares: "Many happy and excellent natures would owe their being to me. No father could claim the gratitude of his child so completely as I should deserve theirs." In short, what Frankenstein is denying here is the very principle on which love must rest—that principle which, in the year of the novel's completion, Shelley was to call "Eldest of things, divine Equality!"

Consequently, the creation proceeds in a necessarily grotesque fashion, the Creator viewing his material not with the eyes of love but with the limited vision of the selfhood, unduly ready to impose itself by the assertion of "differences" and not "similitudes":

> As the minuteness of the parts formed a great hindrance to my speed, I resolved, contrary to my first intention, to make the being of a gigantic stature, that is to say, about eight feet in height, and proportionately large. After having formed this determination and having spent some months in successfully collecting and arranging my materials, I began....
>
> How can I describe my emotions at this catastrophe, or how delineate the wretch whom with such infinite pains and care I had endeavoured to form? His limbs were in proportion, and I had selected his features as beautiful. Beautiful! Great God! His yellow skin scarcely covered the work of muscles and arteries beneath; his hair was of a lustrous black, and flowing; his teeth of a pearly whiteness; but these luxuriances only formed a more horrid contrast with his watery eyes, that seemed almost of the same colour as the dun-white sockets in which they were set, his shrivelled complexion and straight black lips.
>
> (Chapters 4, 5)

And, when the monster turns upon his creator to reproach him, the speech he utters reverberates with the full implications of the ironic version of Genesis that Mary has already given us. "Accursed creator! Why did you form a monster so hideous that even *you* turned from me in disgust? God, in pity, made man beautiful and alluring, after his own image; but my form is a filthy type of yours, more horrid even from the very resemblance" (Chapter 15). In other words, a close reading of *Frankenstein* suggests that, even in the orthodox version of the creation, the deity must be held accountable for a failure of love; for he deliberately (and selfishly) chose to make man an imperfect image of himself.

And the full Shelleyan strategy of rebuttal—barely implicit in *Frankenstein* through Victor Frankenstein's dying speech of continued hope, followed soon afterward by the monster's outburst of pity for his creator—originates from a conception that is surely present both in Mary's novel and in Shelley's own poetry: that the supposed omnipotence of the deity is purely illusory and that his powers (as well as the powers of all those who simulate his show of dominance) are limited most surely by an imaginative failure to perceive that love, as the eternal principle of life, must lie at the foundation of all things.

A critical reading of *Frankenstein*, then, provides a rich insight into some of the central conflicts of the age that we agree to call Romantic (and, indeed, into some of the most pressing contradictions in Mary Shelley's own mind). On the one hand, the over-all curve of Walton's experience seemingly suggests the futility of aspiration: that man, to use Frankenstein's own words, is wisest when he "believes his native town to be the world." On the other hand, when we look more closely into the novel, we see that the presentation of Victor Frankenstein's character reveals a secondary, subversive theme that itself unfolds into a duality. To speak somewhat unfairly of Mary's achievement, we might say that Frankenstein is presented in his defeat as a Byronic oyster who possibly (and unwittingly) contains a Shelleyan pearl. For, while it is clear that at the end of the novel Frankenstein is portrayed as a radically divided Prometheus who is unable, even on his deathbed, to reconcile man's hopeless conflict between his emotional nature and his intellectual aspirations, it is equally implicit that his true failure stems from the poverty of his imagination and from the inadequacy of his love.

Nor, of course, do such analogues in any sense detract from the stature of *Frankenstein* in its own right. Rather, they indicate the novel's remarkable centrality to an age in which its most brilliant minds were compelled to struggle with a profound sense of conflict: that between an entrenched and powerful system tending toward conservatism in almost every field of human experience (the most concrete example of which was the Congress of Vienna), and an enormous surge of unorganized pyschic energy demanding new forms (social, moral, and political) that would be more nearly commensurate with the individual's increased awareness of his needs. And perhaps Shelley himself provides in the preface to *Prometheus Unbound*, the definitive statement on the question of the individual writer's relationship to the climate of his time: "It is impossible that any one who inhabits the same age with such writers as those who stand in the foremost ranks of our own, can conscientiously assure himself that his language and tone of thought may not have been modified by the study of the productions of those extraordinary intellects."—"Extraordinary intellects," indeed, were those two poets who met on the shore of Lake Geneva and who provided, by their very friendship of opposites, the ideational and emotional stimulus to Mary's most famous novel.

ROBERT KIELY

"Frankenstein"

It is something of a miracle that *Frankenstein*, originally published in 1818, has survived its admirers and critics. Although Scott had admired the Germanic flavor of *The Monk*, he praised the author of *Frankenstein* for writing in "plain and forcible English, without exhibiting that mixture of hyperbolical Germanisms with which tales of wonder are usually told." On the other hand, Beckford, who had little use for earnest horror, noted on the flyleaf of his first edition copy of *Frankenstein:* "This is, perhaps, the foulest Toadstool that has yet sprung up from the reeking dunghill of the present times."

Opinion about *Frankenstein* was strong from the beginning, but no critical thinking on the subject was more elaborate and self-conscious than that of Mary Shelley herself. The genesis of this novel was—even for a work of romantic fiction—uncommonly bookish and artificial. It was supposedly begun as part of a literary contest among Shelley, Mary, Byron, and Polidori to write a ghost story in a vein popular in Germany and France. During the first year of her marriage to Shelley, Mary had set herself a formidable and exotic reading assignment which included *Clarissa, The Sorrows of Young Werter, Lara, The Arabian Nights, Wieland, St. Leon, La Nouvelle Héloïse, Vathek, Waverley, The Mysteries of Udolpho, The Italian, The Monk,* and *Edgar Huntley.* She repeatedly acknowledged the influence of Milton and Coleridge during this period of her life and, of course, Godwin and Shelley were major forces in shaping her mind.

Frankenstein seems a little book to have borne up under such a mixed and mighty company of sponsors, midwives, and ancestors. Mary Shelley

From *The Romantic Novel in England.* Copyright © 1972 by the President and Fellows of Harvard College. Harvard University Press.

did not set out, like her father, to write a philosophical novel, yet her most famous work, written at Shelley's suggestion and dedicated to Godwin, is, to a large extent, an expression of her reaction to the philosophy and character of these two men. In places the narrative seems chiefly to provide the occasion for Mary to write a tribute to her father's idealism and a love poem to her husband. The hero of her novel, the young Genevese student of natural science, is a magnetic character, described by one admiring friend as possessing attributes which seem almost divine:

> Sometimes I have endeavoured to discover what quality it is which he possesses that elevates him so immeasurably above any other person I ever knew. I believe it to be an intuitive discernment; a quick but never-failing power of judgment; a penetration into the causes of things, unequalled for clearness and precision; add to this a facility of expression, and a voice whose varied intonations are soul-subduing music.

Yet despite such expressions of love and veneration for the nobility of Frankenstein, Mary expresses through her characters certain reservations about him which have led some readers to interpret the novel as an unconscious repudiation of Shelley. As M. K. Joseph puts it, "With unassuming originality, [Mary's] 'modern Prometheus' challenges the whole myth of Romantic titanism, of Shelley's neo-Platonic apocalypse in *Prometheus Unbound*, and of the artist as Promethean creator." Frankenstein is brilliant, passionate, sensitive, and capable of arousing feelings of profound sympathy in others, yet he is the creator of a monster which causes great suffering and finally destroys his maker. Signs of impatience and outright disgust with the obsessive ambitions of the hero are certainly present in the narrative.

Still, Frankenstein remains the hero throughout; he is the "divine wanderer," his face lighted up by "a beam of benevolence and sweetness," his spirit enlivened by a "supernatural enthusiasm." He is compared not with Faustus but with Prometheus in his desire to grasp "the secrets of heaven and earth." No one suffers more than he from his failure, and, indeed, there is a strong hint that the fault is more nature's than his that his godlike ambitions result in a monstrosity. For Mary, as for Shelley, nature's imperfect character only confirmed a belief in the superiority of mind over matter. After her husband's death, Mary referred to him as "a spirit caged, an elemental being, enshrined in a frail image," and confessed her reverence for the artist who would rather destroy his health than accept the limitations imposed by the body, whose "delicately attuned [mind] shatters the material frame, and whose thoughts are strong enough to throw down and dilapidate the walls of sense and dikes of flesh that the unimaginative contrive to keep in such good repair."

In her novel *The Last Man*, published eight years after *Frankenstein*,

Mary's narrator takes it as a universal truth "that man's mind alone was the creator of all that was good or great to man, and that Nature herself was only his first minister." And in that same novel there is a character named Adrian, even more obviously patterned after Shelley than is Frankenstein, whose "slight frame was overinformed by the soul that dwelt within." The fact that he is "all mind" does eventually make him behave strangely, but the implication is that the fault is the world's or society's, not his.

Applying the same logic to Frankenstein's attempt to manufacture a man, one might argue that the structural faultiness, the grotesqueness of the result, is another example of nature's failure to live up to man's expectations. Even the fact that the monster becomes a murderer and brings about the destruction of his master does not necessarily detract from the grandeur of Frankenstein's dreams. If he has not been able to create human life, he has been able to create a sublime facsimile. To some, a destructive force was still better than no force at all and the creation of a new menace better than a copy of a worn-out consolation. The Shelleys, like their friends Byron and M. G. Lewis, were fascinated by the correspondence between the terrifying and the magnificent, the proximity of ruinous and constructive forces at the highest levels of experience. "Nothing should shake the truly great spirit which is not sufficiently mighty to destroy it," said Shelley in reference to the personal relationships of geniuses. The risk of calamity becomes the measure of all endeavor, and a great catastrophe is preferable to a small success. Viewed in this way the catastrophic abomination represented by Frankenstein's creature is not proof of its creator's folly, but an inverse indication of his potential greatness.

Potentiality is a key concept in the delineation of Frankenstein's character because, like so many romantic heroes, much of his allure derives from what he might have been, what he almost was, rather than from what he is. "What a glorious creature must he have been in the days of his prosperity," says his friend Walton, "when he is thus noble and godlike in ruin! He seems to feel his own worth and the greatness of his fall." The days of Frankenstein's prosperity do not occupy much of the narrative, but it is nonetheless clear that Walton is not altogether right. Though a good and gifted person before his "ruin," it is really afterward, by means of the uniqueness and depth of his suffering, that Frankenstein achieves superiority over other men. Having made a botch of his experiment, he may fail to impress any but the most loyal advocates in the days of his prosperity. But where actual achievement falters, the guilty and disappointed spirit can sketch the dimensions of its unfulfilled intention by describing the magnitude of its torment. We are reminded of Macaulay's remark about Byron: "He continued to repeat that to be wretched is the destiny of all; that to be eminently wretched, is the destiny of the eminent."

II

Superiority through suffering is a major theme of Mary Shelley's novel, a romantic half-tragedy in which the fall from greatness is nearly all fall or, more accurately, where greatness is defined in terms of the personal pain which results from the consciousness of loss which cannot be recalled or comprehended by other men. In unique regret, Frankenstein discovers his true distinction: "I was seized by remorse and the sense of guilt which hurried me away to a hell of intense tortures, such as no language can describe." The failure of language, as always in romantic fiction, is meant to be a sign not of vacuity or of an imaginative limitation of the character or author, but of the singular noncommunicable nature of great experience.

It is unfortunate (though psychologically fitting) that in the popular mind the monster has assumed the name of his creator, because Mary Shelley considered it of some importance that the creature remain un-named. As Elizabeth Nitchie points out, it was the custom in dramatic performances of *Frankenstein* to represent the monster's part on the playbill with "_____." On first remarking this, Mary Shelley was pleased: "This nameless mode of naming the unnameable is rather good." If the phenome-non itself cannot be named, neither can the feelings it evokes in its maker. No one can know what it is like to be the monster or its "parent."

What cannot be described cannot be imitated, and the pain it causes cannot be relieved. The following lines are Frankenstein's, but they might as easily have been spoken by the creature as by its creator:

> Not the tenderness of friendship, nor the beauty of earth, nor of heaven, could redeem my soul from woe: the very accents of love were ineffectual. I was encompassed by a cloud which no beneficial influence could pene-trate. The wounded deer dragging its fainting limbs to some untrodden brake, there to gaze upon the arrow which had pierced it, and to die—was but a type of me.

"Gazing upon the arrow" can be a fairly protracted occupation even when no use is expected to come of it. Mary Shelley spends a great part of her narrative confronting her hero with images which evoke the sublimity of his mental state where ordinary words fail. Frankenstein journeys to Chamonix, where the mountain views elevate him from all "littleness of feeling" and "subdue and tranquilize" his grief though they cannot remove it. Mont Blanc provides him with a moment of "something like joy," but the Alps, though briefly impressive, are not in the end any more able than words to express or alleviate what Frankenstein feels. Trips up the Rhine, across the sea, even into the Arctic, hint at his unrest, but "imperial

Nature," in all her "awful majesty," can no more provide truly adequate images of his misery than she can provide the fulfillment of his ambitious dreams.

At the end of the narrative, Frankenstein accuses himself of over-reaching, but even in doing this, he immodestly compares himself with the prince of overreachers: "Like the archangel who aspired to omnipotence, I am chained in an eternal hell." Rather than looking back on his ambition with disgust, he remembers it with pleasure: "Even now I cannot recollect without passion my reveries while the work was incomplete. I trod heaven in my thoughts, now exulting in my powers, now burning with the idea of their effects." Despite the conventional speeches about the dangers of pride, it becomes more and more evident in the last pages of the novel that Frankenstein, though regretting the *result* of his extraordinary efforts, is not ashamed of having made the effort in the first place. He repeatedly warns Walton, who is engaged in an expedition into the Polar Sea, to content himself with modest ambitions and a quiet life, but when Walton's men threaten to turn the ship back, the dying Frankenstein rallies to urge them on:

> Did you not call this a glorious expedition? And wherefore was it glorious? Not because the way was smooth and placid as a southern sea, but because it was full of dangers and terror... You were hereafter to be hailed as the benefactors of your species; your names adored as belonging to brave men who encountered death for honor and the benefit of mankind.

In his last breath, he begins to warn Walton once more not to make the same mistake he did, but then changes his mind:

> Seek happiness in tranquility and avoid ambition, even if it be only the apparently innocent one of distinguishing yourself in science and discoveries. Yet why do I say this? I have myself been blasted in these hopes, but another may succeed.

That Frankenstein does not die absolutely repentant once again raises the possibility that the monstrous result of his experiment was not the inevitable issue of pride but an accident of circumstance, the result of insufficient knowledge, or an imperfection in nature itself. If one wishes to accept Walton's reverent appraisal of his new friend, it can be said that Frankenstein has the immunity of all scientific and artistic genius from conventional morality, that he is somehow apart from and superior to material circumstances even when he himself seems to have brought them about. Just as Mary saw Shelley "caged" in a "frail image" and surrounded by misfortunes from which his superiority of mind detached and elevated him, so Walton sees Frankenstein as a man with a "double existence." "He may suffer misery and be overwhelmed by disappointments; yet, when he has retired into himself, he will be like a celestial spirit that has a halo around him, within whose circle no grief or folly ventures."

III

Mary learned her lessons in idealism well, and there is in her narrative a level on which her hero is above reproach. But it must be admitted that there is a mundane side to this fantastic tale. If genius can escape or withdraw from the material universe, ordinary mortals cannot. And however great their admiration for genius may be, they cannot fully separate it from the lesser objects of their perception.

Mary Shelley was a young and impetuous woman when she ran off with the poet; she was also an intelligent woman, but her journals and letters reveal that despite her efforts to form herself after her husband's image, common sense often intruded and made the task difficult. She was never intellectually disloyal to Shelley, yet she admitted that her mind could not follow his to the heights. Her novel, like almost everything else about her life, is an instance of genius observed and admired but not shared. In making her hero the creator of a monster, she does not necessarily mock idealistic ambition, but in making that monster a poor grotesque patchwork, a physical mess of seams and wrinkles, she introduces a consideration of the material universe which challenges and undermines the purity of idealism. In short, the sheer concreteness of the ugly thing which Frankenstein has created often makes his ambitions and his character—however sympathetically described—seem ridiculous and even insane. The arguments on behalf of idealism and unworldly genius are seriously presented, but the controlling perspective is that of an earthbound woman.

In making her hero a scientist rather than a poet or philosopher, Mary could hardly have avoided treating the material consequences of his theoretical projects. But, in almost all important respects, Frankenstein's scientific ambitions are at the level where they coincide with the highest desires of artists and metaphysicians, to investigate the deepest mysteries of life, to determine causes and first principles. The early descriptions of Frankenstein's youthful dreams are filled, like more recent forms of "science fiction," with outlandish schemes which combine the highest fancies of the imagination with an elaborate application of technical ingenuity. Though Frankenstein himself scorns the notion, his "scientific" method has a large dose of hocus-pocus in it and comes a good deal closer to alchemy than it does to physiology. The professor whom he most admires disclaims the inflated schemes of ancient pseudo-scientists, but then proceeds to claim for modern scientists the godlike ambitions previously invoked by poets and prophets:

> Modern masters promise very little; they know that metals cannot be transmuted, and that the elixir of life is a chimera. But these philosophers, whose hands seem only to dabble in dirt, and their eyes to pore over the microscope or crucible, have indeed performed miracles. They penetrate into the recesses of nature, and show how she works in her hiding places. They ascend into the heavens... They have acquired new and almost unlimited powers; they can command the thunders of heaven, mimic the earthquake, and even mock the invisible world with its own shadows.

The passage sounds like an answer to the Lord's questions about knowledge and power in the Book of Job. The obvious echoes of Biblical language show, among other things, that science is making religion (or, more particularly, the fear of God) obsolete. But, beyond this, the speech might be passed over as a conventional piece of hyperbole if Mary did not undercut it sharply by proceeding to show her hero trying literally to put his professor's words into practice by penetrating the "recesses of nature." Frankenstein digging about in graveyards and charnel houses, matching eyeballs and sawing bones, is not an inspiring sight. Even less so is the bungled construct of muscles, arteries, and shriveled skin which he had intended as a perfectly proportioned and beautiful being. The gap between the ideal and the real, the ambition and the accomplishment, produces a result as gruesome and absurd as any pseudo-science of the Middle Ages. Still, Mary is not criticizing exalted ambition, but the misapplication of it, the consequences of what Frankenstein himself describes as "unrelaxed and breathless eagerness," a "frantic impulse," a trance-like pursuit of one idea. Through the mouth of her hero, she raises a question which in life she could probably never bring herself to ask her husband: "Is genius forever separate from the reasonable, the reflective, and the probable?"

The question is one which troubled a great many romantic artists and critics. Hazlitt, for one, did not accept such a division as inevitable, and he criticized Shelley in words which parallel almost exactly Frankenstein's own terms of self-criticism after the failure of his experiment:

> Shelley's style is to poetry what astrology is to natural science—a passionate dream, a striving after impossibilities, a record of fond conjectures, a confused embodying of vague abstractions—a fever of the soul, thirsting and craving over what it cannot have, indulging its love of power and novelty at the expense of truth and nature, associating ideas by contraries, and wasting great powers by their application to unattainable objects.

Hazlitt's impatience with Shelley, as expressed in the opening analogy, is based, to a large degree, on the poet's departure from the natural. Shelley himself was deeply aware of the problem, and *Alastor, or the Spirit of Solitude*, was, in part, a criticism of the pursuit of truth under unnatural conditions of isolation. The poet's invocation to Mother Nature could have been spoken by Frankenstein during the research which led to the creation of the monster:

> ...I have made my bed
> In charnels and on coffins, where black Death
> Keeps record of the trophies won from thee;
> Hoping to still these obstinate questionings
> Of thee and thine by forcing some lone ghost,
> Thy messenger to render up the tale
> Of what we are. In lone and silent hours,
> When night makes a weird sound of its own stillness,
> Like an inspired and desperate alchemist
> Staking his very life on some dark hope,
> Have I mixed awful talk and asking looks
> With my most innocent love; until strange tears,
> Uniting with those breathless kisses, made
> Such magic as compels the charmèd night
> To render up thy charge.

The passage describes a kind of necrophilia, an unnatural probing into the secrets of nature; and yet, despite his disapproving moral, the poet appears to luxuriate in the contemplation of the forbidden and fruitless act. It is, after all, the poet-narrator, not Alastor, who is speaking in this passage. As the image of the "inspired and desperate alchemist" suggests, the question remains as to whether a poet of sufficient genius can transform inert and unlikely objects into "gold"; or, to extend the sexual metaphor of the lines, whether the intercourse of mind with dead matter can produce new and vital images of nature. Shelley seems to be reasoning in the negative and rhyming in the affirmative. He argues in the preface to *Alastor*, that no truly great human effort can succeed if it is removed from the nourishing warmth of "human sympathy." Yet neither his poetry nor his life provides consoling solutions to the solitude genius so often creates for itself. Even an early and, for Shelley, relatively simple definition of love must have given Mary uneasy moments.

> Love...is...the universal thirst for a communion not merely of the senses, but of our whole nature, intellectual, imaginative, and sensitive; and which, when individualized, becomes an imperious necessity.... The sexual impulse, which is only one, and often a small party of (its) claims, serves, from its obvious and external nature, as a kind of type or expression of the rest, a common basis, an acknowledged and visible link.

It is not the kind of statement D. H. Lawrence would have admired, nor can its Platonism have been altogether comforting to a companion for whom the "visible link" of sex was the one claim not rivaled by Byron,

Peacock, Hogg, Hunt, or Trelawny.

IV

In describing the way in which Frankenstein's experiment seems most "unnatural," Mary Shelley implies a definition of the natural which is peculiarly feminine in bias. For her, Frankenstein's presumption is not in his attempt to usurp the power of the gods—she quite willingly grants him his "divine" attributes—but in his attempt to usurp the power of women. "A new species would bless me as its creator and source," says Frankenstein in the enthusiasm of his first experiments. "No father could claim the gratitude of his child so completely as I should deserve theirs." He seeks to combine the role of both parents in one, to eliminate the need for woman in the creative act, to make sex unnecessary. At least that would be the net result of his experiment if it were successful, despite the fact that he himself tends to see its consequences in grander and vaguer terms. Thus, while Mary grants her hero the nobility and even the innocence of his intentions, she cannot help but undercut them with her own womanly sense of how things are.

Stripped of rhetoric and ideological decoration, the situation presented is that of a handsome young scientist, engaged to a beautiful woman, who goes off to the mountains alone to create a new human life. When he confesses to Walton that he has "worked hard for nearly two years" to achieve his aim, we may wonder why he does not marry Elizabeth and, with her cooperation, finish the job more quickly and pleasurably. But one must be careful not to imply that Mary's irony is flippant or altogether conscious. Quite to the contrary, her reservations about her hero's presumptuous idealism are so deeply and seriously felt that they produce a symbolic nightmare far more disturbing and gruesome than the monster itself. As soon as the creature begins to show animation and Frankenstein realizes that he has made an abomination, the scientist races to his bedroom, paces feverishly about, and finally falls into a troubled sleep:

> I slept indeed, but I was disturbed by the wildest dreams. I thought I saw Elizabeth, in the bloom of health, walking in the streets of Ingolstadt. Delighted and surprised, I embraced her; but as I imprinted the first kiss on her lips, they became livid with the hue of death; her features appeared to change, and I thought that I beheld the corpse of my dead mother in my arms; a shroud enveloped her form, and I saw the graveworms crawling in the folds of the flannel. I started from my sleep with horror... (and) beheld the wretch—the miserable monster whom I had created.

In this extraordinary rendition of an Oedipal nightmare, Mary shows, without moral comment, the regressive depths of her hero's mind. Frankenstein's crime against nature is a crime against womanhood, an attempt—however unconscious—to circumvent mature sex. For Mary, this is the supreme symbol of egotism, the ultimate turning away from human society and into the self which must result in desolation. Having moved away from family, friends, and fiancée to perform his "creative" act in isolation, Frankenstein later beholds the monster, in a grotesquely exaggerated re-enactment of his own behavior, "eliminate" his younger brother, his dearest friend, and his beloved Elizabeth.

All the crimes are sins against life in the bloom of youth and beauty, but the murder of the woman is the most effectively presented and, in a way, the most carefully prepared. Frankenstein's fears on his wedding night are presumably due to the monster's threat to pursue him even to his marriage chamber. But the immediate situation and the ambiguity of the language contribute to the impression that the young groom's dread of the monster is mixed with his fear of sexual union as a physical struggle which poses a threat to his independence, integrity, and delicacy of character. Frankenstein describes the event in the following manner:

> I had been calm during the day: but so soon as night obscured the shapes of objects, a thousand fears arose in my mind. I was anxious and watchful while my right hand grasped a pistol which was hidden in my bosom; every sound terrified me; but I resolved that I would sell my life dearly, and not shrink from the conflict, until my own life, or that of my adversary, was extinguished.
> Elizabeth observed my agitation for some time in timid and fearful silence; but there was something in my glance which communicated terror to her, and trembling she asked, "What is it that agitates you, my dear Victor? What is it you fear?"
> "Oh! peace, peace, my love," replied I; "this night and all will be safe; but this night is dreadful, very dreadful."
> ... I reflected how fearful the combat which I momentarily expected would be to my wife, and I earnestly entreated her to retire, resolving not to join her until I had obtained some knowledge as to the situation of my enemy.

Frankenstein leaves the room, and it is while he is away that his bride is murdered by the monster on her untried marriage bed. The passage is filled with the language of anxiety, phallic inference, and imagery of conflict, yet it is in Frankenstein's absence—not in an eager assertion of his physical presence—that harm comes to Elizabeth. If we take the monster to be one side of Frankenstein's nature, an alter-ego, then we see his physically potent self as brutish, ugly, and destructive, completely unintegrated with his gentle spirit. To depict a radical separation of mind from sexuality is one way to explore an unsatisfactory rapport between the imagination and the natural world. But what is important in the thematic terms of the novel is not the mere existence of the separation, but the fact that physical life is made ugly (indeed, is made to wither and die prematurely) because it is inadequately tended by the mind. The problem is not abuse but neglect.

The importance of the wedding night scene lies in its sexual connotation insofar as that provides the basic and concrete context in which, once again, to exemplify the hero's withdrawal from physical and emotional contact with living human beings. There are earlier instances of his separating himself from his family and from his friend Clerval, even while protesting, as he has with Elizabeth, that he continues to love them in spirit. The outrage dramatized in this novel is not restricted to a specifically sexual offense—nor is it directed against genius or ambition or idealism. The enemy is an egotism which, when carried to the extreme, annihilates all life around it and finally destroys itself.

V

While the main theme of the novel is the monstrous consequences of egotism, the counter-theme is the virtue of friendship. For, as Frankenstein's crime is seen as a sin against humankind more than against the heavens, it is through human sympathy, rather than divine grace, that it might have been avoided or redeemed. In her treatment of friendship, Mary shows the Coleridgean side of herself. She sees a friend as a balancing and completing agent, one who is sufficiently alike to be able to sympathize and understand, yet sufficiently different to be able to correct, and refine. Above all, the friend, in giving ear to one's dreams and sufferings, provides not only a temporary release from them, but the immediate excuse to order them by putting them into words.

The entire narrative of *Frankenstein* is in the form of three confessions to individuals with whom the speaker has unusually close ties. First, the young explorer Robert Walton writes to his sister in England as he journeys into the Arctic. There he rescues Frankenstein from a shipwreck and listens to his tale, which, in turn, contains a long narrative spoken by the monster to its creator. There is not a great deal of difference in the styles of the three narratives, though the emphasis in each is determined to a large extent by the speaker's relation to the listener. Walton's sister is an affectionate English lady who needs to be reassured that her brother is not in too much danger. He is lonely and he writes to her in detail about everything, trying usually to maintain an air of competence and calm. Frankenstein is a genius on the verge of despair and death, brought to glow again by the admiration of his rescuer. He tells his story to dissuade Walton from ruining himself similarly through excessive ambition, spares no emotion or rhetoric, and condescends to him from the superiority of his suffering. The monster wants pity from his creator; his narrative is the most sentimental of the three and the most pathetically modest in its claims.

Each narrator speaks of the importance of friendship—Walton and the monster because they feel the lack of it, Frankenstein because he has had friends and lost them. In Walton's second letter to his sister, he reports that he has hired a ship and is ready to set sail on his dangerous journey. The one thing that troubles him is that, though he has a well-trained crew, he has no soul companion:

> I have one want which I have never yet been able to satisfy... I have no friend... When I am glowing with the enthusiasm of success, there will be none to participate in my joy; if I am assailed by disappointment, no one will endeavour to sustain me in dejection... I desire the company of a man who could sympathize with me; whose eyes would reply to mine. You may deem me romantic, my dear sister, but I bitterly feel the want of a friend. I have no one near me, gentle yet courageous, possessed of a cultivated as well as a capacious mind, whose tastes are like my own, to approve or amend my plans. How would such a friend repair the faults of your poor brother!

When Walton's ship picks up the nearly frozen body of Frankenstein, the explorer hopes that at last he has found the ideal friend. He nurses, consoles, and entertains the survivor, but when he approaches the subject of friendship, Frankenstein, as always, agrees in theory, but finds a reason not to become involved in the situation at hand:

> I agree with you... we are unfashioned creatures, but half made up, if one wiser, better, dearer, than ourselves—such a friend ought to be—do not lend his aid to perfectionate our weak and faulty natures. I once had a friend, the most noble of human creatures, and, am entitled, therefore, to judge respecting friendship.

Frankenstein condescends to poor Walton even on the subject of friendship. It is too late for him to take up any new ties in life, he explains, because no man could ever be more to him than Clerval was and no woman more than Elizabeth. Of course, as Walton and the reader soon discover, despite Frankenstein's avowals of mutual influence and attachment, neither Clerval nor Elizabeth had any effect on him at all after his childhood and early youth. In fact, it is precisely the qualities which each of them personifies which might have saved Frankenstein from proceeding in his mad experiment. Clerval, though refined and cultivated, is essentially the outgoing, energetic, and enterprising friend who would counsel Franken-stein to climb the mountain rather than brood over it. Elizabeth was the "saintly soul," whose love softened and attracted, and who, whenever with

Frankenstein, subdued him "to a semblance of her own gentleness."

Mary was sufficiently her mother's daughter to assume that a woman, as easily as another man, could be the soul companion, the ideal friend, of a man. She did not regard sexual love as an impediment to ideal friendship, nor, it would seem, as a "small party" of the claims of true love. Elizabeth and Frankenstein almost always address one another as "dear friend," and she and Clerval simply complement different sides of Frankenstein's nature. If it were to come to a choice of one or the other, the novel leaves little doubt that the feminine companion is the more valuable since she can provide both spiritual sympathy and physical affection. It is a great and painful loss for Frankenstein when Clerval is killed, but the death of Elizabeth is the end of everything for him. He dedicates himself to the pursuit and destruction of the monster, follows him to "the everlasting ices of the north" where, surrounded by blankness and waste, he confronts the sterility and uselessness of his life in a setting which anticipates that of the conclusions of Poe's *A. Gordon Pym* and Lawrence's *Women in Love*, and which was itself inspired by *The Ancient Mariner*. Walton writes to his sister that he goes to "the land of mist and snow" partly because Coleridge's poem has instilled in him "a love for the marvelous." But in *Frankenstein*, unlike *The Ancient Mariner*, the icy region is not an early stage of a long and redemptive journey, but an end point, a cold blank, an image of sterility and failure.

An earlier scene of frozen desolation associated with isolation from human—especially feminine—companionship takes place between Frankenstein and the monster on a glacier at the base of Mont Blanc. The monster begs his maker to listen to him and proceeds to explain in detail how he has observed and imitated the ways of man, but is shunned because of his ugliness and is forced to wander over glaciers and hide in caves of ice because these are the only dwellings "man does not grudge." In other words, despite the bizarre details associated with his creation, the monster's lament is much the same as that of the physically presentable Caleb Williams: the world does not see him as he really is. His narrative is punctuated by outcries of loneliness:

Everywhere I see bliss, from which I alone am irrevocably excluded.

When I looked around, I saw and heard of none like me.

I had never yet seen a being resembling me, or who claimed any intercourse with me. What was I?

I am an unfortunate and deserted creature...I have no relation or friend upon earth.

The repetition of this theme, with slight variations, continues throughout the monster's narrative. However ludicrous or grotesque it may seem in the concrete, it is nonetheless in keeping with one of the central arguments of the novel that the monster should ask Frankenstein to make him a wife. This, in fact, is the object of his narration:

> If I have no ties and no affections, hatred and vice must be my portion; the love of another will destroy the cause of my crimes... My vices are the children of a forced solitude that I abhor; and my virtues will necessarily arise when I live in communion with an equal. I shall feel the affections of a sensitive being, and become linked to the chain of existence and events, from which I am now excluded.

The irony of the situation, though heavy-handed, is effective. Having removed himself from human companionship and the sexual means of procreation, Frankenstein brings into being a creature who, though not innately evil, is a torment to himself and to others precisely because he is without companionship and a sexual counterpart. In this respect the monster may well be taken as Frankenstein's alter-ego, his strange and destructive self, which finds no adequate means of communication with others, no true resemblances, no reciprocation, a repressed and hidden beast for whom all acceptable forms of human commerce are unavailable and therefore hateful. Frankenstein himself calls the unnameable creature "my own spirit let loose from the grave... forced to destroy all that was dear to me."

VI

Mary saw, as did her father, the duality in human nature which is capable of bringing misery and ruin to the most gifted of beings. Her novel is not so pessimistic as *Caleb Williams* nor are the solutions implied in it so optimistic as those outlined in *Political Justice*. Neither her father's trust in system nor her husband's unworldliness seemed satisfactory to her. On the contrary, judging from the events of her novel, both alternatives were too likely to lead to that single-mindedness which, when carried to the extreme, was a kind of insanity. It would seem, in fact, that of all the romantic influences on her mind and work, Shelley's undoubtedly stimulated, but Coleridge's comforted; Shelley's provided confusion and enchantment, Coleridge's provided psychological and moral consolation. The ethereal reveries of her hero are loyal attempts to imitate Shelley, but they are among the most strained and unconvincing passages of the novel. Mary's natural inclination was toward synthesis, integration, a constant effort to find balance, relationship, correspondence, to root all ideals in natural process, and to find in nature the external signs of an ideal region. Her heart is with those, described by Coleridge, "who measuring and sounding the rivers of the vale at the feet of their furthest inaccessible falls have learned, that the sources must be far higher and far inward." Despite his supposedly scientific approach to things, Frankenstein's error is to circumvent an elementary principle of nature in trying to achieve his rather vaguely conceived ambition.

In stressing friendship, and especially heterosexual love, as her "river of the vale," the natural symbol of a higher necessity, Mary presents her own concrete version of the theory of correspondence. We must give her more credit than to think that she supposed the problems of all men—including geniuses—would be solved by marriage to a good woman. What she does mean is that no being truly exists—except in an insane wilderness of its own creation—unless it finds and *accepts* a relationship of mutual dependence with another. The rapport with otherness is both the link with the objective world and the condition for self-delineation.

In his tenth essay from *The Friend*, Coleridge says, "In a self-conscious and thence reflecting being, no instinct can exist without engendering the belief of an object corresponding to it, either present or future, real or capable of being realized." Mary Shelley's definition of a monster is precisely that being to which nothing corresponds, the product of a genius who tried to exercise its will without reference to other beings. Even Caleb Williams, at least until Falkland's death, is better off than the monster in that he can draw energy to shape some identity for himself from his strange bond with his master. Godwin wrote in his preface that he amused himself with the parallels between his story and that of Bluebeard: "Caleb Williams was the wife, who in spite of warning, persisted in his attempts to discover the forbidden secret; and, when he had succeeded, struggled as fruitlessly to escape the consequences, as the wife of Bluebeard in washing the key of the ensanguined chamber."

Frankenstein's first act after creating a new life is to disown it. The problem is not, as in *Caleb Williams*, an ambiguous fascination leading to abuse and immediate and obsessive pursuit. As soon as his dream is realized in concrete form, Frankenstein wants nothing to do with it. Despite his claims to scientific interest, he demonstrates no wish whatever to observe and analyze the imperfect results of his experiment. When he does finally pursue the monster, it is not in order to possess, dominate, or torment it, but to annihilate it. Though there is something ludicrous in the way the monster stumbles upon books and learns to read during his lonely wandering, the thematic consistency of the episode is unmistakable. The monster is most impressed by *Paradise Lost*; he compares himself with Adam before the creation of Eve, but, like a good Romantic, he finds Satan an even "fitter emblem" of his condition. Still, neither emblems, nor words can really help or define him any more than ordinary men can. He can find parallels but no connections and he concludes his encounter with books by envying Satan like all the others, for even he "had his companions."

The two dominant themes of *Frankenstein* never truly harmonize, nor does one succeed effectively in canceling out the other. Surely, the most explicit "moral" theme of the novel—expressed by the author with genuine conviction—is that man discovers and fulfills himself through others and destroys himself alone. Yet played against this, not so much as an argument but as an assumption, is the idea that the genius, even in his failures, is unique, noble, and isolated from other men by divine right.

Frankenstein is neither a pure hymn of praise to Godwin and Shelley nor a simple repudiation of them. Mary's uncertainties are not reflected in parody or burlesque, as Beckford's and Lewis's are in *Vathek* and *The Monk*. Her prose style is solemn, inflated, and imitative, an unhappy combination of Godwin's sentence structure and Shelley's abstract vocabulary. Whatever else she may have thought, Mary obviously did not regard her father or husband as silly. Her reservations about them were deep, complex, and mixed with genuine admiration.

After Shelley's death, Mary considered how best to educate her son, and a friend advised that she teach him to think for himself. Mary is said to have answered, "Oh my God, teach him to think like other people!" If the young wife had been able to speak with the emphatic clarity of the widow, she probably would have had fewer nightmares and *Frankenstein* might never have been written. The book is a bad dream entwined with a moral essay. Like all romantic fiction, it resounds with the fascinating dissonance which usually results from intimate encounters between irrational symbols and reasonable statements.

GEORGE LEVINE

"*Frankenstein*" and the Tradition of Realism

The English novel, as a form, has rarely been kind to characters with large aspirations. For the most part, it has preferred to chastise them and to praise those heroes reconciled to unheroic lives. In a way, the limits of praiseworthy aspiration and of the capacity to act effectively on the world are established in *Robinson Crusoe*, which offers us a hero whose heroism consists in survival and learning to use the most ordinary materials to build a home and a thriving economy. That the story is, as a whole, incredible makes it all the more characteristic since its literary strategy is to make the unbelievable seem quite ordinary, and it uses extravagance not to create a hero with the kind of aspirations appropriate to romance, but with great expectations which go no further than getting rich. The conventions of realism, to which, by and large, the central traditions of the novel were moving by the nineteenth century, entail a preoccupation with ordinary materials so that, even in large historical dramas like those of Scott or in fictions, like Dickens's, where fantasy is allowed a much freer rein, the hero who aspires greatly is regarded with distrust, or gently mocked, or frustrated entirely. Most of the great novelists, from Scott and Jane Austen to Thackeray and George Eliot, tend to concern themselves with heroes and heroines whose major problems are not to affect the course of history or even to make a significant public difference, but to achieve, within the limits imposed by an extremely complicated and restrictive bourgeois society, a satisfactory *modus vivendi*.

From *Novel* 1, vol. 7 (Fall 1973). Copyright © 1973 by Novel Corporation.

Only in gothic fiction can we find heroes whose ambitions—like Melmoth the Wanderer's—outstrip the limits of that society and are not unequivocally judged. Only there can we find directly and unprejudicially dealt with the large emotional energies which are impatient with the quotidian.

Yet it is striking that the great nineteenth-century non-realistic fictions like *Frankenstein* or *Wuthering Heights*, or even lesser works like *Melmoth the Wanderer* and *Uncle Silas*, and certainly the romances of Scott, all tend to share certain attitudes toward heroism which we have hitherto too easily located in traditions of realism. Close examination of any of these works makes clear how inadequate the term realism is for any but the crudest sorts of notation, and how naturally "realistic" methods slip over into romance, or gothicism, or other non-realist categories. It is possible, I think, to take a work like *Frankenstein* and see it as representative of certain attitudes and techniques that become central to the realist tradition itself. As it works frankly in a world freed from some of the inhibiting restrictions of "belief" and "fact," it allows us to see at work quite openly some of the tensions that always threaten to destroy the realist world of the ordinary in which belief is compatible with desire.

I

Frankenstein has the qualities of a genuine hero—or so, at least, the narrative of his story specifically tells us. He is clearly conceived as a figure sharing many of the qualities of Milton's Satan, some of Coleridge's Ancient Mariner, and some, too, of Percy Shelley. The sea captain, Walton, the monster, and Frankenstein himself testify to his potential greatness. "What a glorious creature must he have been in the days of his prosperity," writes Walton, "when he is thus noble and godlike in ruin!" (London: Oxford University Press, 1971, p. 210). And Frankenstein, as if to make clear to Walton and to us that the analogy with the fallen angel is not exaggerated, is quoted, immediately afterwards, as saying: "I trod heaven in my thoughts, now exulting in my powers, now burning with the idea of their effects. From my infancy I was imbued with high hopes and a lofty ambition; but how am I sunk! Oh! my friend, if you had known me as I once was, you would not recognise me in this state of degradation. Despondency rarely visited my heart; a high destiny seemed to bear me on, until I fell, never, never again to rise" (p. 211). And the monster, overcome by remorse at his creator's death, cries out on seeing his body, "Oh, Frankenstein! generous and self-devoted being! what does it avail that I now ask thee to pardon me?" (p. 219). "I have devoted my creator, the select specimen of all that is worthy of love and admiration among men, to misery" (p. 222). There is nothing ambivalent about these commendations (although there is a curious note in the monster's word "self-devoted" to which I shall have to return). Frankenstein apparently combined extraordinary powers with physical and spiritual beauty, great ambition with great tenderness.

But one of the major ironies of the novel, *Frankenstein*, is that it seems, by the direction of its three separate narratives, and the fates it spells out, to be explicitly anti-heroic, to challenge the ambition and actions which make Frankenstein such a special sort of man. It uses some of the conventions of the gothic and sensation novels to reject those traditions and assert the value of harmonious and quiet domestic life. The assertion of these values is, however, incomplete, conditional on an awareness of what they cost, and is made, in any case, in a manner that is both complicated and moving and altogether of a different species from similar kinds of assertion in works which salaciously exploit excess to assert some final pietistic moralism. It calls to mind not *Fanny Hill* (pornography has intimate relations with gothicism), which pretends to be concerned with the corrupting power of civilization on rural innocence, or even Lewis's *The Monk* (which is, in about equal parts, a pornographic, gothic, and psychological novel), but, as it is intended to do, Coleridge's "Rime of the Ancient Mariner" (Walton says that his interest in discovering mysteries was inspired by Coleridge's poem). That poem carries us through an extraordinary supernatural and symbolic journey, only to end in a way that, in another context, would seem merely banal:

> O sweeter than the Marriage-feast
> 'Tis sweeter far to me
> To walk together to the Kirk
> With a goodly company.
>
> To walk together to the Kirk
> And all together pray,
> While each to his great father bends,
> Old men, and babes, and loving friends,
> And Youths and Maidens gay.
>
> Farewell, farewell! but this I tell
> To thee, thou wedding guest!
> He prayeth well who loveth well
> Both man and bird and beast.
>
> He prayeth best who loveth best,
> All things both great and small:
> For the dear God, who loveth us,
> He made and loveth all.

Frankenstein does not look back to the sensation novel but forward to realistic books like Dostoevsky's *Crime and Punishment* or Conrad's *The Secret Sharer* which—like Coleridge's poem—explore the psychology of unorthodox aspirations and complicate traditional pieties with metaphysical mystery.

Coleridge's description of the task undertaken in the *Lyrical Ballads* by him and Wordsworth is remarkably appropriate to *Frankenstein* and suggests as well how the fantastic *Frankenstein* is, in fact, connected with the traditions of realism which were most fully developed after it. Coleridge and Wordsworth were to undertake the writing of poems of two sorts:

> In the one, the incidents and agents were to be, in part at least, supernatural; and the excellence aimed at was to consist in the interesting of the affections by the dramatic truth of such emotions, as would naturally accompany such situations, supposing them real.... For the second class, subjects were to be chosen from ordinary life; the characters and incidents were to be such as will be found in every village and its vicinity, where there is a meditative and feeling mind to seek after them, or to notice them, when they present themselves. [Coleridge was to write about] persons and characters supernatural, or at least romantic, [but with] a semblance of truth sufficient to procure ... that willing suspension of disbelief which constitutes poetic faith.
>
> (*Biographia Literaria*, chapter 14)

Percy Shelley's description, using the voice of the true author in the Preface to the 1818 edition, echoes Coleridge in a way that is surely not coincidental:

> I have not considered myself as merely weaving a series of supernatural terrors. The event on which the intent of the story depends is exempt from the disadvantages of a mere tale of spectres or enchantment. It was recommended by the novelty of the situations which it developes; and, however impossible as a physical fact, affords a point of view to the imagination for the delineating of human passions more comprehensive and commanding than any which the ordinary relations of existing events can yield.
>
> I have thus endeavoured to preserve the truth of the elementary principles of human nature, while I have not scrupled to innovate upon their combinations.

And, though these are Percy's not Mary's words, it is not unreasonable to take with some seriousness the following: "yet my chief concern in this respect has been limited to the avoiding [of] the enervating effects of the novels of the present day, and to the exhibition of the amiableness of domestic affection, and the excellence of universal virtue" (pp. 13–14).

As many critics have noted, one of the most interesting aspects of *Frankenstein* is that, for the most part, it eschews the supernatural. Mary's originating idea for the story was developed from what was taken to be fact: "They talked," she wrote of Byron and Shelley in her introduction to the 1831 edition of the novel, "of the experiments of Dr. Darwin (I speak not of what the Doctor really did, or said that he did, but, as more to my purpose, of what was then spoken of as having been done by him), who preserved a piece of vermicelli in a glass case, till by some extraordinary means it began to move with voluntary motion. Not thus, after all, would life be given. Perhaps a corpse would be re-animated; galvanism had given token of such things: perhaps the component parts of a creature might be manufactured, brought together, and endued with vital warmth" (p. 9). In any case, beyond the fatal donnée—that it was possible to induce life into dead matter—*Frankenstein* fairly severely confines itself to the possible, if not always to the probable. It maintains a remarkable consistency and coherence of characterization and its surface details are either recognizable in ordinary experience or follow almost inevitably from the fact of the monster's existence. Given the initial idea, there is very little of the improbable in it. I don't mean to claim that it thus belongs within the traditions of realism, but rather that its effects and its power derive from its rejection of arbitrariness, indeed, from the almost austere way in which Mary Shelley insists on following out the consequences of her initial imagination. The scenery of the Alps, the mad chase across the Arctic ocean, the traditional abstract emotiveness of the language all link the novel with novels of sensation—as does the imagination of the hero himself. But by focusing so intensely on the landscape of the hero's mind, and on the product of its energies, and by eschewing any easy intervention of supernatural force, Mary Shelley sets out with astonishing clarity some of the moral implications of the heroic ideal. She writes, in fact, a brilliant psychological novel in which the psychology is the action itself, and while free to insist on the Wordsworthian, Coleridgean, and Shelleyan morals of the importance of community, domestic affections, love, and sensitivity to nature, she writes a story whose moral ambivalences of action are the real terror.

Frankenstein is one of the first in a long tradition of fictional overreachers, of characters who act out in various ways the myth of Faust, and transport it from the world of mystery and miracle to the commonplace. He is destroyed not by some metaphysical agency, some supernatural intervention—as God expelled Adam from Eden or Mephistopheles collected his share of the bargain (though echoes of these events are everywhere)—but by his own nature and the consequences of living in or rejecting human community. Frankenstein is in a way the indirect father of lesser, more humanly recognizable figures, like Becky Sharp or Pip or Lydgate, people who reject the conventional limits imposed upon them by society and who are punished for their troubles. *Frankenstein* embodies one of the central myths of realistic fiction in the nineteenth century, even in the contrast between its sensational style and its apparently explicit moral implications. It embodies characteristically a simultaneous awe and reverence toward greatness of ambition, and fear and distrust of those who act on such ambition. That ambivalence is almost always disguised in realistic fiction, where the manner itself seems to reject the possibility of greatness and the explicit subject is frequently the evil of aspiring to it: in gothic fiction the energies to be suppressed by the realist ideal, by the model of Flemish painting, by worldly wise compromise with the possible, are released. Gothic fiction, as Lowry Nelson has observed, "by its insistence on singularity and exotic setting... seems to have freed the minds of readers from direct involvement of their superegos and allowed them to pursue daydreams and wish fulfillment in regions where inhibitions and guilt could be suspended" (*Yale Review*, 1962–63, p. 238). The mythology of virtue rewarded, which was curiously central to English realism, is put to question in the gothic landscape where more powerful structures than social convention give shape to wish; and, as Nelson suggests, reader and writer alike were freed to pursue the possibilities of their own potential evil. It is striking how difficult it is to locate in realistic fiction any positive and active evil. The central realist mythology is spelled out in characters like George Eliot's Tito Melema, whose wickedness is merely a gradual sliding into the consequences of a natural egoism. In gothic fiction, but more particularly in *Frankenstein*, evil is both positively present and largely inexplicable. Although ostensibly based on the ideas of Godwin's rationalist ethics which see evil as a consequence of maltreatment or injustice, there is no such comfortable explanation for the evil of Frankenstein himself. Where did his decision to create the monster come from? Mere chance. Evil is a deadly and fascinating mystery originating in men's minds as an inexplicable but inescapable aspect of human goodness.

It is a commonplace of criticism of *Frankenstein* as of Conrad's *The Secret Sharer*, that the hero and his antagonist are one. Leggatt is the other side of the captain; the monster and Frankenstein are doubles, two aspects of the same being. This seems an entirely just reading given that Frankenstein creates the monster and that, as they pursue their separate lives, they increasingly resemble and depend upon each other so that by the end Frankenstein pursues his own monster, their positions reversed, and the monster plants clues to keep Frankenstein in pursuit. As Frankenstein's creation, the monster can be taken as an expression of an aspect of Frankenstein's self: the monster is a sort of New Critical art object, leading an apparently independent organic life of its own and yet irremediably and subtly tied to its creator, re-enacting in mildly disguised ways, his creator's feelings and experiences. We will have to return to this aspect of the novel again, but I want to point out here certain other doublings or duplications in the novel.

The world of *Frankenstein* has a kind of objective existence which only partially disguises—much less convincingly than a realistic novel would—its quality as projection of a subjective state. The laws governing this world are almost the laws of dream in which the control of action is only partially, if at all, ordinary causation. Characters and actions move around central emotional preoccupations. Clearly, for example, Walton is an incipient Frankenstein, in his lesser way precisely in Frankenstein's position: ambitious for glory, embarked on a voyage of scientific discovery, putting others to risk for his work, isolated from the rest of mankind by his ambition, and desperately lonely. Frankenstein becomes his one true friend, and he is a friend who dies just at the point when their friendship is becoming solidified. And, of course, he is the man to whom Frankenstein tells his story, partly, like the Ancient Mariner, to keep him from the same fate. Moreover, the lesson he learns is not merely the explicit one, that he must sacrifice his ambition to others, but that he must also reject the vengeance that Frankenstein wishes upon him. Frankenstein's last wish is that Walton promise to destroy the monster; yet when the monster appears, Walton does not kill him but rather listens to his story and is moved to compassion which he tries to force himself to reject. He cannot kill the monster, who speaks in a way that echoes Frankenstein's own ideas and sentiments; and, though this is not stated, in rejecting the vengeance which consumed Frankenstein, he is finally freed into a better (and perhaps a lesser) life—but one to which he returns in bitterness and dejection.

Clerval, too, Frankenstein's friend from boyhood, echoes an aspect of Frankenstein's self. Clerval is, surely, Frankenstein without the monster. Frankenstein describes himself as having been committed from his youth to the "metaphysical, or, in its highest sense, the physical secrets of the world." Meanwhile, Clerval occupied himself, so to speak, "with the moral relations of things. The busy stage of life, the virtues of heroes, and actions of men, were his theme; and his hope and his dream was to become one among those whose names are recorded in story, as the gallant and adventurous benefactors of our species" (pp. 37–38). Except, of course, for the emphasis on political action, this description would serve for Frankenstein as well. Moreover, as Frankenstein himself notes, both he and Clerval were softened into gentleness and generosity by the influence of Elizabeth: "I might have become sullen in my study, rough through the ardour of my nature, but that she was there to subdue me to a semblance of her own gentleness. And Clerval . . . might not have been so perfectly humane . . . so full of kindness and tenderness amidst his passion for adventurous exploit, had she not unfolded to him the real loveliness of beneficence, and made the doing good

the end and aim of his soaring ambition" (p. 38). Clerval, whose father
denies him a university education, feels, like Frankenstein himself, a
repugnance to the meanness of business. On the night Frankenstein is to
depart for Ingolstadt and the university, he reads in Clerval's "kindling eye
and in his animated glance a firm but restrained resolve, not to be chained
to the miserable details of commerce" (p. 44). Both men reject the occupations of ordinary life, both are consumed with great ambitions, both are
kept humane by the influence of the same woman, and, in the end, both are
destroyed by Frankenstein's own creation, by the aspect of Frankenstein
which ignores "the moral relations of things." Moreover, when Clerval dies,
Frankenstein is not only accused of the murder (and seems unwilling to
exculpate himself though he knows he has evidence that will do so), but he
falls almost mortally ill—as though he himself has been the victim.

   These kinds of redoublings are characteristic of the whole novel. Not
only all the major characters, but the minor characters as well seem to be
echoes of each other. Every story seems a variation on every other. Both
Elizabeth and Justine are found by the Frankenstein family and rescued
from poverty, and both accuse themselves, in different ways, of the murder
of Frankenstein's youngest brother. When she hears of his death, Elizabeth
exclaims, "O God, I have murdered my darling child" (p. 72). Justine, too, is
a kind of sister of Frankenstein. She so adored Madame Frankenstein that
she "endeavoured to imitate her phraseology and manners, so that even
now," Elizabeth writes, "she often reminds me of her" (p. 65). And after she
is convicted, Justine "confesses" to the murder.

   And then there are the parents. Frankenstein himself is a father, the
creator of the monster, and the novel is in part an examination of the
responsibility of the father to the son. The monster asks Frankenstein for
the gift of a bride to alleviate his solitude. Frankenstein's father in effect
gives Frankenstein a bride, and a sister. The night before Elizabeth is
brought into the Frankenstein house, his mother "had said playfully,—'I
have a pretty present for my Victor—tomorrow he shall have it.' And when,
on the morrow, she presented Elizabeth to me as her promised gift, I, with
childish seriousness, interpreted her words literally, and looked upon
Elizabeth as mine—mine to protect, love, and cherish. All praises bestowed
on her, I received as made to a possession of my own. We called each other
familiarly by the name of cousin. No word, no expression could body forth
the kind of relation in which she stood to me—my more than sister, since till
death she was to be mine only" (pp. 35–36). Frankenstein's father, in
bestowing the gift and in caring for him, behaves to his son as the monster
would have Frankenstein behave. Interestingly, in this extraordinary novel
of intricate relations, when Frankenstein's father arrives after Clerval's
death to help his son, Frankenstein at first assumes that his visitor is to be

the murderer: "Oh take him away! I cannot see him," he cries. "For God's sake, do not let him enter." This strange hallucination focuses again on the bond that connects all the characters in the novel, and suggests how deeply incestuous and Oedipal the relationships are. It suggests, too, how close to the surface of this world are motives derived not from external experience, but from emotional and psychic energies beneath the surface of things.

Despite the potentially easy patterning, there is no simple way to define the relation between parents and offspring in this novel. Frankenstein's father is loved and generous, and marries the daughter of an unsuccessful merchant who, in his pride, almost brings his whole family down. The father of Safie betrays his daughter and her lover and is the cause of the fall of the DeLacey family. Felix DeLacey, in order to save Safie, brings his whole family to the brink of ruin. Frankenstein ignores his creation and, in effect, destroys his family as a consequence. Father and sons are almost equally responsible and irresponsible: what is consistent is only the focal concern on the relationship itself.

Within the novel, almost all relations have the texture of blood kinship. Percy Shelley's notorious preoccupation with incest is manifest in Mary's work. The model is Eden, where Eve is an actual physical part of Adam, and the monster's situation is caused precisely because he has no blood relations, no kinship. Frankenstein, on his death bed, makes clear why there is such an intense, reduplicative obsession throughout the novel on the ties of kinship:

> I thank you, Walton ... for your kind intentions towards so miserable a wretch; but when you speak of new ties, and fresh affections, think you that any can replace those who are gone? Can any man be to me as Clerval was; or any woman another Elizabeth? Even where the affections are not strongly moved by any superior excellence, the companions of our childhood always possess a certain power over our minds, which hardly any later friend can obtain. They know our infantine dispositions, which, however they may be afterwards modified, are never eradicated; and they can judge of our actions with more certain conclusions as to the integrity of our motives. A sister or a brother can never, unless indeed such symptoms have been shown early, suspect the other of fraud or false dealing, when another friend, however strongly he may be attached, may, in spite of himself, be contemplated with suspicion.
>
> (pp. 211–212)

In the original version of the novel, Elizabeth was, as the Oxford editor M. K. Joseph points out, Frankenstein's cousin, "the daughter of his father's sister" (p. 236n), and throughout the revised version, Frankenstein continues to refer to her as cousin. Every death in the novel is a death in the family, literal or figurative: what Frankenstein's ambition costs him is the family connection which makes life humanly possible. William is his brother. Justine looks like his mother, and is another kind of sister, though a subservient one. Clerval is a "brother." Elizabeth is both bride and sister (and cousin). And as a consequence of these losses, his father dies as well. Frankenstein kills his family, and is, in his attempt to obliterate his own creation, his own victim. As he dies, he severs the monster's last link with life so that, appropriately, the monster then moves out across the frozen wastes to immolate himself. The family is an aspect of the self and the self cannot survive bereft of its family.

Thus, even while it wanders across the Alps, to the northern islands of Scotland, to the frozen wastes of the Arctic, *Frankenstein* is a claustrophobic novel. It presents us not with the landscape of the world but of a single mind, and its extraordinary power, despite its grotesqueness and the awkwardness of so much of its prose, resides in its mythic exploration of that mind, and of the consequences of its choices, the mysteries of its impulses. Strangely, the only figure who stands outside of that mind is Walton, who is nevertheless, as I have already argued, another "double" of Frankenstein. Walton provides the frame which allows us to glimpse Frankenstein's story. He is the "wedding guest," who can hear the story only because he is so similar to Frankenstein, and who can engage us because while he is outside the story he is still, like us, implicated in it. He is the link between our world and Frankenstein's, and he is saved by Frankenstein and by his difference from him, to return to his country and, significantly, his sister—his one connection with the human community.

The apparent simplicity and order of Mary Shelley's story only intensifies its extraordinary emotional energy and complexity. Although, for example, it is not unreasonable to argue, as Shelley did, that it aims at exhibiting "the amiableness of domestic affection, and the excellence of universal virtue," we can see that the strongly ordering hand of the novelist has allowed the expression of powerful tensions and energies which realistic techniques would tend to repress and, which, having their source in the irrational, will not resolve themselves into any simple meanings. Comparing *Frankenstein* to Charles Brockden Brown's *Wieland,* Christopher Small argues the same point:

> Mary's imaginative response was in many respects similar to Brown's, but what she got from him was not so much perhaps any specific elements of her story as a readiness to accept what her imagination offered. Indeed, she went much further than he did. In Brown, the unconscious material so profusely thrown up remains disorganized, much of the time incoherent, and this was paradoxically an effect of his failure to allow it full force or to trust the products of his imagination. A pervasive scepticism or, at bottom, a moral timidity caused him to shy away from their full development and

consequently to land as often as not in the most ludicrous banality. Mary, of far greater resolution and single-mindedness...was able to bind many strands into a single whole, and to give her creation a life outside and beyond herself.

(*Ariel Like a Harpy: Shelley, Mary and "Frankenstein,"*
Letchworth, England, 1972, p. 99)

Frankenstein, like other great romances, notably *Wuthering Heights*, is a more shapely and orderly book than most realistic novels, but the order is the means by which Mary's "readiness to accept what her imagination offered" is expressed. As Northrop Frye has suggested, the freer the imagination is allowed to roam, the more formally shapely will be the structure of the work. Imagination is structural power. Or at least it is that in *Frankenstein* and *Wuthering Heights* which, freed from the initial commitment to plausibility and to reason, take the shape of the writers' most potent imaginations and desires.

The simplicity of the structure, Walton's tale enfolding Franken-stein's, which, in turn, enfolds that of the monster, implies a clarity and firmness of moral ordering which is not present in the actual texture of the novel. Walton would seem the ultimate judge of the experience, as the outsider: yet he explicitly accepts Frankenstein's judgment of it, and largely exculpates him. The monster's own defense and explanation, lodged in the center of the story, is, however, by far the most convincing—though it is also a special—reading, and Frankenstein himself confesses that he has failed in his responsibility to his creature. In the end, however, we are not left with a judgment but with Walton's strangely uncolored report of the monster's last speech and last action. If anyone, the monster has the last word: and that word expresses a longing for self-destruction, for the pleasure which will come in the agony of self-immolation, and for an ultimate peace in extinction.

Even the structural parallels to *Paradise Lost* do not help to clarify the moral significance of the action because Frankenstein must be seen as both the creator and the fallen angel, and the monster as both Adam and Satan. Whereas Frankenstein insistently excuses himself (or, at best, fails to admit his guilt publicly) and sees the monster as embodied evil, the fact is that (as each admits about the other on occasion) they are both agents of good *and* evil. Although there is little evidence besides the love he inspires and his own sense of his virtue to prove Frankenstein's goodness, he is clearly not a wicked man in the tradition of melodrama or the gothic. Unlike Melmoth the Wanderer, he has made no pact with the devil. His vices are the defects of his virtues: it was the desire both for glory and to aid mankind that led him to create the monster. As the monster describes him, ambiguously but with clear evidence of admiration: "O Generous and self-devoted being."

As in much realistic fiction, there is no wholly evil character in *Frankenstein*, but, at the same time, there is evil in the world. Frankenstein locates it in the monster; the monster locates it in Frankenstein and, more abstractly, in man. The monster, of course, in his hideousness and in his violent acts, can be seen as the objectification of evil in Frankenstein's mind. But this is far too simple. Frankenstein is sickened with guilt at the murders and feels, in a way and justly, responsible for them. Yet, until after the death of Elizabeth, on the night of their wedding, he never admits to anyone that he has created the monster, and he produces time after time (even when it costs Justine her life) elaborate rationalizations to keep from confessing. Looked at abstractly, Frankenstein's guilt might be said to reside in the act of creating the monster. But there are few occasions in the book where this view becomes the focus. The arguments of the monster and the action of the narrative suggest far more concretely and powerfully that the evil resides not so much in the creation of the monster—which is where the modern popularized myth of Frankenstein places the blame—but in Frankenstein's failure to take the responsibility for what he has created. His first response to the monster on seeing his hideous but quite touching filial grin is to flee: "He held up the curtain of the bed; and his eyes, if eyes they may be called, were fixed on me. His jaws opened, and he muttered some inarticulate sounds, while a grin wrinkled his cheeks. He might have spoken, but I did not hear; one hand was stretched out, seemingly to detain me, but I escaped, and rushed down stairs. I took refuge in the courtyard" (p. 58). Throughout the novel Frankenstein hides from the consequences of his actions so that, to make him face his responsibilities, his own creation must make those actions more and more inescapable. Frankenstein does not see his creation a second time until after it has killed his brother.

There is no evidence in the early stages of anything essentially evil in the monster, and on the strength of his own narrative six chapters later, it is clear that the monster, like Frankenstein himself, was full of benevolence and affection. His only crime is his ugliness, and this is entirely the work of Frankenstein who has been careless in his haste of creation. The monster is evil not because of what he intrinsically is, but because of the consequences of Frankenstein's obsession with creating him. In his obsession, Frankenstein has cut himself off from his family and from the human community; in his reaction to that obsession, Frankenstein cuts himself off from his creation. To be sure, Frankenstein has overreached himself: "Oh! no mortal could support the horror of that countenance" (p. 58). Implicitly, that is, only God should undertake the responsibility of creation. But the true sin is not against God, is not really the Promethean theft of fire from Heaven, but against himself and the human community. Frankenstein cannot face directly that aspect of himself which could create the monster—his own capacity for evil. He sins against his father and his son, and in so doing, he sins against himself. The true sin is his refusal even to attempt to recognize and then to cope with his own capacity for evil. Interestingly, he never learns to do so, but tries to destroy that capacity while, in so doing, he only revitalizes it (and this is, of course, made objectively true by the monster's need to be pursued). To his death he is obsessed with vengeance and destruction as, in his youth, he had been obsessed with creation and benevolence. In this strange book, these are two aspects of the same thing.

The real mystery in *Frankenstein* then has little to do with the mysteries of the gothic machinery. Rather, it has to do with the problem of where the evil came from in the first place. As we shall see, the novel provides a Godwinian explanation for the monster's actual evil, but the underlying structure of the book implies an irrational and dangerous world, which cannot be comprehended by rational theory and which is strained with enormous energies latent and repressed. The surrender to the passionate, however generous and benevolent the apparent intentions, releases those energies; and these break loose in ways altogether independent of any character. Frankenstein, after all, has suffered none of the injustices from which the monster suffers. He has been loved, encouraged by his family, and given the gift of a lifelong companion. Yet he is the original agent of evil. Frankenstein's final reason for not creating a bride for his monster is that he fears—and the whole narrative implies the justice of these fears—that the new monster will not feel herself bound by the original monster's own good intentions. But beyond this mystery, which novelists committed to the realist tradition tended to ignore, or explain in terms of egoism, the explicit moral ideals of *Frankenstein* are very close to those of realism: the ideals of compromise, moderation, commitment to family and community.

Where in Frankenstein's story there seems no rational explanation for the entrance of evil into the world, in the monster's the explanation is clear. The monster's story implies the primacy of responsibility to family and community and his arguments are keenly rational, Godwinian polemics which, in almost every case, are superior to the responses of Frankenstein, who is ruled by vague but powerful emotions. "Yet you, my creator, detest and spurn me . . . ," cries the monster, "to whom thou art bound by ties only dissoluble by the annihilation of one of us. You purpose to kill me. How dare you sport thus with life?" (p. 99). Amidst all the extraordinary reversals in this novel, perhaps the most startling is the way the monster becomes, at least in dramatized action, the intellectual and, indeed, moral superior of Frankenstein. The audacity of a murderer accusing his pursuer of "sporting with life"! The monster nevertheless vows his devotion and docility to Frankenstein: "I am thy creature, and I will be even mild and docile to my natural lord and king, if thou wilt also perform thy part, the which thou owest me.... Remember, that I am thy creature; I ought to be thy Adam; but I am rather the fallen angel, whom thou drivest from joy for no misdeed. Everywhere I see bliss, from which I alone am irrevocably excluded. I was benevolent and good; misery made me a fiend. Make me happy, and I shall again be virtuous" (p. 100). I suppose that this sort of moral lecturing, hectoring, and condescension might have tried the spirit of greater men than Frankenstein. But Frankenstein's response is to reject as specious ideas what much of the narrative enforces. The case is all the monster's—except that in his Godwinian naïveté, he doesn't fully understand the power of irrational energies which he himself enacts. The monster is, however, simply pleading against the injustice of man and his institutions, and for what each nineteenth-century fictional orphan wants—new parents, someone to love and rely on, justice, a place in which to define himself and be happy.

"Make me happy, and I shall again be virtuous." The point is a political one, of course, and much of the monster's experience exemplifies the view that evil enters man's spirit as a result of the injustice of other men (though this is a circular and inconclusive argument). Man is born naturally good, and there is every evidence that the monster's heart is in the right place (after all, it was put there by Frankenstein). The monster represents a kind of Dickensian reading (almost Carlylean but that Carlyle, if an admirer of Rousseau, still found it difficult to believe in man's natural goodness) of the French Revolution. Abused, abandoned, maltreated, deprived, he turns in vengeance on his master and on everything associated with his master. The violent energies released by the revolution enact, in the Terror, the evil that has its apparent source in the masters' injustice. The center of evil is parental irresponsibility and selfishness, and the ideal of goodness is the father's bond to his son and the reciprocal bond of son to father. As the aristocracy in France betrayed the people, so Frankenstein betrayed his creation and, at the same time, in cutting himself off from his own family, betrayed his father as well.

The model of the family is imposed, in *Frankenstein*, on society itself. Thus, like Thackeray's Henry Esmond (who, in marrying the woman who takes the place of his mother, acts out in definitive form the ideal implied in *Frankenstein*), like Dickens's Florence Dombey, like George Eliot's Daniel Deronda, the monster seeks a bond to take the place of the natural one with his creator, without which he is doomed to rootlessness and a meaningless existence. Without such connections, the monster asks himself questions like those of any good modern anti-hero: "Who was I? What was I? Whence did I come? What was my destination?" (p. 128). As we look through the novel, we discover that the injustice to the monster is acted out in many other relations and, certainly, in human institutions. Justine is forced by her father confessor to confess a crime she didn't commit, and she is hanged.

Safie's father betrays her and her lover and the DeLacey family is wrongly condemned: Felix turns on the monster who had been assisting him and his family for months and the monster discovers "the system" on which society is based—"The division of property, of immense wealth and squalid poverty, of rank, descent and noble blood."

None of the characters comfortable in domestic harmony can believe that the world is governed unjustly until disaster strikes. And this is true even of the monster, who enjoys domestic bliss only by peering into the DeLaceys' window. When Elizabeth weeps for Justine before the hanging, she is comforted by Frankenstein's father, who says, "If she is, as you believe, innocent, rely on the justice of our law" (p. 81). But experience brings knowledge and one of the novel's themes is the danger of knowledge. In the realistic novel, knowledge entails disenchantment, a recognition of one's own limits, of the injustice pervasive in society, and of the power of society over one's own ambitions. Thus, the characteristic realistic hero ends his story in some sort of compromise (though he is usually eased, in his fate, by marriage to a lovely creature). But *Frankenstein*, working in a different mode, does not allow a lapse into worldly wisdom and moderation. It deals with the motif of knowledge and innocence and disenchantment on a scale far larger than that of the conventional *bildungsroman*. Frankenstein's quest for knowledge can be seen as a dramatic metaphor for the universal condition of lost innocence as a result of the knowledge of experience. It is not merely Frankenstein in this novel who becomes disenchanted: each major character learns something of the nature of his own illusions. As the reality of death (which is really the product of Frankenstein's knowledge) enters the almost idyllic household of Frankenstein's family, the romance of domestic harmony gives way to a deep gloom. What happens to Frankenstein in his pursuit of knowledge happens, inescapably, to everyone no matter how safe or how good he may seem.

Frankenstein may point the moral of his story to Walton: "Learn from me, if not by my precepts, at least by my example, how dangerous is the acquirement of knowledge, and how much happier that man is who believes his native town to be the world, than he who aspires to become greater than his nature will allow" (p. 53). But this moral—particularly appropriate to the realistic novel—is argued very ambivalently. Even the monster repeats the argument (as he must, being Frankenstein's alter ego): "Increase of knowledge only discovered to me more clearly what a wretched outcast I was" (p. 131). As his knowledge grows, he cries out: "Oh, that I had for ever remained in my native wood, nor known nor felt beyond the sensation of hunger, thirst, and heat!" (p. 120). Yet Mary Shelley knows, as the monster learned, that there is no returning to innocence, once it is lost. "Of what a strange nature is knowledge! It clings to the mind, when it has once seized on it, like a lichen on the rock. I wished sometimes to shake off all thought and feeling; but I learned that there was but one means to overcome the sensation of pain, and that was death" (p. 120). And Frankenstein, near the end, cannot even insist unambiguously on the moral of his story. His last speech is a masterpiece of doubt: "Farewell, Walton!" he says. "Seek happiness in tranquility, and avoid ambition, even if it be only the apparently innocent one of distinguishing yourself in science and discoveries. Yet why do I say this? I have myself been blasted in these hopes, yet another may succeed." Death is the only resolution and yet it resolves nothing since knowledge and innocence are continuing aspects of human experience. The tension worked out in *Frankenstein* between ambition and natural harmony is not resolved.

II

If we read the novel as anti-heroic (which it frequently is, quite explicitly) we miss its peculiar power, its relevance to more conventionally mimetic novels that followed it and, I think, to our present condition in a society which seems almost damned by its own ambition. Frankenstein is not the stock figure of the mad scientist that he has become in modern science fiction films, partly because his potential destructiveness is an inevitable aspect of quite remarkable powers for goodness and of generous intentions, but partly also because the novel he lives in forces us to recognize that we cannot destroy the monster without destroying ourselves, that we cannot forget what we know. The novel faces frankly, moreover (in a way that even Dickens tried not to do) that the monstrous in us can be both beautiful and generous. It struggles to be anti-intellectual, but cannot be. It struggles to assert the supremacy of domestic peace, but cannot altogether succeed. By following out the consequences of the gothic form, by freeing her characters from the full constricting effects both of nature and society, Mary Shelley reveals to us quite clearly the tensions that underlay the Victorian fictional compromise. The ideal of familial responsibility and love is always partly violated because one's fullness as a separate human being entails that violation. And as for the family, so for society. We can't live without it, but we can't live with it.

As a hero, Frankenstein is freed from the restraints of society usually imposed by the very texture of realism. He actually succeeds in creating what he desires, only to find that he doesn't desire it. But we can see here that the freedom is as illusory as Dorothea Brooke's or Isabel Archer's, that the pressures which, in realistic novels, seem to be imposed by a constricting society, are here imposed by the minimal condition of man—the condition, that is, of sentience and of family ties. "Alas!" says Frankenstein, "why does man boast of sensibilities superior to those apparent in the brute; it only renders them more necessary beings" (p. 97). Social pressures in fiction can frequently, if not always, be taken as objectifications of subjective states of feeling and being. In Hardy's *Jude the Obscure*, for example, it is possible to blame Jude's fate on a backward and oppressive society. But the full power of the book lies in the fact that Jude is destroyed as much by his own instincts as by society. Hardy's consistent lament at the unsuitability of man to the natural world is altogether in keeping with Frankenstein's vision here. And Lydgate's fall, we remember, though it has extraordinarily complicated social sources and implications, is as much the result of his own nature as of society's. *Frankenstein* gives us an opportunity to examine the energies of restraint and self-destruction that are built into the human condition precisely because it is not a social novel, because it does not work in the realist mode which depends so heavily on surfaces and the complexities of social relations and the multiplicity of things. In both worlds, freedom is illusory, responsibility is inevitable.

In both worlds, as I have already suggested, the domestic ideal is central, and in both worlds, the hero's relation to it is ambivalent. Frankenstein alternately desires, above all things, to return to the bosom of his family, and then yearns to do something great which will cut him off from the family. That Walton can be saved makes him a lesser man, and there is even a hint that he will not be saved: "Thus are my hopes blasted by cowardice and indecision; I come back ignorant and disappointed. It requires more philosophy than I possess to bear this injustice with patience" (p. 215). Yet he is absolved of guilt while Frankenstein must see himself as the most guilty of beings as long as he does not face the reality of his actions and desires. Only confession, some public recognition of guilt, could possibly have reabsorbed Frankenstein into the human community. But even at Frankenstein's death, with his confession to Walton, we do not have the full absolution because the past is irrevocable and indestructible except in death itself. As he attempts to face what he has done, he moves beyond guilt to a position largely inconceivable in realistic fiction. He does not, he says, find his past conduct "blameable." Guilt is an aspect of repression, and where the realist mode entails repression, Mary Shelley's mode frees her characters into a full accordance with their own deepest feelings. Frankenstein almost callously accepts his past and his ambitions: in the cool language of moral calculus he simply comes to recognize the impossibility of his having avoided disaster. Here is his quiet retrospect on his career, and we can note in the cool abstract language and in the logical balancing of the sentences how far this is from a statement possible within the realist conventions:

> During these last days I have been occupied in examining my past conduct; nor do I find it blameable. In a fit of enthusiastic madness I created a rational creature, and was bound towards him, to assure, as far as was in my power, his happiness and well-being. This was my duty; but there was another still paramount to that. My duties towards the beings of my own species had greater claims to my attention, because they included a greater proportion of happiness or misery.
>
> (p. 217)

It is partly to avoid the horror of this kind of insight that the realist novel erects its defenses against excess and ambition, and employs a prose both less calculating and abstract and more preoccupied with quotidian details.

Frankenstein spells out both the horror of going ahead and the emptiness of return. In particular, it spells out the price of heroism, a price which most nineteenth-century novelists were not willing to pay. Heroism is personal satisfaction writ large. That is, it implies the importance and the power of the individual human being, not in the web of responsibilities which constitute personal action within his family and society and which deter him from all but the most compromised and therefore moderate satisfactions, but in the testing and fulfillment of personal powers. To test is to risk loss and, of course, disenchantment with self. To risk the test is to cut the cord, to assert one's selfhood as a being independent of others. The alternative to the test is repression of self, the establishment of constraints for the sake of order and peace. *Frankenstein* is, in a way, about cutting the cord, and in its treatment of the problem it offers no comforting solution, only the knowledge that there is no way to return to the womb.

This leads to one final point about Frankenstein as a hero, and as a type of the realist hero. His unattractiveness to the reader as a hero is, I think, the result of three qualities. The first is precisely his obsession with great action. As he is obsessed he is also necessarily cruel and turns away from his responsibilities; and, as we have seen, it is with a new sense of these responsibilities that he dies. The second is that he is really unequal to his own ambitions. He has the technical power to create the monster, but he has not the moral power to cope with his creation. In this respect, he is rather like Dostoevsky's Raskolnikov, though dispassionately treated, without the psychological intimacy that makes us participate in Raskolnikov's weaknesses so that we can recognize them as our own (and this, I think, is one of the great weaknesses of Mary Shelley's book). But the third is more central to my immediate concern here. It is the nature of his behavior when he undergoes one of his regular spasms of desire to return to the virtues of domesticity, "the amiableness of domestic affection." On these occasions, Frankenstein is the passive hero.

As an ambitious hero, he wants to change things, to improve them, and much of the novel, as I have pointed out, regards the mechanisms of society as cruel and unjust. But the notion of domestic affections and of the need for communal and family ties runs deeply through the novel, and as Frankenstein longs for these, his ambition drops away and he falls into inaction. There are any number of examples of this sort of thing. The whole narrative reveals that Frankenstein, as an active figure, does only two things: he acts obsessively in creating the monster (and it should be noted that even here he insists on his passivity before fate—this provides the moral excuse); and, at the end, he acts obsessively (and ineffectually) in pursuing him. This last act is an attempt to destroy the fruits of his own ambitions. The passivity is most painful when he retreats from recognition of the evil he has created and allows Justine to die. But his initial flight from the monster is also a supreme passive act: if you don't see it, it's not there, as Jack Burden says in *All the King's Men*. After Frankenstein flees from the aborted attempt to create a mate for the monster, he glides into one of the scenes that will become typical of Victorian fiction. He finds himself on a boat which drifts beyond his control in a storm, and he comes ashore at precisely the place where the monster has just killed Clerval. His response to this is to fall into one of his characteristic illnesses that render him powerless, that return him to the helplessness of infancy and to the care of his father and family. We find in *Frankenstein*, in other words, that the passivity of the hero is not only to be explained by the ideals of prudence and domestic harmony and natural affection, or the ideal of the civilized community, but by the irrational need to escape the consequences of adulthood, to retreat to the innocence and helplessness of the womb where the heroic expression of selfhood is denied and replaced by the comfort of dependence and the absorption of the love of others.

Thus *Frankenstein* provides us with a hero whose being, in every aspect, expresses precisely those tensions which are to preoccupy later English novelists, and Frankenstein enacts not only the role of the realist hero but the alternatives to that role which do much to explain the characteristic shape of realist fiction. The failure of Frankenstein to destroy his knowledge and to retreat to innocence foreshadows, I think, the ultimate self-destruction of realist techniques. Of course, this is a dangerously oversimple generalization, and puts rather a heavy burden on a novel which makes no such claims. But studying *Frankenstein* can help us to understand some of the powerful and inexplicit energies that lie beneath the surface of realist fiction in England and can help explain both the pervasive resistance to and distrust of ambition and energy in its heroes—their strange dullness and inadequacy—and the equally strange and subversive fascination with ambition and evil energies. Who would prefer Amelia Sedley to Becky Sharp, or Little Nell to Quilp, or Daniel Deronda to Grandcourt? The irrational is latent in every important English realist novel, and within every hero there is a Frankenstein—or his monster—waiting to get out.

PETER BROOKS

"Godlike Science/ Unhallowed Arts": Language, Nature, and Monstrosity

Mary Shelley's *Frankenstein* continues to solicit and disturb us not only through its creation of a decisive image of Gothic horror, but also by the pathos of a monsterism in doomed dialectic with nature and with culture. It is above all in the question of language, both as explicit theme of the novel and as implicit model of the novel's complex organization, that the problem of the monstrous is played out. We might approach the network of issues dramatized in the novel first through Victor Frankenstein's crucial interview with his monstrous creation, the interview which leads to the Monster's telling his tale to Frankenstein, the story-within-a-story (itself a story-within-a-story-within-a-story, when we consider the role of Robert Walton as initial and ultimate narrator). Following the first murders committed by his Monster—William strangled, Justine judicially done to death through maliciously falsified evidence—Frankenstein seeks solace in the mountains above Chamonix. He penetrates into the "glorious presence-chamber of imperial Nature," climbs to Montanvert and the Mer de Glace, hoping to recapture a remembered effect of "a sublime ecstasy that gave wings to the soul, and allowed it to soar

From *The Endurance of Frankenstein*, edited by George Levine and U. C. Knoepflmacher. Copyright © 1979 by University of California Press.

from the obscure world to light and joy." His ascension takes him to a "wonderful and stupendous scene," overlooking the Mer de Glace, facing the "awful majesty" of Mont Blanc; his heart once again opens to joy, and he exclaims, in the tones of the Ossianic bard, "Wandering spirits, if indeed ye wander, and do not rest in your narrow beds; allow me this faint happiness, or take me, as your companion, away from the joys of life." Whereupon a superhuman shape comes bounding over the ice. It is, of course, no spirit of the departed, nor any beneficent spirit of nature, but the Monster himself, who has at last tracked down his creator, and will force him into parley.

It is worth noting here that virtually every time "nature" is invoked in the novel, as moral presence presiding over human life, it appears to produce only the monstrous. Thus, earlier, as Frankenstein returns to Geneva after learning of William's death, a tremendous thunderstorm breaks out over the Lake, a "noble war" in the sky that elevates his soul so that he cries out: "William, dear angel! this is thy funeral, this thy dirge!" No sooner is the apostrophe uttered than Frankenstein perceives in a flash of lightning the figure of the Monster nearby and with this apparition comes the moral certainty that here is William's murderer. We will find other instances in the fate of Henry Clerval, the poet figure in the Wordsworthian mold, nourished on "the very poetry of nature," and the creation of the Monster itself. But already it may be apparent that the call upon nature the Preserver—the moral support and guardian of man—produces instead the Destroyer, the monstrous, what Frankenstein calls "my own vampire."

Frankenstein's initial reaction to the encounter with the Monster consists in curses and an abortive attempt to do battle with him. Still the Monster pleads for a hearing. A hearing that need not be a seeing: when Frankenstein commands, "Begone! relieve me from the sight of your detested form," the Monster responds by placing his huge hands over Frankenstein's eyes: "Thus I relieve thee, my creator . . . thus I take from thee a sight which you abhor. Still thou canst listen to me, and grant me thy compassion." The Monster understands that it is not visual relationship that favors him—indeed, his only favorable reception by a human being has come from a blind man—but rather the auditory, the interlocutory, the relationship of language.

For the Monster is eloquent. From his first words, he shows himself to be a supreme rhetorician of his own situation, one who controls the antitheses and oxymorons that express the pathos of his existence: "Remember, that I am thy creature; I ought to be thy Adam; but I am rather the fallen angel, whom thou drivest from joy for no misdeed. Everywhere I see bliss, from which I alone am irrevocably excluded. I was benevolent and good; misery made me a fiend. Make me happy, and I shall again be virtuous." When we learn of the Monster's self-education—and particularly his three master-texts: *Paradise Lost*, Plutarch's *Lives*, and *Werther*—we understand the sources of his eloquence, and of the conception of a just order of things that animates his plea to his creator. But it is of primary importance to register Mary Shelley's radical and saving decision to stage a deformed and menacing creature who, rather than using grunts and gestures, speaks and reasons with the highest elegance, logic, and persuasiveness. In the Monster's use of language the novel poses its most important questions, for it is language alone that may compensate for a deficient, monstrous nature.

I

Frankenstein is touched by the Monster's eloquence. When he looks at this "filthy mass that moved and talked," he feels horror and hatred; yet by the end of the Monster's tale he avows: "His words had a strange effect upon me. I compassionated him." Through the medium of language, a first relationship is created. Like Coleridge's Wedding Guest, Frankenstein is compelled to hear out the tale of this cursed being. The force of the compulsion here is no "glittering eye," but the power of language itself to link speaker and listener. In the narrative situation of the Monster facing and speaking to his creator, we have an instance of what we might call, in the terms of Jacques Lacan, the imaginary versus the symbolic order. The imaginary order is that of the speculary, of the mirror-stage, and is based on deception, the subject's relation to itself as other. The symbolic order is that of language, the systematic and trans-subjective order of the signifier, the cultural system into which individual subjects are inserted. In any speculary relationship the Monster will always be the "filthy mass;" only in the symbolic order may he realize his desire for recognition.

The Monster hence produces a tale, based, like any tale, on the "narrative contract" between narrator and narratee. Its very possibility depends on an order of cultural symbolic which implies that network of intersubjective relations from which the Monster protests he has been excluded. The close of his narrative suggests the importance of language as relation. In arguing that Frankenstein create a female monster to be a companion to him, the Monster asserts that only in communication with a similar being can he "become linked to the chain of existence and events, from which I am now excluded." The wish for a *semblable* may itself belong to the imaginary order, as an instance of speculary narcissism and deception. The term *chain*, however, identifies meaning as residing in a systematic network of relation, in the symbolic order. It suggests Lacan's exposition of the "signifying chain" of language. Exclusion from this chain could be the very definition of monsterism. The fact of the interlocutionary relationship established by the tale-within-the-tale (within-the-tale) implies the Monster's lack and his desire. Only through those linked signs whose rules he has mastered can the Monster hope to enter "the chain of existence and events," to *signify*.

Language is also the principal theme of the Monster's story of his life up to this point. His first experience with humankind has laid bare the hopelessness of speculary relationship, its necessary result in alienation and rejection: the shepherd he encounters in a hut flees shrieking from his sight. Retreating into the hovel adjoining the De Lacey cottage, he then begins his education, seeing, but himself unseen. From his hiding place, he discovers that "these people possessed a method of communicating their experience and feelings to one another by articulate sounds." What particularly impress him are the emotional effects wrought by these sounds, which "sometimes produced pleasure or pain, smiles or sadness, in the minds and countenances of the beholders. This was indeed a godlike science."

Mary Shelley's Monster is in many respects an Enlightenment natural man, or noble savage; his first ideas demonstrate the processes of Lockean sensationalism and Hartleyan associationism. His discovery of language implies Rousseau's argument, in the *Essai sur l'origine des langues*, that language springs from passion rather than need: need cannot form the necessary social context for voiced language, since its effect is to scatter men; and need can make do with the barest repertory of visual signs, gestures, imperatives. Passion, on the other hand, brings men together, and the relation of desire calls forth voice. It is hence no accident that what language first reveals to the Monster is human love, and that his rhetorical plea to his creator ends with the demand for a creature whom he might love.

The Monster also discovers an important corollary to Rousseau's postulate of the emotional origin of language: the radical figurality of language, its founding statute as misnaming, transference. The sign is not consubstantial with the thing it names: "the words they uttered, not having any apparent connection with visible objects, I was unable to discover any clue by which I could unravel the mystery of their reference." The Monster in this manner uncovers the larger question of the arbitrariness, or immotivation, of the linguistic sign, postulated by Ferdinand de Saussure as the foundation of modern linguistics. And the consequences of this recognition will be consonant with Saussure's: the understanding that the "godlike science" of language depends, not on simple designation, on passage from the signifier to the signified, but rather on the systematic organization of signifiers. The Monster intuitively grasps that language will be of importance to him because by its very nature it implies the "chain of existence and events" within which he seeks a place, defines the interdependency of senders and receivers of messages in that chain, and provides the possibility of emotional effect independent of any designation.

The Monster unerringly discovers language to be on the side of culture rather than nature, and to imply the structures of relation at the basis of culture. The discovery is a vital one, for the side of "nature" is irreparably marked by lack, by monsterism. Against the Monster's hearing of the cottagers' language is set his discovery of his own features mirrored in a pool—a sinister parody of Eve's discovery of her fair features in the pool of Eden, on the day of her creation, in Book IV of *Paradise Lost*. In *Frankenstein*, the reflected image convinces the beholder "that I was in reality the monster that I am." This speculary *cogito*, where the Monster witnesses his outward identity as alien to his inner desire, estranged, determined by the view and judgment of the Other, clinches the importance of language as the symbolic order that must compensate for nature. The Monster understands that he must not show himself to the cottagers until he has mastered their language, "which knowledge might enable me to make them overlook the deformity of my figure."

The thematization of language becomes so rich at this point in the narrative that one is forced to abridge discussion. There is, first of all, a criss-crossing of languages implicit in the text: with the arrival of Safie, we have a lesson in French being offered to a Turkish Arab, in a German-speaking region, the whole rendered for the reader in English. This well-ordered Babel calls attention to the fact and problem of transmission and communication, the motive for language, and reminds us that the framing structure of the novel—Walton's letters to his sister, to which we shall return—evokes the same concerns. The Monster learns language through overhearing the instruction of Safie by Felix and Agatha; though excluded, he is learning the means by which to be included. Since the Monster needs language to compensate for a deficient nature, it is fitting that the first use to which he puts his new science is reading, the written word being for Rousseau precisely the supplementary and mediate state of language, its transmissible (hence also potentially deceitful) form, which does not demand presence for its operation. The three texts which the Monster finds and reads—Plutarch's *Lives*, Goethe's *Werther*, and *Paradise Lost*—cover the public, the private, and the cosmic realms, and three modes of love; they constitute a possible Romantic *cyclopedia universalis*. The Monster's literalist reading of *Paradise Lost* poses in acute, emblematic, and literary terms his problem: he appears to be a unique creation, like Adam "united by no link to any other being in existence," yet by his condition more resembling Satan. The paradox of his origin and nature will be resolved by another piece of writing, Frankenstein's lab journal, which substitutes for myths of creation a literal account of the Monster's manufacture, a "disgusting" tale of an "accursed origin," by which the Monster discovers that he has indeed been created in another's image, but as a "filthy type." The "godlike science" has led him to learn of his origins in Victor Frankenstein's "unhallowed arts."

Thus far language, and especially writing, must appear to the Monster, as it did to Rousseau, ambiguous in effect, like the Promethean gift of fire, so strange in its production of "opposite effects." Yet it remains the necessary compensation, the only hope for linkage to humankind. The Monster will try its effects first on the blind De Lacey. And here the godlike power of the science does reveal itself, as De Lacey responds: "I am blind, and cannot judge of your countenance, but there is something in your words which persuades me that you are sincere." Mutual sympathy, benefaction, protection, and relation are close to being sealed through language, when Felix, Agatha, and Safie enter and throw the situation brutally back into the speculary order: Agatha faints, Safie flees, and Felix "tore me from his father, to whose knees I clung." The result is Fall. The Monster becomes explicitly satanic—"I, like the arch-fiend, bore a hell within me," sets fire to the De Laceys' abandoned cottage, and sets forth into the world in search of his creator, the *deus absconditus* who alone now can restore, through a second creation, the Monster to the chain of living sympathies. It is during this search that the Monster commits his first murder. This act implicates the question of relation through its displacement of Oedipal conflict: the Monster strangles William when the boy protests that his "papa" is M. Frankenstein; he then stands fascinated, erotically medused by the portrait of William's and Victor's mother hanging round William's neck. The result of his baffled desire is the perverse planting of the portrait on Justine Moritz, thus condemning the mother substitute ("not indeed so beautiful as her whose portrait I held; but of an agreeable aspect, and blooming in the loveliness of youth and health"), whose possession is forever denied to him.

At its completion, the Monster's narrative implies that use of language has failed to gain him entry into the "chain of existence and events," but has rather made him fully aware of his unique and accursed origin. In his confrontation with humankind, speculary relationship and the imaginary order appear to have reasserted their dominion. Yet if language has failed to accomplish the Monster's desire, it has nonetheless provided the means for construction of a story within Frankenstein's story that will subvert the entire set of relations of which Frankenstein is part. The Monster's use of language has contextualized desire itself as a systematic chain of signifiers whose rhetorical effect cannot be denied by the narratee. The symbolic order is operational.

In the passage from the Monster's narrative back to Frankenstein's, desire reveals its functioning as metonymy, explicated by Lacan as a perpetual "sliding" of the inaccessible signified under the signifier. Desire is born from an original lack or want, in the discrepancy between need and demand, which in the relationship of Monster to creator (as in the infant-mother relationship) is essentially the demand for recognition. In constructing his narrative appeal, the Monster has made language the vehicle of desire, has built a construct of signifiers which figures his initial want and lack without fulfilling it, so that language itself as relation becomes the medium of his truth, which is want to relation. The metonymic sliding passes desire on to his interlocutor, charged now with crossing the "bar" between signifier and signified, finding access to the meaning of desire. Frankenstein is forced to accept the establishment of relation and the contagion of desire: "His tale, and the feelings he now expressed, proved him to be a creature of fine sensations; and did I not as his maker owe him all the portion of happiness that it was in my power to bestow?" This response is the basis for a contract or even convenant: the Monster will desist from acts of vengeance against mankind, while Frankenstein will undertake creation of a female monster.

The covenant is violated by the creator himself when he destroys the nearly completed form of the Monster's companion. This violent rupture may serve notice that Frankenstein has come to understand that the Monster's expressed wish is a figure for something else that could endanger the whole dialectic of desire and repression. He has agreed to create the monsteress because, while he is moved by the Monster's narrative, he cannot "sympathize with him." This creation, then, would be a *substitute* for the Monster's inclusion within the human chain; Frankenstein may obscurely recognize that the Monster's desire for his mate may itself be a substitute for his real, his absolute demand, which is for recognition by his creator. To create the monsteress would be to create the possibility of that demand being laid bare, and this in turn would confront Frankenstein too blindingly with the monstrous element in his own nature, would force him to recognize what he wishes to deny. The Monster would be his *symptom* ("my own spirit let loose from the grave"), which in Lacanian terms is metaphor, the figure of access to repressed truth.

Whatever the value of such a speculative interpretation, Frankenstein's decision to break his promise to the Monster explicitly concerns the "chain of existence and events." It occurs to Frankenstein that the inevitable result of "those sympathies for which the daemon thirsted" will be a race of monstrous progeny that may wreak havoc on mankind. Precisely because the special creation demanded by the Monster has as its purpose the inception of an affective chain *outside* humanity—a new family, a new society—it raises the frightening possibility of a new and uncontrollable signifying chain, one with unknown rules and grammar. Milton's Eve after the Fall considers that the divine command to reproduce now means "propagated curse." The idea of the propagation of his aberrant signifier, through unforeseeably monstrous messages, leads Frankenstein to destroy what the Monster considers his authentic desired signified, and to accept the consequences in terms of his own chain of affections—consequences that are immediately ghastly.

The Monster is now hopelessly condemned to the order of words that does not match the order of things, that has not produced the desired referent but has only brought knowledge of the unappeasable lack or difference that defines his monsterism. The godlike science itself proves deceptive: his eloquence can achieve no more than a state of permanently frustrated desire for meaning; his language is metonymic advance without a terminus. The way in which, out of his frustration, he seeks vengeance on Frankenstein exactly mirrors this situation. He does not strike directly at his creator—at the sacred name that is the signified of all signifiers—but, by displacement, by metonymy, at closely related elements in Frankenstein's own chain of existence and events: at his friend Clerval, at Elizabeth when she becomes Frankenstein's bride. Despite the Monster's words, "I will be with you on your wedding night," Frankenstein seems obtusely blind as to the threatened object. The reader understands at once that it must be Frankenstein's bride who will be sacrificed to the bride denied to the Monster.

One could pause over Frankenstein's blindness, the convergence of Eros and death on his wedding night, and the apparent fear of erotic union. "Oh! peace, peace, my love," he murmurs to Elizabeth, "this night, and all will be safe: but this night is dreadful, very dreadful." Elizabeth may be the interdicted because incestuous bride: she has been raised as sister to Frankenstein, and has furthermore assumed the nurturing role of Frankenstein's dead mother. The necrophilic embrace which is all that Frankenstein obtains follows the logic of his creative project, which has usurped the power to make life from the dead. Fulfillment with Elizabeth would mark Frankenstein's achievement of a full signified in his life, accession to plenitude of being—which would leave no place in creation for his daemonic projection, the Monster. That projection must act out Frankenstein's sadistic impulses in destruction of the being who would bring rest, and arrest, to Frankenstein's movement of desire, must maintain the lack that led to the Monster's creation in the first place.

Frankenstein and his Monster are in fact by now engaged in an exacerbated dialectic of desire, in which each needs the other because the other represents for each the lack or gap within himself. Frankenstein sets out in pursuit of the Monster intending to destroy him, but also with a firm intuition that the Monster's death will be his own death—that in destroying the daemonic side of himself, he will also destroy the whole of self. For, like the Monster, he too bears "a Hell within me," and destruction of the representative of that hell will entail destruction of the ego, now mastered by its sadistic drives. The Monster flees from Frankenstein, yet never escapes completely, intent that Frankenstein maintain his pursuit, the only form of recognition by his creator that he can exact, his last tenuous link to the signifying chain. Hence as he flees the Monster leaves his mark and trace to guide his pursuer, messages carved in trees, even caches of food to sustain the chase. "Come on, my enemy," reads one inscription, in a nice balance of hatred and affection. The pursuit finally leads toward the very heart of non-meaning, toward the lifeless pole, the immaculate icecap.

II

What we have said about the Monster's efforts to achieve recognition and to enter the signifying chain may pose with new force the question with which we began, the relation of the monstrous on the one hand to nature, on the other to culture. The question of origins has been of utmost importance to the Monster since his first initiation into language. Like Oedipus, he has felt that his very definition depended on the discovery of his generation: "Who was I? What was I? Whence did I come?" His origin turns out to be not the defining plenitude of parenthood—the two who make one—but an undecidable borderline instance. He appears to have been generated at the very frontier between nature and the supernatural, from Frankenstein's studies in physics and chemistry, which are always on the verge of becoming metaphysics and alchemy. When Frankenstein discovers the principle of animation (the Promethean revelation which the text never speaks, but maintains as a central interdiction and dumbness), he must proceed through death to create a new life. "Life and death," he recalls, "appeared to me ideal bounds, which I should first break through, and pour a torrent of light into our dark world." Thus he works within the very "citadel of nature," with its first principles, but he is engaged in an overreaching quest which from its inception bears the mark of the counternatural. For his "loathesome" task he collects "with profane fingers" pieces of the dead; he becomes "insensible to the charms of nature," and the seasons pass unnoticed. The Monster comes into existence as a product of nature—his ingredients are one hundred percent natural—yet by the fact and process of his creation he is unnatural. Yet since he is a unique creation, without precedence or replication, he has no cultural context. He remains, so to speak, postnatural and precultural.

Despite the ambiguities and profanity of his creation, the Monster comes into existence potentially good, an Enlightenment savage with essentially benevolent instincts. The story of his education is a classic study of right natural instinct perverted and turned evil by the social milieu, a counterexample to such pedagogical utopias as Rousseau's *Emile*. He understands perfectly what has happened to him: "I am malicious because I am miserable," he says; and we must believe that the establishment of links between himself and the human community would restore his benevolence. Natural goodness is real but not sturdy; rejection and isolation easily turn us back to an original accursedness, to the satanic *non serviam*: "Evil henceforth be thou my good."

"Nature" in *Frankenstein* appears to be a fragile moral concept of ambiguous implication. It is as if the Monster, generated within the sanctum of nature, at home in its most sublime settings, might himself represent the final secret of nature, its force of forces. The novel dissents from the optimistic assumption that nature is support and comfort and source of right moral feeling—"The guide, the guardian of my heart, and soul/Of all my moral being," as Wordsworth writes in "Tintern Abbey." This dissent is suggested most forcefully through the figure of Henry Clerval, who balances Frankenstein's pursuit of science with study of the poets and is described as "a being formed in 'the very poetry of nature'" (the quotation is from Leigh Hunt). Frankenstein quotes Wordsworth in a description of Clerval:

> The sounding cataract
> Haunted *him* like a passion: the tall rock,
> The mountain, and the deep and gloomy wood,
> Their colours and their forms, were then to him
> An appetite; a feeling, and a love,
> That had no need of a remoter charm,
> By thought supplied, or any interest
> Unborrow'd from the eye.

The lines from "Tintern Abbey" are usually taken to represent the poet's first, immediate, unreflective relation to nature, now lost to him but apparent in his sister Dorothy, to whom he can say that "Nature never did betray/The heart that loved her." As Peter Scott [has pointed out], Clerval cleaves to nature with a Wordsworthian child-like love and trust; yet when he falls victim to the Monster the ensuing scenario curiously implicates nature. Frankenstein has defied the Monster by destroying the nearly complete monsteress, and has rowed out to cast the *disjecta membra* into the sea. He then loses consciousness, a storm blows up, his skiff is blown off course and finally comes to ground on the Irish coast, where he is arrested as a murderer and confronted with Clerval's corpse. Nature does not protect Clerval from its own malignant possibilities. It contains more than sounding cataracts and sublime mountains: there are also unaccommodated monsters and disseminated pieces of monstrous creation.

Nature is not one thing, and those who think it so are caught in a self-destructive blindness. This Frankenstein eventually recognizes, when he cries out to the Genevan magistrate who refuses to credit his tale of the Monster, "Man . . . how ignorant art thou in thy pride of wisdom!" Nature is preserver and destroyer. It possesses the awesome and ambiguous Power evoked in P. B. Shelley's "Mont Blanc," a poem written in the same summer that Mary Shelley composed *Frankenstein*, which takes us back to the scene on the Mer de Glace, where, in "the glorious presence-chamber of imperial nature," Victor evokes the spirit of the majestic mountain and instead summons forth his created daemon. The daemonic virtuality of Power in "Mont Blanc" "dwells apart." *Frankenstein* brings it into human existence, as the destructive potential of the creative drive, or Eros, of nature's creature man.

The fact of monsterism suggests that nature in *Frankenstein* has something of the radical amorality described by Sade. For Sade, nature permits everything and authorizes nothing. Since all tastes and pleasures are in nature, no perversion can outrage and no crime alter nature; if one searches for an underlying pattern or principle in nature, what one finds is destruction itself. Therefore man's destruction—torture, murder—merely does nature's work. The impassibility of nature, the regulatory principle of life which yet refuses to offer any ethical principle, is a source of anguish for Sade; and his compilation of pleasures and crimes *contra naturam* can be read as an ever-frustrated effort to make a human mark on nature, to break nature's bonds, to reach through to some transcendent principle. There are perhaps parallels to be found in Victor Frankenstein's manic quest to push nature to a frontier where it becomes meta-nature, where it releases its own principle of being. Certainly Frankenstein's assault on and in the citadel of nature produces a monsterism that both reveals and mocks the arcane principle. The overriding fact of nature in the book—dominating Mont Blanc, the Lake of Geneva, the Hebrides, and all the other sublime natural settings—is the fact and possibility of monsterism itself. It is to this, I believe, that the Monster returns in his peroration, as he says farewell to Walton and to the dead Frankenstein: "Blasted as thou wert, my agony was still superior to thine." He attributes his superior torture to remorse; yet surely it first of all derives from the condition of monstrosity itself. This is the supreme agony, and the properly monstrous blot upon nature: that nature should be capable of producing the monstrous. It is a nature that eludes any optimistic Romanticism, and finally most resembles Freud's "uncanny": the Monster perfectly illustrates the *Unheimliche*, a monstrous potentiality so close to us—so close to home—that we have repressed its possibility, and assigned an *un* as the mark of censorship on what is indeed too *heimisch* for comfort.

The ambiguous and paradoxical nature of nature in *Frankenstein*—its seemingly equal potential as essentially good and as self-negatingly evil—cannot be resolved within the orders of the real or the imaginary, but only within the symbolic order, and only in structural terms. That is, the creations of nature will be bad or good only through the play of difference and relation, only in terms of their place in the signifying chain. This is what the Monster has understood by the time he makes his appeal to his creator for a *semblable*, what indeed he has already grasped when he intuits the possibilities of the "godlike science." In the play of sameness and difference that founds the system of our signs for things, then in grammar and syntax, we have the basis of relation and the possibility of exchange of tokens, communication. The Monster's failure—what establishes him irremediably *as* monster—is his inability, despite his eloquence, to find relation.

There finally remains as interlocutor for the Monster only Walton, who has been warned by Frankenstein that though the Monster is "eloquent and persuasive," he is not to be listened to. By the time of his confrontation with Walton that closes the book, the Monster states his recognition that his effort to enter into the signifying chain is at an end: "the miserable series of my being is wound to its close." This expression, "the series of my being," is used twice in the final scene. The now obsolete sense of series as "sequence," "order," suggests the meaning of "chain" in the word's etymology, and well implies the metonymic "sliding" of the Monster's effort to reach satisfaction of desire, the movement ever forward that can reach no point of arrest and no ultimate structuring relationship. It is a textual movement that can never cover over and fill in its central lack, that can reach an end only in extinction.

Yet in a larger context, the "series" does not stop with the Monster's self-immolation. The fact of monstrosity has established its own chain, with its own syntax and significance. The contamination of monsterism is a kind of accursed signifier that has come to inhabit the novel's principal actors. We must here reflect on the significance of the outer frame of the novel, which encloses Frankenstein's narrative as his encloses the Monster's. Walton's initial letters to his sister strike the very note of the Monster's narrative: Walton has "no friend...no one to participate my joy...to sustain me in dejection." He is reduced to committing his thoughts to paper, "a poor medium for the communication of feeling" when really "I desire the company of a man who could sympathize with me; whose eyes would reply to mine." In the uninhabited polar regions he meets his first friend in a man who has had similar visions of Promethean discovery and fame, and whose understanding of friendship—since the death of Clerval—articulates

Walton's own feelings: "I agree with you . . . we are unfashioned creatures, but half made up, if one wiser, better, dearer than ourselves—such a friend ought to be—do not lend his aid to perfectionate our weak and faulty natures." Friendship is thus defined as specularity and as complementarity, the longing of two incomplete creatures for fullness in androgynous fusion. But this dream is no more to be realized than the Monster's hope of union. Walton loses Frankenstein to death. And he loses his dream of Promethean discovery, as his mutinous sailors vote to turn southward. His hopes are "blasted"—the term applied to Frankenstein's aspirations, and which the Monster will at the last apply to himself.

All aspirations, then, lie blasted and wasted at the end, as if the original act of overreaching, of sacrilegious creation, had tainted the world. Each tale interlocked within tale touches its listener with the taint of monsterism: Frankenstein receives it from the Monster's tale—his life, contracted to the Monster's desire, becomes torment thereafter—and Walton receives it from Frankenstein's. Walton remains, like the Ancient Mariner—or perhaps, more accurately, like the Wedding-Guest—the bearer of a tale of unnatural wisdom, the bearer of the taint of monsterism. The fate of this monsterism can perhaps best be described as textual. The ostensible recipient of Walton's letters (and hence of the interpolated manuscript of Frankenstein, itself containing the Monster's narrative) is Margaret Saville, Walton's sister. (Is there, once again, a suggestion of incest in the choice of the object of affection?) But she has no more existence in the novel than a postal address. She is inscribed as a kind of lack of being, leaving us with only a text, a narrative tissue that never wholly conceals its lack of ultimate reference and its interminable projection forward to no destination.

The absent Mrs. Saville, faceless addressee of all the textual material that constitutes Frankenstein, is exemplary of the situation of language and desire as they have been dramatized in the novel. If the Monster's story demonstrates that the godlike science of language is a supplement to a deficient nature, an attempt to overcome a central gap or lack of being, the inner and outer frames—Frankenstein's narrative and Walton's letters—indicate that language never can overcome the gap, that the chain established has no privileged limits, no mode of reference, but signifies purely as a chain, a system or series in which everything is mutually interrelated and interdependent but without any transcendent signified. There is no transcendent signified because the fact of monsterism is never either justified nor overcome, but is simply passed along the chain, finally to come to inhabit the reader himself who, as animator of the text, is left with the contamination of monsterism. Desire—Walton's, Frankenstein's, the Monster's—cannot overcome the monstrous but only reproduce it. Monsterism comes rather to be contextualized; the text remains as indelible record of the monstrous, emblem of language's murderous lack of transcendent reference.

In his essay on the *Unheimliche*, Freud speculates on the special capacity of literature to evoke and to control the feeling of the uncanny. Literature appears to be a kind of controlled play with the daemonic. It may belong to the logic of literature that Mary Shelley's daemon should understand that his place lies within the symbolic order of language, that the daemon should fail of arriving at meaning, and become rather the very image of a desire that can never fix or pin down meaning, but merely pass on the desire and the curse of meaning. Yet here we find the logic of desire in literature, desire of the text and for the text. The text solicits us through the promise of a transcendent signified, and leaves us, on the threshold of pleasure, to be content with the play of its signifiers. At the same time, it contaminates us with a residue of meaning that cannot be explained or rationalized, but is passed on as affect, as taint.

SANDRA M. GILBERT AND SUSAN GUBAR

Horror's Twin: Mary Shelley's Monstrous Eve

Many critics have noticed that
Frankenstein (1818) is one of the key Romantic "readings" of *Paradise Lost*.
Significantly, however, as a woman's reading it is most especially the story of
hell: hell as a dark parody of heaven, hell's creations as monstrous imitations
of heaven's creations, and hellish femaleness as a grotesque parody of
heavenly maleness. But of course the divagations of the parody merely
return to and reinforce the fearful reality of the original. For by parodying
Paradise Lost in what may have begun as a secret, barely conscious attempt
to subvert Milton, Shelley ended up telling, too, the central story of *Paradise
Lost*, the tale of "what misery th' inabstinence of Eve/Shall bring on men."

Mary Shelley herself claims to have been continually asked "how I . . .
came to think of and to dilate upon so very hideous an idea" as that of
Frankenstein, but it is really not surprising that she should have formulated
her anxieties about femaleness in such highly literary terms. For of course
the nineteen-year-old girl who wrote *Frankenstein* was no ordinary nineteen-
year-old but one of England's most notable literary heiresses. Indeed, as "the
daughter of two persons of distinguished literary celebrity," and the wife of a
third, Mary Wollstonecraft Godwin Shelley was the daughter and later the
wife of some of Milton's keenest critics, so that Harold Bloom's useful
conceit about the family romance of English literature is simply an accurate
description of the reality of her life.

In acknowledgment of this web of literary/familial relationships, critics have traditionally studied *Frankenstein* as an interesting example of Romantic myth-making, a work ancillary to such established Promethean masterpieces as Shelley's *Prometheus Unbound* and Byron's *Manfred*. ("Like almost everything else about [Mary's] life," one such critic remarks, *Frankenstein* "is an instance of genius observed and admired but not shared.") Recently, however, a number of writers have noticed the connection between Mary Shelley's "waking dream" of monster-manufacture and her own experience of awakening sexuality, in particular the "horror story of Maternity" which accompanied her precipitous entrance into what Ellen Moers calls "teen-age motherhood." Clearly they are articulating an increasingly uneasy sense that, despite its male protagonist and its underpinning of "masculine" philosophy, *Frankenstein* is somehow a "woman's book," if only because its author was caught up in such a maelstrom of sexuality at the time she wrote the novel.

In making their case for the work as female fantasy, though, critics like Moers have tended to evade the problems posed by what we must define as *Frankenstein*'s literariness. Yet, despite the weaknesses in those traditional readings of the novel that overlook its intensely sexual materials, it is still undeniably true that Mary Shelley's "ghost story," growing from a Keatsian (or Coleridgean) waking dream, is a Romantic novel about—among other things—Romanticism, as well as a book about books and perhaps, too, about the writers of books. Any theorist of the novel's femaleness and of its significance as, in Moers's phrase, a "birth myth" must therefore confront this self-conscious literariness. For as was only natural in "the daughter of two persons of distinguished literary celebrity," Mary Shelley explained her sexuality to herself in the context of her reading and its powerfully felt implications.

For this orphaned literary heiress, highly charged connections between femaleness and literariness must have been established early, and established specifically in relation to the controversial figure of her dead mother. As we shall see, Mary Wollstonecraft Godwin read her mother's writings over and over again as she was growing up. Perhaps more important, she undoubtedly read most of the reviews of her mother's *Posthumous Works*, reviews in which Mary Wollstonecraft was attacked as a "philosophical wanton" and a monster, while her *Vindication of the Rights of Woman* (1792) was called "A scripture, archly fram'd for propagating w[hore]s." But in any case, to the "philosophical wanton's" daughter, all reading about (or of) her mother's work must have been painful, given her knowledge that that passionate feminist writer had died in giving life to *her*, to bestow upon Wollstonecraft's death from complications of childbirth the melodramatic cast it probably had for the girl herself. That Mary Shelley was conscious, moreover, of a strangely intimate relationship between her feelings toward her dead mother, her romance with a living poet, and her own sense of vocation as a reader and writer is made perfectly clear by her habit of "taking her books to Mary Wollstonecraft's grave in St. Pancras' Church-yard, there," as Muriel Spark puts it, "to pursue her studies in an atmosphere of communion with a mind greater than the second Mrs. Godwin's [and] to meet Shelley in secret."

Her mother's grave: the setting seems an unusually grim, even ghoulish locale for reading, writing, or lovemaking. Yet, to a girl with Mary Shelley's background, literary activities, like sexual ones, must have been primarily extensions of the elaborate, gothic psychodrama of her family history. If her famous diary is largely a compendium of her reading lists and Shelley's that fact does not, therefore, suggest unusual reticence on her part. Rather, it emphasizes the point that for Mary, even more than for most writers, reading a book was often an emotional as well as an intellectual event of considerable magnitude. Especially because she never knew her mother, and because her father seemed so definitively to reject her after her youthful elopement, her principal mode of self-definition—certainly in the early years of her life with Shelley, when she was writing *Frankenstein*—was through reading, and to a lesser extent through writing.

Endlessly studying her mother's works and her father's, Mary Shelley may be said to have "read" her family and to have been related to her reading, for books appear to have functioned as her surrogate parents, pages and words standing in for flesh and blood. That much of her reading was undertaken in Shelley's company, moreover, may also help explain some of this obsessiveness, for Mary's literary inheritance was obviously involved in her very literary romance and marriage. In the years just before she wrote *Frankenstein*, for instance, and those when she was engaged in composing the novel (1816–17), she studied her parents' writings, alone or together with Shelley, like a scholarly detective seeking clues to the significance of some cryptic text.

To be sure, this investigation of the mysteries of literary genealogy was done in a larger context. In these same years, Mary Shelley recorded innumerable readings of contemporary gothic novels, as well as a program of study in English, French, and German literature that would do credit to a modern graduate student. But especially, in 1815, 1816, and 1817, she read the works of Milton: *Paradise Lost* (twice), *Paradise Regained*, *Comus*, *Areopagetica*, *Lycidas*. And what makes the extent of this reading particularly impressive is the fact that in these years, her seventeenth to her twenty-first, Mary Shelley was almost continuously pregnant, "confined," or nursing. At the same time, it is precisely the coincidence of all these disparate activities—her family studies, her initiation into adult sexuality, and her literary self-education—that makes her vision of *Paradise Lost* so significant.

For her developing sense of herself as a literary creature and/or creator seems to have been inseparable from her emerging self-definition as daughter, mistress, wife, and mother. Thus she cast her birth myth—her myth of origins—in precisely those cosmogenic terms to which her parents, her husband, and indeed her whole literary culture continually alluded: the terms of *Paradise Lost*, which (as she indicates even on the title page of her novel), she saw as preceding, paralleling, and commenting upon the Greek cosmogeny of the Prometheus play her husband had just translated. It is as a female fantasy of sex and reading, then, a gothic psychodrama reflecting Mary Shelley's own sense of what we might call bibliogenesis, that *Frankenstein* is a version of the misogynistic story implicit in *Paradise Lost*.

It would be a mistake to underestimate the significance of *Frankenstein's* title page, with its allusive subtitle ("The Modern Prometheus") and carefully pointed Miltonic epigraph ("Did I request thee, Maker, from my clay/To mould me man? Did I solicit thee/From darkness to promote me?"). But our first really serious clue to the highly literary nature of this history of a creature born outside history is its author's use of an unusually *evidentiary* technique for conveying the stories of her monster and his maker. Like a literary jigsaw puzzle, a collection of apparently random documents from whose juxtaposition the scholar-detective must infer a meaning, *Frankenstein* consists of three "concentric circles" of narration (Walton's letters, Victor Frankenstein's recital to Walton, and the monster's speech to Frankenstein), within which are embedded pockets of digression containing other miniature narratives (Frankenstein's mother's story, Elizabeth Lavenza's and Justine's stories, Felix's and Agatha's story, Safie's story), etc. As we have noted, reading and assembling documentary evidence, examining it, analyzing it and researching it comprised for Shelley a crucial if voyeuristic method of exploring origins, explaining identity, understanding sexuality. Even more obviously, it was a way of researching and analyzing an emotionally unintelligible text, like *Paradise Lost*. In a sense, then, even before *Paradise Lost* as a central item on the monster's reading list becomes a literal event in *Frankenstein*, the novel's literary structure prepares us to confront Milton's patriarchal epic, both as a sort of research problem and as the framework for a complex system of allusions.

The book's dramatic situations are equally resonant. Like Mary Shelley, who was a puzzled but studious Miltonist, this novel's key characters—Walton, Frankenstein, and the monster—are obsessed with problem-solving. "I shall satiate my ardent curiosity with the sight of a part of the world never before visited," exclaims the young explorer, Walton, as he embarks like a child "on an expedition of discovery up his native river" (letter 1). "While my companions contemplated . . . the magnificent appearance of things," declares Frankenstein, the scientist of sexual ontology, "I delighted in investigating their causes" (chap. 2). "Who was I? What was I? Whence did I come?" (chap. 15) the monster reports wondering, describing endless speculations cast in Miltonic terms. All three, like Shelley herself, appear to be trying to understand their presence in a fallen world, and trying at the same time to define the nature of the lost paradise that must have existed before the fall. But unlike Adam, all three characters seem to have fallen not merely from Eden but from the earth, fallen directly into hell, like Sin, Satan, and—by implication—Eve. Thus their questionings are in some sense female, for they belong in that line of literary women's questionings of the fall into gender which goes back at least to Anne Finch's plaintive "How are we fal'n?" and forward to Sylvia Plath's horrified "I have fallen very far!"

From the first, however, *Frankenstein* answers such neo-Miltonic questions mainly through explicit or implicit allusions to Milton, retelling the story of the fall not so much to protest against it as to clarify its meaning. The parallels between those two Promethean overreachers Walton and Frankenstein, for instance, have always been clear to readers. But that both characters can, therefore, be described (the way Walton describes Frankenstein) as "fallen angels" is not as frequently remarked. Yet Frankenstein himself is perceptive enough to ask Walton "Do you share my madness?" at just the moment when the young explorer remarks Satanically that "One man's life or death were but a small price to pay...for the dominion I [wish to] acquire" (letter 4). Plainly one fallen angel can recognize another. Alienated from his crew and chronically friendless, Walton tells his sister that he longs for a friend "on the wide ocean," and what he discovers in Victor Frankenstein is the fellowship of hell.

In fact, like the many other secondary narratives Mary Shelley offers in her novel, Walton's story is itself an alternative version of the myth of origins presented in *Paradise Lost*. Writing his ambitious letters home from St. Petersburgh [sic], Archangel, and points north, Walton moves like Satan away from the sanctity and sanity represented by his sister, his crew, and the allegorical names of the places he leaves. Like Satan, too, he seems at least in part to be exploring the frozen frontiers of hell in order to attempt a return to heaven, for the "country of eternal light" he envisions at the Pole (letter 1) has much in common with Milton's celestial "Fountain of Light" (*PL* 3. 375). Again, like Satan's (and Eve's) aspirations, his ambition has violated a patriarchal decree: his father's "dying injunction" had forbidden him "to embark on a seafaring life." Moreover, even the icy hell where Walton encounters Frankenstein and the monster is Miltonic, for all three of these diabolical wanderers must learn, like the fallen angels of *Paradise Lost*, that "Beyond this flood a frozen Continent/Lies dark and wild.../ Thither by harpy-footed Furies hal'd,/At certain revolutions all the damn'd/Are brought . . . From Beds of raging Fire to starve in Ice" (*PL* 2. 587–600).

Finally, another of Walton's revelations illuminates not only the likeness of his ambitions to Satan's but also the similarity of his anxieties to those of his female author. Speaking of his childhood, he reminds his sister that, because poetry had "lifted [my soul] to heaven," he had become a poet and "for one year lived in a paradise of my own creation." Then he adds ominously that "You are well-acquainted with my failure and how heavily I bore the disappointment" (letter 1). But of course, as she confesses in her introduction to *Frankenstein*, Mary Shelley, too, had spent her childhood in "waking dreams" of literature; later, both she and her poet-husband hoped she would prove herself "worthy of [her] parentage and enroll [herself] on the page of fame." In a sense, then, given the Miltonic context in which Walton's story of poetic failure is set, it seems possible that one of the anxious fantasies his narrative helps Mary Shelley covertly examine is the fearful tale of a female fall from a lost paradise of art, speech, and autonomy into a hell of sexuality, silence, and filthy materiality, "A Universe of death, which God by curse/Created evil, for evil only good,/Where all life dies, death lives, and Nature breeds,/Perverse, all monstrous, all prodigious things" (*PL* 2. 622–25).

Walton and his new friend Victor Frankenstein have considerably more in common than a Byronic (or Monk Lewis-ish) Satanism. For one thing, both are orphans, as Frankenstein's monster is and as it turns out all the major and almost all the minor characters in *Frankenstein* are, from Caroline Beaufort and Elizabeth Lavenza to Justine, Felix, Agatha, and Safie. Victor Frankenstein has not always been an orphan, though, and Shelley devotes much space to an account of his family history. Family histories, in fact, especially those of orphans, appear to fascinate her, and wherever she can include one in the narrative she does so with an obsessiveness suggesting that through the disastrous tale of the child who becomes "an orphan and a beggar" she is once more recounting the story of the fall, the expulsion from paradise, and the confrontation of hell. For Milton's Adam and Eve, after all, began as motherless orphans reared (like Shelley herself) by a stern but kindly father-god, and ended as beggars rejected by God (as she was by Godwin when she eloped). Thus Caroline Beaufort's father dies leaving her "an orphan and a beggar," and Elizabeth Lavenza also becomes "an orphan and a beggar"—the phrase is repeated (chap. 1)—with the disappearance of her father into an Austrian dungeon. And though both girls are rescued by Alphonse Frankenstein, Victor's father, the early alienation from the patriarchal chain-of-being signalled by their orphanhood prefigures the hellish fate in store for them and their family. Later, motherless Safie and fatherless Justine enact similarly ominous anxiety fantasies about the fall of woman into orphanhood and beggary.

Beyond their orphanhood, however, a universal sense of guilt links such diverse figures as Justine, Felix, and Elizabeth, just as it will eventually link Victor, Walton, and the monster. Justine, for instance, irrationally confesses to the murder of little William, though she knows perfectly well she is innocent. Even more irrationally, Elizabeth is reported by Alphonse Frankenstein to have exclaimed "Oh, God! I have murdered my darling child!" after her first sight of the corpse of little William (chap. 7). Victor, too, long before he knows that the monster is actually his brother's killer, decides that his "creature" has killed William and that therefore he, the creator, is the "true murderer": "the mere presence of the idea," he notes, is "an irresistable proof of the fact" (chap. 7). Complicity in the murder of the child William is, it seems, another crucial component of the Original Sin shared by prominent members of the Frankenstein family.

At the same time, the likenesses among all these characters—the common alienation, the shared guilt, the orphanhood and beggary—imply relationships of redundance between them like the solipsistic relationships among artfully placed mirrors. What reinforces our sense of this hellish solipsism is the barely disguised incest at the heart of a number of the marriages and romances the novel describes. Most notably, Victor Frankenstein is slated to marry his "more than sister" Elizabeth Lavenza, whom he confesses to having always considered "a possession of my own" (chap. 1). But the mysterious Mrs. Saville, to whom Walton's letters are addressed, is apparently in some sense *his* more than sister, just as Caroline Beaufort was clearly a "more than" wife, in fact a daughter, to her father's friend Alphonse Frankenstein. Even relationless Justine appears to have a metaphorically incestuous relationship with the Frankensteins, since as their servant she becomes their possession and more than sister, while the female monster Victor half-constructs in Scotland will be a more than sister as well as a mate to the monster, since both have the same parent/creator.

Certainly at least some of this incest-obsession in *Frankenstein* is, as Ellen Moers remarks, the "standard" sensational matter of Romantic novels. Some of it, too, even without the conventions of the gothic thriller, would be a natural subject for an impressionable young woman who had just spent several months in the company of the famously incestuous author of *Manfred*. Nevertheless, the streak of incest that darkens *Frankenstein* probably owes as much to the book's Miltonic framework as it does to Mary Shelley's own life and times. In the Edenic cosiness of their childhood, for instance, Victor and Elizabeth are incestuous as Adam and Eve are, literally incestuous because they have the same creator, and figuratively so because Elizabeth is Victor's pretty plaything, the image of an angelic soul or "epipsyche" created from his own soul just as Eve is created from Adam's rib. Similarly, the incestuous relationships of Satan and Sin, and by implication of Satan and Eve, are mirrored in the incest fantasies of *Frankenstein*, including the disguised but intensely sexual waking dream in which Victor Frankenstein in effect couples with his monster by applying "the instruments of life" to its body and inducing a shudder of response (chap. 5). For Milton, and therefore for Mary Shelley, who was trying to understand Milton, incest was an inescapable metaphor for the solipsistic fever of self-awareness that Matthew Arnold was later to call "the dialogue of the mind with itself."

If Victor Frankenstein can be likened to both Adam and Satan, however, who or what is he *really*? Here we are obliged to confront both the moral ambiguity and the symbolic slipperiness which are at the heart of all the characterizations in *Frankenstein*. In fact, it is probably these continual and complex reallocations of meaning, among characters whose histories echo and re-echo each other, that have been so bewildering to critics. Like figures in a dream, all the people in *Frankenstein* have different bodies and somehow, horribly, the same face, or worse—the same two faces. For this reason, as Muriel Spark notes, even the book's subtitle "The Modern Prometheus" is ambiguous, "for though at first Frankenstein is himself the Prometheus, the vital fire-endowing protagonist, the Monster, as soon as he is created, takes on [a different aspect of] the role." Moreover, if we postulate that Mary Shelley is more concerned with Milton than she is with Aeschylus, the intertwining of meanings grows even more confusing, as the monster himself several times points out to Frankenstein, noting "I ought to be thy Adam, but I am rather the fallen angel," (chap. 10), then adding elsewhere that "God, in pity, made man beautiful . . . after His own image; but my form is a filthy type of yours. . . . Satan had his companions . . . but I am solitary and abhorred" (chap. 15). In other words, not only do Frankenstein and his monster both in one way or another enact the story of Prometheus, each is at one time or another like God (Victor as creator, the monster as his creator's "Master"), like Adam (Victor as innocent child, the monster as primordial "creature"), and like Satan (Victor as tormented overreacher, the monster as vengeful fiend).

What is the reason for this continual duplication and reduplication of roles? Most obviously, perhaps, the dreamlike shifting of fantasy figures from part to part, costume to costume, tells us that we are in fact dealing with the psychodrama or waking dream that Shelley herself suspected she had written. Beyond this, however, we would argue that the fluidity of the narrative's symbolic scheme reinforces in another way the crucial significance of the Miltonic skeleton around which Mary Shelley's hideous progeny took shape. For it becomes increasingly clear as one reads *Frankenstein* with *Paradise Lost* in mind that because the novel's author is such an inveterate student of literature, families, and sexuality, and because she is using her novel as a tool to help her make sense of her reading, *Frankenstein* is ultimately a mock *Paradise Lost* in which both Victor and his monster, together with a number of secondary characters, play all the neo-biblical parts over and over again—all except, it seems at first, the part of Eve. Not just the striking omission of any obvious Eve-figure from this "woman's book" about Milton, but also the barely concealed sexual components of the story as well as our earlier analysis of Milton's bogey should tell us, however, that for Mary Shelley the part of Eve *is* all the parts.

On the surface, Victor seems at first more Adamic than Satanic or Eve-like. His Edenic childhood is an interlude of prelapsarian innocence in which, like Adam, he is sheltered by his benevolent father as a sensitive plant might be "sheltered by the gardener, from every rougher wind" (chap. 1). When cherubic Elizabeth Lavenza joins the family, she seems as "heaven-sent" as Milton's Eve, as much Victor's "possession" as Adam's rib is Adam's. Moreover, though he is evidently forbidden almost nothing ("My parents [were not] tyrants . . . but the agents and creators of many delights"), Victor hints to Walton that his deific father, like Adam's and Walton's, did on one occasion arbitrarily forbid him to pursue his interest in arcane knowledge. Indeed, like Eve and Satan, Victor blames his own fall at least in part on his father's apparent arbitrariness. "If . . . my father had taken the pains to explain to me that the principles of Agrippa had been entirely exploded. . . . It is even possible that the train of my ideas would never have received the fatal impulse that led to my ruin" (chap. 2). And soon after asserting this he even associates an incident in which a tree is struck by Jovian thunderbolts with his feelings about his forbidden studies.

As his researches into the "secrets of nature" become more feverish, however, and as his ambition "to explore unknown powers" grows more intense, Victor begins to metamorphose from Adam to Satan, becoming "as Gods" in his capacity of "bestowing animation upon lifeless matter," laboring like a guilty artist to complete his false creation. Finally, in his conversations with Walton he echoes Milton's fallen angel, and Marlowe's, in his frequently reiterated confession that "I bore a hell within me which nothing could extinguish" (chap. 8). Indeed, as the "true murderer" of innocence, here cast in the form of the child William, Victor perceives himself as a diabolical creator whose mind has involuntarily "let loose" a monstrous and "filthy demon" in much the same way that Milton's Satan's swelled head produced Sin, the disgusting monster he "let loose" upon the world. Watching a "noble war in the sky" that seems almost like an intentional reminder that we are participating in a critical rearrangement of most of the elements of *Paradise Lost*, he explains that "I considered the being whom I had cast among mankind . . . nearly in the light of my own vampire, my own spirit let loose from the grave and forced to destroy all that was dear to me" (chap. 7).

Even while it is the final sign and seal of Victor's transformation from Adam to Satan, however, it is perhaps the Sin-ful murder of the child William that is our first overt clue to the real nature of the bewilderingly disguised set of identity shifts and parallels Mary Shelley incorporated into *Frankenstein*. For as we saw earlier, not just Victor and the monster but also Elizabeth and Justine insist upon responsibility for the monster's misdeed. Feeling "as if I had been guilty of a crime" (chap. 4) even before one had been committed, Victor responds to the news of William's death with the same self-accusations that torment the two orphans. And, significantly, for all three—as well as for the monster and little William himself—one focal point of both crime and guilt is an image of that other beautiful orphan, Caroline Beaufort Frankenstein. Passing from hand to hand, pocket to pocket, the smiling miniature of Victor's "angel mother" seems a token of some secret fellowship in sin, as does Victor's post-creation nightmare of transforming a lovely, living Elizabeth, with a single magical kiss, into "the corpse of my dead mother" enveloped in a shroud made more horrible by "grave-worms crawling in the folds of the flannel" (chap. 5). Though it has been disguised, buried, or miniaturized, femaleness—the gender definition of mothers and daughters, orphans and beggars, monsters and false creators—is at the heart of this apparently masculine book.

Because this is so, it eventually becomes clear that though Victor Frankenstein enacts the roles of Adam and Satan like a child trying on costumes, his single most self-defining act transforms him definitively into Eve. For as both Ellen Moers and Marc Rubenstein have pointed out, after much study of the "cause of generation and life," after locking himself away from ordinary society in the tradition of such agonized mothers as Wollstonecraft's Maria, Eliot's Hetty Sorel, and Hardy's Tess, Victor Frankenstein has a baby. His "pregnancy" and childbirth are obviously manifested by the existence of the paradoxically huge being who emerges from his "workshop of filthy creation," but even the descriptive language of his creation myth is suggestive: "incredible labours," "emaciated with confinement," "a passing trance," "oppressed by a slow fever," "nervous to a painful degree," "exercise and amusement would . . . drive away incipient disease," "the instruments of life" (chap. 4), etc. And, like Eve's fall into guilty knowledge and painful maternity, Victor's entrance into what Blake would call the realm of "generation" is marked by a recognition of the necessary interdependence of those complementary opposites, sex and death: "To examine the causes of life, we must first have recourse to death," he observes (chap. 4), and in his isolated workshop of filthy creation—filthy because obscenely sexual—he collects and arranges materials furnished by "the dissecting room and the slaughterhouse." Pursuing "nature to her hiding places" as Eve does in eating the apple, he learns that "the tremendous secrets of the human frame" are the interlocked secrets of sex and death, although, again like Eve, in his first mad pursuit of knowledge he knows not "eating death." But that his actual orgasmic animation of his monster-child takes place "on a dreary night in November," month of All Souls, short days, and the year's last slide toward death, merely reinforces the Miltonic and Blakean nature of his act of generation.

Even while Victor Frankenstein's self-defining procreation dramatically transforms him into an Eve-figure, however, our recognition of its implications reflects backward upon our sense of Victor-as-Satan and our earlier vision of Victor-as-Adam. Victor as Satan, we now realize, was never really the masculine, Byronic Satan of the first book of *Paradise Lost*, but always, instead, the curiously female, outcast Satan who gave birth to Sin. In his Eve-like pride ("I was surprised . . . that I alone should be reserved to discover so astonishing a secret" [chap. 4], this Victor-Satan becomes "dizzy" with his creative powers, so that his monstrous pregnancy, bookishly and solipsistically conceived, reenacts as a terrible bibliogenesis the moment when, in Milton's version, Satan "dizzy swum/In darkness, while [his] head flames thick and fast/Threw forth, till on the left side op'ning wide" and Sin, Death's mother-to-be, appeared like "a Sign/Portentous" (*PL* 2: 753–61). Because he has conceived—or, rather, misconceived—his monstrous offspring by brooding upon the *wrong* books, moreover, this Victor-Satan is paradigmatic, like the falsely creative fallen angel, of the female artist, whose anxiety about her own aesthetic activity is expressed, for instance, in Mary Shelley's deferential introductory phrase about her "hideous progeny," with its plain implication that in her alienated attic workshop of filthy creation she has given birth to a deformed book, a literary abortion or miscarriage. "How [did] I, then a young girl, [come] to think of and to *dilate* upon so very hideous an idea?" is a key (if disingenuous) question she records. But we should not overlook her word play upon *dilate*, just as we should not ignore the anxious pun on the word *author* that is so deeply embedded in *Frankenstein*.

If the adult, Satanic Victor is Eve-like both in his procreation and his anxious creation, even the young, prelapsarian, and Adamic Victor is—to risk a pun—*curiously* female, that is, Eve-like. Innocent and guided by silken threads like a Blakeian lamb in a Godwinian garden, he is consumed by "a fervent longing to penetrate the secrets of nature," a longing which—expressed in his explorations of "vaults and charnelhouses," his guilty observations of "the unhallowed damps of the grave," and his passion to understand "the structure of the human frame"—recalls the criminal female curiosity that led Psyche to lose love by gazing upon its secret face, Eve to insist upon consuming "intellectual food," and Prometheus's sister-in-law Pandora to open the forbidden box of fleshly ills. But if Victor-Adam is also Victor-Eve, what is the real significance of the episode in which, away at school and cut off from his family, he locks himself into his workshop of filthy creation and gives birth by intellectual parturition to a giant monster? Isn't it precisely at this point in the novel that he discovers he is not Adam but Eve, not Satan but Sin, not male but female? If so, it seems likely that what this crucial section of *Frankenstein* really enacts is the story of Eve's discovery not that she must fall but that, having been created female, she *is* fallen, femaleness and fallenness being essentially synonymous. For what Victor Frankenstein most importantly learns, we must remember, is that he is the "author" of the monster—for him alone is "reserved . . . so astonishing a secret"—and thus it is he who is "the true murderer," he who unleashes Sin and Death upon the world, he who dreams the primal kiss that incestuously kills both "sister" and "mother." Doomed and filthy, is he not, then, Eve instead of Adam? In fact, may not the story of the fall be, for women, the story of the discovery that one is not innocent and Adam (as one had supposed) but Eve, and fallen? Perhaps this is what Freud's cruel but metaphorically accurate concept of penis-envy really means: the girl-child's surprised discovery that she is female, hence fallen, inadequate. Certainly the almost grotesquely anxious self-analysis implicit in Victor Frankenstein's (and Mary Shelley's) multiform relationships to Eve, Adam, God, and Satan suggest as much.

The discovery that one is fallen is in a sense a discovery that one is a monster, a murderer, a being gnawed by "the never-dying worm" (chap. 8) and therefore capable of any horror, including but not limited to sex, death, and filthy literary creation. More, the discovery that one is fallen—self-divided, murderous, material—is the discovery that one has released a "vampire" upon the world, "forced to destroy all that [is] dear" (chap. 7). For this reason—because *Frankenstein* is a story of woman's fall told by, as it were, an apparently docile daughter to a censorious "father"—the monster's narrative is embedded at the heart of the novel like the secret of the fall itself. Indeed, just as Frankenstein's workshop, with its maddening, riddling answers to cosmic questions is a hidden but commanding attic womb/room where the young artist-scientist murders to dissect and to recreate, so the murderous monster's single, carefully guarded narrative commands and controls Mary Shelley's novel. Delivered at the top of Mont Blanc—like the North Pole one of the Shelley family's metaphors for the indifferently powerful source of creation and destruction—it is the story of deformed Geraldine in "Christabel," the story of the dead-alive crew in "The Ancient Mariner," the story of Eve in *Paradise Lost*, and of her degraded double Sin— all secondary or female characters to whom male authors have imperiously denied any chance of self-explanation. At the same time the monster's narrative is a philosophical meditation on what it means to be born without a "soul" or a history, as well as an exploration of what it feels like to be a "filthy mass that move[s] and talk[s]," a thing, an other, a creature of the second sex. In fact, though it tends to be ignored by critics (and film-makers), whose emphasis has always fallen upon Frankenstein himself as the archetypal mad scientist, the drastic shift in point of view that the nameless monster's monologue represents probably constitutes *Frankenstein's* most striking technical *tour de force*, just as the monster's bitter self-revelations are Mary Shelley's most impressive and original achievement.

Like Victor Frankenstein, his author and superficially better self, the monster enacts in turn the roles of Adam and Satan, and even eventually hints at a sort of digression into the role of God. Like Adam, he recalls a time of primodial innocence, his days and nights in "the forest near Ingolstadt," where he ate berries, learned about heat and cold, and per-ceived "the boundaries of the radiant roof of light which canopied me" (chap. 11). Almost too quickly, however, he metamorphoses into an outcast and Satanic figure, hiding in a shepherd's hut which seems to him "as exquisite . . . a retreat as Pandemonium . . . after the lake of fire" (chap. 11). Later, when he secretly sets up housekeeping behind the De Laceys' pigpen, his wistful observations of the loving though exiled family and their pastoral abode ("Happy, happy earth! Fit habitation for gods . . . " [chap. 12]) recall Satan's mingled jealousy and admiration of that "happy rural seat of various view" where Adam and Eve are emparadised by God and Milton (*PL* 4. 247). Eventually, burning the cottage and murdering William in demonic rage, he seems to become entirely Satanic: "I, like the arch-fiend, bore a hell within me" (chap. 16); "Inflamed by pain, I vowed eternal hatred . . . to all mankind" (chap 16). At the same time, in his assertion of power over his "author," his mental conception of another creature (a female monster), and his implicit dream of founding a new, vegetarian race somewhere in "the vast wilds of South America," (chap. 17), he temporarily enacts the part of a God, a creator, a master, albeit a failed one.

As the monster himself points out, however, each of these Miltonic roles is a Procrustean bed into which he simply cannot fit. Where, for instance, Victor Frankenstein's childhood really was Edenic, the monster's anxious infancy is isolated and ignorant, rather than insulated or innocent, so that his groping arrival at self-consciousness—"I was a poor, helpless, miserable wretch; I knew and could distinguish nothing; but feeling pain invade me on all sides, I sat down and wept" (chap. 11)—is a fiercely subversive parody of Adam's exuberant "all things smil'd,/With fragrance and with joy my heart o'erflowed./Myself I then perus'd, and Limb by Limb/Survey'd, and sometimes went, and sometimes ran/With supple joints, as lively vigor led" (*PL* 8. 265–69). Similarly, the monster's attempts at speech ("Sometimes I wished to express my sensations in my own mode, but the uncouth and inarticulate sounds which broke from me frightened me into silence again" (chap. 11) parody and subvert Adam's ("To speak I tri'd, and forthwith spake,/My Tongue obey'd and readily could name/Whate'er I saw" (*PL* 8. 271–72). And of course the monster's anxiety and confusion ("What was I? The question again recurred to be answered only with groans" [chap. 13]) are a dark version of Adam's wondering bliss ("who I was, or where, or from what cause,/[I] Knew not.... [But I] feel that I am happier than I know" (*PL* 8. 270–71, 282).

Similarly, though his uncontrollable rage, his alienation, even his enormous size and superhuman physical strength bring him closer to Satan than he was to Adam, the monster puzzles over discrepancies between his situation and the fallen angel's. Though he is, for example, "in bulk as huge/ As whom the Fables name of monstrous size,/*Titanian*, or *Earth-born*, that warr'd on *Jove*," and though, indeed, he is fated to war like Prometheus on Jovean Frankenstein, this demon/monster has fallen from no heaven, exercised no power of choice, and been endowed with no companions in evil. "I found myself similar yet at the same time strangely unlike to the beings concerning whom I read and to whose conversation I was a listener," he tells Frankenstein, describing his schooldays in the De Lacey pigpen (chap. 15). And, interestingly, his remark might well have been made by Mary Shelley herself, that "devout but nearly silent listener" (xiv) to masculine conversations who, like her hideous progeny, "continually studied and exercised [her] mind upon" such "histories" as *Paradise Lost*, Plutarch's *Lives*, and *The Sorrows of Werter* [*sic*] "whilst [her] friends were employed in their ordinary occupations" (chap. 15).

In fact, it is his intellectual similarity to his authoress (rather than his "author") which first suggests that Victor Frankenstein's male monster may really be a female in disguise. Certainly the books which educate him— *Werter*, Plutarch's *Lives*, and *Paradise Lost*—are not only books Mary had herself read in 1815, the year before she wrote *Frankenstein*, but they also typify just the literary categories she thought it necessary to study: the contemporary novel of sensibility, the serious history of Western civilization, and the highly cultivated epic poem. As specific works, moreover, each must have seemed to her to embody lessons a female author (or monster) must learn about a male-dominated society. Werter's story, says the monster—and he seems to be speaking for Mary Shelley—taught him about "gentle and domestic manners," and about "lofty sentiments ... which had for their object something out of self." It functioned, in other words, as a sort of Romantic conduct book. In addition, it served as an introduction to the virtues of the proto-Byronic "Man of Feeling," for admiring Werter and never mentioning Lotte, the monster explains to Victor that "I thought Werter himself a more divine being than I had ever... imagined," adding in a line whose female irony about male self-dramatization must surely have been intentional, "I wept [his extinction] without precisely understanding it" (chap. 15).

If *Werter* introduces the monster to female modes of domesticity and self-abnegation, as well as to the unattainable glamour of male heroism, Plutarch's *Lives* teaches him all the masculine intricacies of that history which his anomalous birth has denied him. Mary Shelley, excluding herself from the household of the second Mrs. Godwin and studying family as well as literary history on her mother's grave, must, again, have found in her own experience an appropriate model for the plight of a monster who, as James Rieger notes, is especially characterized by "his unique knowledge of what it is like to be born free of history." In terms of the disguised story the novel tells, however, this monster is not unique at all, but representative, as Shelley may have suspected she herself was. For, as Jane Austen has Catherine Morland suggest in *Northanger Abbey*, what is woman but man without a history, at least without the sort of history related in Plutarch's *Lives*? "History, real solemn history, I cannot be interested in," Catherine declares " ... the men all so good for nothing, and hardly any women at all— it is very tiresome" (*NA* I, chap. 14).

But of course the third and most crucial book referred to in the miniature *Bildungsroman* of the monster's narrative is *Paradise Lost*, an epic myth of origins which is of major importance to him, as it is to Mary Shelley, precisely because, unlike Plutarch, it does provide him with what appears to be a personal history. And again, even the need for such a history draws Shelley's monster closer not only to the realistically ignorant female defined by Jane Austen but also to the archetypal female defined by John Milton. For, like the monster, like Catherine Morland, and like Mary Shelley herself, Eve is characterized by her "unique knowledge of what it is like to be born free of history," even though as the "Mother of Mankind" she is fated to "make" history. It is to Adam, after all, that God and His angels grant explanatory visions of past and future. At such moments of high historical colloquy Eve tends to excuse herself with "lowliness Majestic" (before the fall) or (after the fall) she is magically put to sleep, calmed like a frightened animal "with gentle Dreams... and all her spirits compos'd/To meek submission" (*PL* 12. 595–96).

Nevertheless, one of the most notable facts about the monster's ceaselessly anxious study of *Paradise Lost* is his failure even to mention Eve. As an insistently male monster, on the surface of his palimpsestic narrative he appears to be absorbed in Milton's epic only because, as Percy Shelley wrote in the preface to *Frankenstein* that he drafted for his wife, *Paradise Lost* "most especially" conveys "the truth of the elementary principles of human nature," and conveys that truth in the dynamic tensions developed among its male characters, Adam, Satan, and God. Yet not only the monster's uniquely ahistorical birth, his literary anxieties, and the sense his readings (like Mary's) foster that he must have been parented, if at all, by *books*; not only all these facts and traits but also his shuddering sense of deformity, his nauseating size, his namelessness, and his orphaned, motherless isolation link him with Eve and with Eve's double, Sin. Indeed, at several points in his impassioned analysis of Milton's story he seems almost on the verge of saying so, as he examines the disjunctions among Adam, Satan, and himself (chap. 15):

> Like Adam, I was apparently united by no link to any other being in existence; but his state was far different from mine in every other respect. He had come forth from the hands of God a perfect creature, happy and prosperous, guided by the especial care of his Creator; he was allowed to converse with and acquire knowledge from beings of a superior nature, but I was wretched, helpless, and alone. Many times I considered Satan as the fitter emblem of my condition, for often, like him, when I viewed the bliss of my protectors, the bitter gall of envy rose within me.... Accursed creator! Why did you form a monster so hideous that even *you* turned from me in disgust? God, in pity, made man beautiful and alluring, after his own image; but my form is a filthy type of yours, more horrid even from the very resemblance. Satan had his companions, fellow devils, to admire and encourage him, but I am solitary and abhorred.

It is Eve, after all, who languishes helpless and alone, while Adam converses with superior beings, and it is Eve in whom the Satanically bitter gall of envy rises, causing her to eat the apple in the hope of adding "what wants/In Female Sex." It is Eve, moreover, to whom deathly isolation is threatened should Adam reject her, an isolation more terrible even than Satan's alienation from heaven. And finally it is Eve whose body, like her mind, is said by Milton to resemble "less/His Image who made both, and less [to express]/The character of that Dominion giv'n/O'er other Creatures ..." (*PL* 8. 543–46). In fact, to a sexually anxious reader, Eve's body might, like Sin's, seem "horrid even from [its] very resemblance" to her husband's, a "filthy" or obscene version of the human form divine.

As we argued earlier, women have seen themselves (because they have been seen) as monstrous, vile, degraded creatures, second-comers, and emblems of filthy materiality, even though they have also been traditionally defined as superior spiritual beings, angels, better halves. "Woman [is] a temple built over a sewer," said the Church father Tertullian, and Milton seems to see Eve as both temple and sewer, echoing that patristic misogyny. Mary Shelley's conscious or unconscious awareness of the monster woman implicit in the angel woman is perhaps clearest in the revisionary scene where her monster, as if taking his cue from Eve in *Paradise Lost* book 4, first catches sight of his own image: "I had admired the perfect forms of my cottagers . . . but how was I terrified when I viewed myself in a transparent pool. At first I started back, unable to believe that it was indeed I who was reflected in the mirror; and when I became fully convinced that I was in reality the monster that I am, I was filled with the bitterest sensations of despondence and mortification" (chap. 12). In one sense, this is a corrective to Milton's blindness about Eve. Having been created second, inferior, a mere rib, how could she possibly, this passage implies, have seemed anything but monstrous to herself? In another sense, however, the scene supplements Milton's description of Eve's introduction to herself, for ironically, though her reflection in "the clear/Smooth Lake" is as beautiful as the monster's is ugly, the self-absorption that Eve's confessed passion for her own image signals is plainly meant by Milton to seem morally ugly, a hint of her potential for spiritual deformity: "There I had fixt/Mine eyes till now, and pin'd with vain desire,/Had not a voice thus warn'd me, What thou seest,/What there thou seest fair Creature is thyself . . ." (*PL* 4. 465–68).

The figurative monstrosity of female narcissism is a subtle deformity, however, in comparison with the literal monstrosity many women are taught to see as characteristic of their own bodies. Adrienne Rich's twentieth-century description of "a woman in the shape of a monster/A monster in the shape of a woman" is merely the latest in a long line of monstrous female self-definitions that includes the fearful images in Djuna Barnes's *Book of Repulsive Women*, Denise Levertov's "a white sweating bull of a poet told us/our cunts are ugly" and Sylvia Plath's "old yellow" self of the poem "In Plaster." Animal and misshapen, these emblems of self-loathing must have descended at least in part from the distended body of Mary Shelley's darkly parodic Eve/Sin/Monster, whose enormity betokens not only the enormity of Victor Frankenstein's crime and Satan's bulk but also the distentions or deformities of pregnancy and the Swiftian sexual nausea expressed in Lemuel Gulliver's horrified description of a Brobdignagian breast, a passage Mary Shelley no doubt studied along with the rest of *Gulliver's Travels* when she read the book in 1816, shortly before beginning *Frankenstein*.

At the same time, just as surely as Eve's moral deformity is symbolized by the monster's physical malformation, the monster's physical ugliness represents his social illegitimacy, his bastardy, his namelessness. Bitchy and dastardly as Shakespeare's Edmund, whose association with filthy female-ness is established not only by his devotion to the material/maternal goddess Nature but also by his interlocking affairs with those filthy females Goneril and Regan, Mary Shelley's monster has also been "got" in a "dark and vicious place." Indeed, in his vile illegitimacy he seems to incarnate that bestial "unnameable" place. And significantly, he is himself as nameless as a woman is in patriarchal society, as nameless as unmarried, illegitimately pregnant Mary Wollstonecraft Godwin may have felt herself to be at the time she wrote *Frankenstein*.

"This nameless mode of naming the unnameable is rather good," Mary commented when she learned that it was the custom at early dramatizations of *Frankenstein* to place a blank line next to the name of the actor who played the part of the monster. But her pleased surprise was disingenuous, for the problem of names and their connection with social legitimacy had been forced into her consciousness all her life. As the sister of illegitimate and therefore nameless Fanny Imlay, for instance, she knew what bastardy meant, and she knew it too as the mother of a premature and illegitimate baby girl who died at the age of two weeks without ever having been given a name. Of course, when Fanny dramatically excised her name from her suicide note Mary learned more about the significance even of insignificant names. And as the stepsister of Mary Jane Clairmont, who defined herself as the "creature" of Lord Byron and changed her name for a while with astonishing frequency (from Mary Jane to Jane to Clara to Claire), Mary knew about the importance of names too. Perhaps most of all, though, Mary's sense of the fearful significance of legitimate and illegitimate names must have been formed by her awareness that her own name, Mary Wollstonecraft Godwin, was absolutely identical with the name of the mother who had died in giving birth to *her*. Since this was so, she may have speculated, perhaps her own monstrosity, her murderous illegitimacy, consisted in her being—like Victor Frankenstein's creation—a reanimation of the dead, a sort of galvanized corpse ironically arisen from what should have been "the cradle of life."

This implicit fantasy of the reanimation of the dead in the monstrous and nameless body of the living returns us, however, to the matter of the monster's Satanic, Sin-ful and Eve-like moral deformity. For of course the crimes that the monster commits, once he has accepted the world's definition of him as little more than a namelessly "filthy mass," all reinforce his connection with Milton's unholy trinity of Sin, Eve/Satan, and Death. The child of two authors (Victor Frankenstein and Mary Shelley) whose mothers have been stolen away by death, this motherless monster is after all made from dead bodies, from loathsome parts found around cemeteries, so that it seems only "natural" for him to continue the Blakeian cycle of despair his birth began, by bringing further death into the world. And of course he brings death, in the central actions of the novel: death to the childish innocence of little William (whose name is that of Mary Shelley's father, her half-brother, and her son, so that one can hardly decide to which male relative she may have been alluding); death to the faith and truth of allegorically named Justine; death to the legitimate artistry of the Shelleyan poet Clerval; and death to the ladylike selflessness of angelic Elizabeth. Is he acting, in his vile way, for Mary Shelley, whose elegant femininity seemed, in view of her books, so incongruous to the poet Beddoes and to literary Lord Dillon? "She has no business to be a woman by her books," noted Beddoes. And "your writing and your manners are not in accordance," Dillon told Mary herself. "I should have thought of you—if I had only read you—that you were a sort of... Sybil, outpouringly enthusiastic... but you are cool, quiet and feminine to the last degree.... Explain this to me."

Could Mary's coolness have been made possible by the heat of her monster's rage, the strain of her decorous silence eased by the demonic abandon of her nameless monster's ritual fire dance around the cottage of his rejecting "Protectors"? Does Mary's cadaverous creature want to bring more death into the world because he has failed—like those other awful females, Eve and Sin—to win the compassion of that blind and curiously Miltonic old man, the Godlike musical patriarch De Lacey? Significantly, he is clinging to the blind man's knees, begging for recognition and help— "Do not you desert me in the hour of trial!"—when Felix, the son of the house, appears like the felicitous hero he is, and, says the monster, "with supernatural force [he] tore me from his father... in a transport of fury, he dashed me to the ground and struck me violently with a stick... my heart sank within me as with bitter sickness" (chap. 15). Despite everything we have been told about the monster's physical vileness, Felix's rage seems excessive in terms of the novel's overt story. But as an action in the covert plot—the tale of the blind rejection of women by misogynistic/Miltonic patriarchy—it is inevitable and appropriate. Even more psychologically appropriate is the fact that having been so definitively rejected by a world of fathers, the monster takes his revenge, first by murdering William, a male child who invokes his father's name ("My papa is a syndic—he is M. Frankenstein—he will punish you") and then by beginning a doomed search for a maternal, female principle in the harsh society that has created him.

In this connection, it begins to be plain that Eve's—and the monster's—motherlessness must have had extraordinary cultural and personal significance for Mary Shelley. "We think back through our mothers if we are women," wrote Virginia Woolf in *A Room of One's Own*. But of course one of the most dramatic emblems of Eve's alienation from the masculine garden in which she finds herself is her motherlessness. Because she is made in the image of a man who is himself made in the image of a male creator, her unprecedented femininity seems merely a defective masculinity, a deformity like the monster's inhuman body. In fact, as we saw, the only maternal model in *Paradise Lost* is the terrifying figure of Sin. (That Eve's punishment for *her* sin is the doom of agonized maternity—the doom of painfully becoming no longer herself but "Mother of Human Race"— appears therefore to seal the grim parallel.) But all these powerful symbols would be bound to take on personal weight and darkness for Shelley, whose only real "mother" was a tombstone—or a shelf of books—and who, like all orphans, must have feared that she had been deliberately deserted by her dead parent, or that, if she was a monster, then her hidden, underground mother must have been one too.

For all these reasons, then, the monster's attitude toward the possibility (or impossibility) of finding a mother is unusually conflicted and complex. At first, horrified by what he knows of the only "mother" he has ever had—Victor Frankenstein—he regards his parentage with loathing. Characteristically, he learns the specific details of his "conception" and "birth" (as Mary Shelley may have learned of hers) through reading, for Victor has kept a journal which records "that series of disgusting circumstances" leading "to the production of [the monster's] . . . loathsome person." Later, however, the ill-fated miniature of Caroline Beaufort Frankenstein, Victor's "angel mother," momentarily "attract[s]" him. In fact, he claims it is because he is "forever deprived of the delights that such beautiful creatures could bestow" that he resolves to implicate Justine in the murder of William. His reproachful explanation is curious, though ("The crime had its source in her; be hers the punishment"), as is the sinister rape fantasy he enacts by the side of the sleeping orphan ("Awake, fairest, thy lover is near—he who would give his life but to obtain one look of affection from thine eyes" [chap. 16]). Clearly feelings of rage, terror, and sexual nausea, as well as idealizing sentiments, accrete for Mary and the monster around the maternal female image, a fact which explains the later climactic wedding-night murder of apparently innocent Elizabeth. In this fierce, Miltonic world, *Frankenstein* says, the angel woman and the monster woman alike must die, if they are not dead already. And what is to be feared above all else is the reanimation of the dead, specifically of the maternal dead. Perhaps that is why a significant pun is embedded in the crucial birth scene ("It was on a dreary night of November") that, according to Mary Shelley, rose "unbidden" from her imagination. Looking at the "demoniacal corpse to which I had so miserably given life," Victor remarks that "A *mummy* again endued with animation could not be so hideous as that wretch" (chap. 5). For a similarly horrific (and equally punning) statement of sexual nausea, one would have to go back to Donne's "Loves Alchymie" with its urgent, misogynistic imperative: "Hope not for minde in women; at their best/Sweetnesse and wit, they are but/*Mummy* possest."

Interestingly, the literary group at Villa Diodati received a packet of books containing, among other poems, Samuel Taylor Coleridge's recently published "Christabel," shortly before Mary had her monster-dream and began her ghost story. More influential than "Loves Alchymie"—a poem Mary may or may not have read—"Christabel"'s vision of femaleness must have been embodied for the author of *Frankenstein* not only in the witch Geraldine's withered side and consequent self-loathing ("Ah! What a stricken look was hers!") but also in her anxiety about the ghost of Christabel's dead mother ("Off, wandering mother! Peak and pine!") and in Christabel's "Woe is me/She died the hour that I was born." But even without Donne's puns or Coleridge's Romanticized male definition of deathly maternity, Mary Shelley would have absorbed a keen sense of the agony of female sexuality, and specifically of the perils of motherhood, not just from *Paradise Lost* and from her own mother's fearfully exemplary fate but also from Wollstonecraft's almost prophetically anxious writings.

Maria, or the Wrongs of Woman (1797), which Mary read in 1814 (and possibly in 1815) is about, among other "wrongs," Maria's search for her lost child, her fears that "she" (for the fantasied child is a daughter) may have been murdered by her unscrupulous father, and her attempts to reconcile herself to the child's death. In a suicide scene that Wollstonecraft drafted shortly before her own death, as her daughter must have known, Maria swallows laudanum: "her soul was calm . . . nothing remained but an eager longing . . . to fly . . . from this hell of disappointment. Still her eyes closed not. . . . Her murdered child again appeared to her . . . [But] 'Surely it is better to die with me, than to enter on life without a mother's care!' " Plainly, *Frankenstein*'s pained ambivalence toward mothers and mummies is in some sense a response to *Maria*'s agonized reaching—from beyond the grave, it may have seemed—toward a daughter. "Off, wandering mother! Peak and pine!" It is no wonder if Coleridge's poem gave Mary Wollstonecraft Godwin Shelley bad dreams, no wonder if she saw Milton's "Mother of Human Race" as a sorrowful monster.

Though *Frankenstein* itself began with a Coleridgean and Miltonic nightmare of filthy creation that reached its nadir in the monster's revelation of filthy femaleness, Mary Shelley, like Victor Frankenstein himself, evidently needed to distance such monstrous secrets. Sinful, motherless Eve and sinned-against, daughterless Maria, both paradigms of woman's helpless alienation in a male society, briefly emerge from the sea of male heroes and villains in which they have almost been lost, but the ice soon closes over their heads again, just as it closes around those two insane figure-skaters, Victor Frankenstein and his hideous offspring. Moving outward from the central "birth myth" to the icy perimeter on which the novel began, we find ourselves caught up once more in Walton's naive polar journey, where

Frankenstein and his monster reappear as two embattled grotesques, distant and archetypal figures solipsistically drifting away from each other on separate icebergs. In Walton's scheme of things, they look again like God and Adam, Satanically conceived. But now, with our more nearly complete understanding of the bewildered and bewildering perspective Mary Shelley adopted as "Milton's daughter," we see that they were Eve and Eve all along.

Nevertheless, though Shelley did manage to still the monster's suffering and Frankenstein's and her own by transporting all three from the fires of filthy creation back to the ice and silence of the Pole, she was never entirely to abandon the sublimated rage her monster-self enacted, and never to abandon, either, the metaphysical ambitions Frankenstein incarnated. In The Last Man she introduced, as Spark points out, "a new, inhuman protagonist," PLAGUE (the name is almost always spelled entirely in capitals), who is characterized as female and who sees to it that "disaster is no longer the property of the individual but of the entire human race." And of course PLAGUE's story is the one that Mary claims to have found in the Sibyl's cave, a tale of a literally female monster that was merely foreshadowed by the more subdued narrative of "The Modern Prometheus."

Interestingly, PLAGUE's story ends with a vision of last things, a vision of judgment and of paradise nihilistically restored that balances Frankenstein's vision of first things. With all of humanity wiped out by the monster PLAGUE, just as the entire Frankenstein family was destroyed by Victor's monster, Lionel Verney, the narrator, goes to Rome, that cradle of patriarchal civilization whose ruins had seemed so majestically emblematic to both Byron and Shelley. But where Mary's husband had written of the great city in a kind of ecstasy, his widow has her disinherited "last man" wander lawlessly about empty Rome until finally he resolves, finding "parts of a manuscript... scattered about," that "I also will write a book... [but] for whom to read?—to whom dedicated? And then with silly flourish (what so capricious and childish as despair?) I wrote,

DEDICATION
TO THE ILLUSTRIOUS DEAD
SHADOWS, ARISE, AND READ YOUR FALL!
BEHOLD THE HISTORY OF THE LAST MAN.

His hostile, ironic, literary gesture illuminates not only his own career but his author's. For the annihilation of history may well be the final revenge of the monster who has been denied a true place in history: the moral is one that Mary Shelley's first hideous progeny, like Milton's Eve, seems to have understood from the beginning.

PAUL SHERWIN

"Frankenstein": Creation as Catastrophe

As Frankenstein gets under way, we are lured by the promise of a new beginning: Walton's pathbreaking journey to the North Pole. Bound for Archangel to assemble a crew, Walton is inspired by the cold northern wind to envision a perpetually warm and radiant paradise at the summit of the globe. To be there would be to capture the heavens in a glance, to tap earth's central power source, and to stand within the magic circle of the poets he once sought to emulate but whose sublimity he could not match. Such extravagance is easier to credit if we keep in mind the uneasiness it is intended to dispel: "There is something at work in my soul, which I do not understand." Perhaps for his own good, and certainly at the dramatically right moment, the quest founders somewhere in the frozen wastes between Archangel and the Pole, just where Walton is waylaid by Frankenstein, who is feverishly pursuing the path of the Creature's departure. It may be more accurate to say that the quest is deflected. For although Walton is relegated to the periphery of the fiction, ushering in and out a wondrous tale that preempts his own, he is profoundly implicated as well. The tale, of course, is a monitory example meant for him, but it is also a riddle of fate that means him: the mystery that he is and that becomes his by virtue of his fascinated participation in Frankenstein's story. In short, Walton is in the critical position, and nowhere is his situation better evidenced than at the end of the novel. Frankenstein, burdened by his tale's monstrous residue, concludes his narrative by

From *PMLA* (October 1981). Copyright © 1981 by *PMLA*.

enjoining Walton to slay the Creature after his death. Yet the climactic encounter with the Creature unsettles everything even more and leaves Walton powerless to act. The final word and deed belong to the Creature, who vows to undo the scene of his creation once he bounds from the ship: "I shall...seek the most northern extremity of the globe; I shall collect my funeral pile, and consume to ashes this miserable frame, that its remains may afford no light...my ashes will be swept into the sea by the winds." To Walton, however, belongs the burden of the mystery as he watches this self-destroying artifact vanish into darkness and distance and contemplates a catastrophe at the Pole.

I

Mary Shelley might well have titled her novel *One Catastrophe after Another*. For Frankenstein, who is dubiously in love with his own polymorphously disastrous history, the fateful event to which every other catastrophe is prelude or postscript is the creation. According to the archaic model implicit in his narrative, transcendence is equivalent to transgression, and his presumptuous deed is invested with the aura of a primal sin against nature that somehow justifies the ensuing retributive bother. Condemned by nature's gods to limitless suffering, the aspiring hero learns his properly limited human place. *Frankenstein*, however, knows differently. A reading alert to the anti-Gothic novel Mary Shelley inscribes within her Gothic tale will discover that nothing is simple or single. *The* critical event is impossible to localize, terms such as "justice" and "injustice" do not so much mean as undergo vicissitudes of meaning, and all the narrators are dispossessed of their authority over the text. As the central misreader, Frankenstein is the chief victim of the text's irony, the humor becoming particularly cruel whenever he thinks he is addressing the supernatural powers that oversee his destiny, for his invocatory ravings never fail to conjure up his own Creature. Indeed, the evacuation of spiritual presence from the world of the novel suggests that *Frankenstein* is more a house in ruins than the house divided that its best recent critics have shown it to be. The specter of deconstruction rises: doubtless future interpreters will describe a text that compulsively subverts its own performance and that substitutes for its missing center the senseless power play of a catastrophic Gothic machine. Yet the Gothic is always already demystified, the ruin of an anterior world of large spiritual forces and transcendent desires that the most relentless of demystifiers cannot will away. *Frankenstein*, although arguably a Gothic fiction, remains a living novel because it is a haunted house, ensouled by the anxious spirit that perturbs all belated romances.

While the unconsummated spirit raised by *Frankenstein* cannot be put to rest, one might suppose that *das Unheimliche* can be contained within the spacious edifice of Freudian psychoanalysis. Freud's antithetical system provides an interpretive context for many of the anomalies disclosed by an ironic reading: the dissonance of overt and implicit meanings, the obscure sense of having trespassed on sacred ground, the appalling secret that craves expression yet must be protected as though it were a holy thing. In addition, the novel's catastrophic model functions in a way strikingly similar to the Freudian psychic apparatus. Instead of hubris, there is the drive's excess; instead of a downcast hero assaulted by phantasmagoria, there is the boundless anxiety occasioned by the proliferation of repressed desire; and instead of the restrictive gods, there is the exalted secondary process, intended to keep the apparatus stable by binding or incarcerating mobile energy. More telling, the catastrophic model is an almost exact duplicate of the oedipal scenario, the most privileged psychoanalytic thematic and the dynamic source of Freud's mature topography of the psyche. The way is opened for a recentering of the novel's unresolved intellectual and emotional turmoil.

Of course, the Freudian way has increasingly become, and always was, a wildly extravagant detour or series of detours, and staking out a position in the psychoanalytic field can be as agonizing as "choosing" a neurosis. Still, when one reads that Walton is about to enact the favorite dream of his youth, seeking a passage through the ice to the warm Pole, where he may "discover the wondrous power which attracts the needle," or that Frankenstein struggles "with a child's blindness" to break through "the fortifications and impediments that seemed to keep human beings from entering the citadel of nature," it is hard not to translate such statements into the formulations of a recognizably classical psychoanalysis. I should acknowledge here that I am averse to reducing the questing drive in *Frankenstein* to a desire for primordial union with, or active possession of, the maternal body and that I think it is a dangerous critical error to conceive the novel as a tale told by an idiot, signifying. I do, however, consider the orthodox Freudian approach a formidable antagonist to the sort of psychoanalytic interpretation I venture in the second section of this essay; and I should like to sketch my own "Freudian" romancing of *Frankenstein*, before proceeding to unweave it, in part because none of the many analytic runs at the text in recent years seems to me as persuasive as it might be and in part because something in me is deeply responsive to such a reading. Psychoanalysis, it may be said, is properly attuned to an important element in the life of the mind; its problem is that it fancies that part the whole.

A reading of the oedipal drama the novel reenacts can begin with a notice of the first overt catastrophe recorded in Frankenstein's narrative: his witnessing, at fifteen, the terrible power of a lightning bolt during a thunderstorm. When the adult Frankenstein describes the event, which occurred at a time when his enthusiasm for alchemy had redoubled the urgency of his endeavors to penetrate nature's secrets, his excited rhetoric betrays the insistent presence of a forgotten childhood scene. "I remained, while the storm lasted, watching its progress with curiosity and delight. As I stood at the door, on a sudden I beheld a stream of fire issue from an old and beautiful oak ... and so soon as the dazzling light vanished the oak had disappeared, and nothing remained but a blasted stump." In the original version of the text it is the father who discourses on the nature of lightning and who controls the symbolically castrating bolt that cripples desire: "he constructed a small electrical machine, and exhibited a few experiments ... which drew down that fluid from the clouds." The son is, as it were, shocked into the latency stage; a sudden influx of self-revulsion impels him to denounce "natural history and all its progeny as a deformed and abortive creation ... which could never even step within the threshold of real knowledge. . . . an unusual tranquility and gladness of soul ... followed the relinquishing of my ancient and latterly tormenting studies."

The next critical event in Frankenstein's history is his mother's death, and a period of mourning delays his departure for the university. Once there, he abruptly resumes his former studies, reconverted by Professor Waldman's panegyric on modern chemists: "these philosophers ... penetrate into the recesses of nature. . . . They ascend into the heavens ... they can command the thunders of heaven." The difficult work of mourning—the guilt-ridden withdrawal of attachment to the mother, a process allied to the transferal of Frankenstein's love to Elizabeth and his decision to leave home—is undone. Waldman's vision of the master who can refind the lost object and command limitless power has the characteristically unsettling impact of a pubescent irruption of libido, and the idea of the mother, set free by death for fantasy elaboration, becomes the focus of the regressive descent into phantasmagoria that constitutes Frankenstein's reanimation project. Within the secretive darkness of vaults and charnels, he dabbles in filth, his heart sickening at the work of his hands as he disturbs, "with profane fingers, the tremendous secrets of the human frame." The imagery has an unmistakably anal and masturbatory cast. At once feces and phallus, the filth is also the maternal presence he is assembling from phantasmal body parts and buried wishes. In sum, Frankenstein's descent is a grotesque act of lovemaking, the son stealing into the womb that bore him in order to implant his seed. Having fully re-membered the form of his desire, the mother restored by a far more radical rescue than the one by which the father claimed her, he is ready to draw rebellious Promethean fire down from the heavens and realize his grandiose conception, the creation proper.

Or so Frankenstein dreams: the time never can be right for this obsessional neurotic:

> With an anxiety that almost amounted to agony, I collected the instruments of life around me, that I might infuse a spark of being into the lifeless thing that lay at my feet.... my candle was nearly burnt out, when ... I saw the dull yellow eye of the creature open, and a convulsive motion agitated its limbs. How can I describe my emotions at this catastrophe...?

What is most strange here is that the Creature is a sleeping beauty until its orgasmic stirring rouses Frankenstein to recognize the monstrosity before him. We confront the antithetical aspects not only of the fantasy mother but of the son's desire. The Creature is thus a befouled version of the son who would usurp the father's prerogatives, the would-be transcendent father of himself who now beholds the squalor of his actual origins and wishes. But such an interpretation is still oversimplified. The scene scatters the self into every possible familial position; the Creature, on the contrary, is a massively overdetermined representation of the entire scene as well as of the related Oedipus complex. We can infer that the Creature also embodies the fantasy father because it is as much a ubiquitous gaze under which Frankenstein cowers as a nightmare image that bewilders his sight. The convulsive agitation of the aroused Creature suggests ejaculation; yet although this "filthy mass" represents a monstrously oversized phallus, its dread-provoking *corps morcelé* bears the stigma of castration, calling to mind the Lacanian castrated phallus. This difficulty can be resolved if the Creature is viewed as Frankenstein's renounced phallic self, the self he yields to the father, perhaps detached in the very achievement of orgasm, at once the moment of the organ's autonomy and a repetition of the father's act of begetting. Whatever the interpretation, when Frankenstein mimics the Creature's convulsions after his flight and subsequent nightmare, the appropriate description, given his regressed condition, is anal evacuation, which Freud claims is the child's typical response to the primal scene. Here we may note that Mary Shelley writes in the Introduction of "the working of some powerful engine," but Frankenstein has a spark, not a bolt, and as he begins to infuse life, his candle has dwindled. Already defeated by his own scene of origins, Frankenstein is barred from the compensatory replay he intends. Instead the creation precipitously repeats the occasion of his mental trouble, the traumatic fixation he is fated to suffer again and again.

It is not until several chapters later and some two years after the creation that the novel, approaching another dangerous crossing, is disturbed into strength. By now the abandoned or liberated Creature has embarked on its career of murderous inroads into Frankenstein's family romance, and the creator, increasingly abandoned to morbid anxiety, gravitates to the Alps, whose "savage and enduring scenes" become the stage for an attempted reworking of his defining scene. Alternately plunging and mounting for three days, he is at last urged to penetrate the mists rising like incense from the ravine of Arve toward the surrounding heights, coming to a halt in a spectacular setting where "a power mighty as Omnipotence" manifests itself. As in the lightning scene of his youth, he stands apart, gazing ecstatically. From the recess of a rock, he looks across the troubled surface of *La Mer de Glace*, the glacier poured down from the summits in an eternally solemn procession, and in the distance the stupendous bright dome of Mont Blanc rises "in awful majesty" before him. Power, throughout this section of the novel, is envisioned as the power to wound: "the ... silence of this glorious presence-chamber of imperial Nature was broken ... by ... the cracking ... of the accumulated ice, which, through the silent working of immutable laws, was ever and anon rent and torn, as if it had been but a plaything." To be where Power is would mean to be above the turmoil of desire, the desire of and for the mother (*la mère*), whom the father controls and possesses by right. Restaging his primal-scene fantasy under the gaze of the terrific god of the Alps, Frankenstein has a dual aim. While he would seem to be propitiating the father, submitting to the law that freezes or castrates desire, he may also be seeking a way out of his oedipal impasse by identifying with a transcendent paternal principle that enables the son, in his turn, to put on the power of the father.

The scene dissipates when Frankenstein's call to the "wandering spirits" of his mountain god summons the Creature, his own errant spirit. Rising up to demand a mate from *his* father, the Creature forces Frankenstein into the unamiable role of a jealously restrictive frustrate father, a lame parody of his dread paternal imago. A possible explanation for this failed oedipal normalization is that the excessive harshness of the agency whose function is to suppress the complex actually reinforces Frankenstein's most primitive longings. But such an overweening superego is too deeply contaminated by unregenerate desire to be construed as autonomous. Rather, it is a phantasmic derivative of the complex, a shadowy type of that relentless internal danger which the Creature consummately represents. At least the Creature is almost a representation. Though actualized in the world of the fiction, out of narrative necessity, the Creature is so uncannily fearful that it cannot in fact be seen. Yet how is one to comprehend a representation that transcends representation, that is apparently the thing itself? Frankenstein's astonishing psychic achievement, in Freudian terms, is the construction of a primal repression, whose constitutive role in psychic development is to structure the unconscious as an articulate erotogenic zone. His sorrow is that this catastrophically global repression, or rerepression, is so radically alienated from the ego that it disqualifies any attempt at integration, insistently transmitting its full affective charge and thus preventing the institution of a firm psychic apparatus.

The developing plot of the novel elaborates the grim psychic consequences of Frankenstein's deepening subjugation to his dark double. The Creature is cast as the active partner in what amounts to a bizarre conspiracy, rehearsing in another register the scandalous history of the creator's desire, with Frankenstein bound to what Melanie Klein calls the "depressive position." As a recognizable human world recedes and the Creature becomes a progressively more enthralling superpower, Frankenstein joins in the frenetic dance of death that impels these mutually fascinated antagonists across the waste places of the earth. By now wholly the Creature's creature, he must be considered a florid psychotic, pursuing the naked form of his desire in a fantastic nowhere that is his own. Of course, the consummating thrust of the sword eludes Frankenstein, who is drained by his interminable quest, but the Creature, that monstrous embodiment of his unremitting parental nightmare, can say "I am satisfied."

I am not, nor in fact is the Creature, though admittedly the coherence and audacity of this psychoanalytic reading give it considerable authority. While it is true that by the end of Frankenstein's narrative creator and Creature form a kind of symbiotic unit whose significance various orthodox analytic schools are well suited to explain, such pathological relatedness can be as cogently elucidated by Hegel's master-slave dialectic or by its derivatives in Lacan and Girard. This fearful symmetry, moreover, stems largely from a perverse misreading that Frankenstein sets in motion and that the traditional psychoanalytic critic refines on.

Consider a privileged psychoanalytic moment in the text, Frankenstein's nightmare after the creation and his subsequent response:

> I thought I saw Elizabeth, in the bloom of health, walking in the streets. ...Delighted and surprised, I embraced her; but as I imprinted the first kiss on her lips, they became livid with the hue of death; her features appeared to change, and I thought that I held the corpse of my dead mother in my arms; a shroud enveloped her form, and I saw the graveworms crawling in the folds of the flannel. I started from my sleep with horror... every limb became convulsed: when, by the dim and yellow light of the moon...I beheld...the miserable monster whom I had created. He held up the curtain of the bed; and his eyes, if eyes they may be called, were fixed on me. His jaws opened, and he muttered some inarticulate sounds, while a grin wrinkled his cheeks. He might have spoken, but I did not hear, one hand was stretched out, seemingly to detain me, but I escaped....I took refuge in the courtyard...fearing each sound as if it were to announce the approach of the demoniacal corpse.... A mummy again endued with animation could not be so hideous....

Restricting the interpretive game to a psychoanalytic strategy and overlooking those automatic signals (Elizabeth as streetwalker, the mummy-mommy pun) with which a prevalent mode of subcriticism clutters the mind, what can we deduce from the passage? Most simply, there is a treacherous wishing-dreading circuit that links Elizabeth and the Creature to the mother, the central term of the triad. As symbolic counter, Elizabeth is the mother's corpse, and in embracing this cousin-sister-bride Frankenstein reaches through her to take hold of the maternal body he intends to possess. The hungry phallic worms only faintly disguise his wish, and when it comes too close to fulfillment he wakens excitedly on the bed of his desire, where he is confronted by the Creature as demoniacal corpse, its negativity a token of the repression that distorts the wish even in the dream. Once this basic fantasy material is unearthed, numerous variations on the dream scenario are possible: Elizabeth is killed off because she tempts Frankenstein to a sublimated version of his true desire; Frankenstein's lust is overwhelmed by his fear of being sucked into the cloaca of the vampirish mother; and the Creature is alternatively or simultaneously the accusatory phallic father, the rephallicized mother, and (in view of the multiplication of genital symbols in the dream) the castrated self.

At issue is where and how closely such a commentary touches the passage. Clearly a psychoanalytic reading is attuned to Frankenstein's anxious, conflict-ridden experience, but the bewilderment of his desire and his relationships is at most tangentially allied to sexuality and not at all to incest, which is a poor trope for the disturbing center of the dream. To reopen the text we must reverse the process by which the analyst translates the teasingly idiomatic world of the dream into a too familiar context of anticipated meanings. At the outset we need to recall that Frankenstein has devoted two years to his animation project; that, aside from a few detours into the abyss, he has been soaring in a rarefied atmosphere where it is impossible to breathe; and that now he is responding to the dissolution of his hopes as well as to the embarrassing fact of the Creature, a singular enormity for which there is no place in his experiential horizon. His response is revealing: first literal flight, then flight into sleep, and finally flight from both the dream and the Creature. The dream itself, the way it is lived, beautifully testifies to the disorienting shock of Frankenstein's reentry into reality. The dreamer does not know what is happening to him. He exists discontinuously, overwhelmed by sudden, appalling contrasts and baffled by the uncertain boundaries between the real and the phantasmal. When the imagery of the dream's core, derived from the creator's descent into the house of the dead, is brought together with the family world he bracketed during the creation, the most canny (heimlich) of worlds, the effect is peculiarly poignant. Elizabeth is present because she is a fit emblem of the dream of loveliness that has slipped away from him, and the mother is there mainly because she is the only dead person who matters to him. Waking, within the dream, into emptiness and worse, Frankenstein beholds the idealized form of his mother, preserved intact by his memory as by the shroud in the dream, falling prey to anonymous malforming powers. He has nothing to hold onto except the body of death, and as he wakens he spills out of one nightmare into another, finding himself face to face with the abomination he has created.

For Frankenstein there is an inescapable connection between the intruding "graveworms" of the dream and the monster that invades his curtained bed. Only after the Creature's narrative cuts into his and compels us to reread the passage do we appreciate how mistaken Frankenstein is. He will not hear and cannot see. Reading a sinister intention into this newborn's clumsy gestures, he is terrified by a shadow of his own casting, a bad interpretation that climaxes all the traumatic events and that irrevocably determines the creation as The Bad Event. The process of misreading is most clearly exemplified when he next encounters the Creature, during a nocturnal storm in the Alps. The figure is suddenly illuminated by a bolt of lightning. A series of staccato flashes enables Frankenstein to make out the Creature's dizzying course as it leaps from crag to crag, and in the intervals of darkness, while his eye is recovering from each blinding glance, he reflects. None but this "devil" could have strangled his little brother or framed the saintly Justine for the murder. "No sooner did that idea cross my imagination, than I became convinced of its truth." Unlike those who convict Justine on the basis of mere appearance, Frankenstein has the facts right, but his imputation of diabolical designs to the Creature is a gross distortion, as is his summary judgment, which marks him as the prototypical psychoanalytic reader of his own text: "I conceived the being . . . in the light of my own vampire, my own spirit let loose from the grave, and forced to destroy all that was dear to me." The proper analytic rejoinder is that Frankenstein is an overreacting, moralizing misreader, rather like the self-blinded ego that travesties the id. The analogy is admissible, however, only if it is restricted to an illustrative function. Reading it literally, the critic perpetuates Frankenstein's interpretive error, violating the Creature's spiritual integrity and evading the aesthetic problem this figure poses.

The overriding ironies are that it is the psychoanalytic reader, not the Creature, who reenacts the history of Frankenstein's desire in another register and that what enables the analyst to articulate this desire so persuasively is what discredits the interpretation. Both protagonist and critic are family-obsessed (or, rather, preoccupied with that aspect of the familial which is an adjunct to the personal), backward-looking, fatalistic, fixated on a terrible secret. They exist within the same disturbed conceptual horizon, conceiving experience and the experiential universe in solipsistic terms. Once again the alchemist is reborn in the scientist: the projector would look or crash through the phenomenal to an occult, transcendent reality. An apparent difference is that while Frankenstein, who is by turns indifferent to and sickened by appearances, views reality as the elixir that will grant him power over things, the analyst sees appearances, no matter how superficially hideous, as a deceptively appealing screen and reality as a squalor. Yet that squalor is the critic's secret of secrets, the means of pouring the light of meaning into the dark world of desire and so of overpowering the text. For both, however, the act of knowledge is as devastating for knower and known as the attempt to "sieze the inmost Form" in Blake's "The Crystal Cabinet." The image—world or text—shatters, and one is left holding onto a corpse. That form of alienation, for the orthodox psychoanalytic critic, is the literal, dead letter of the Freudian corpus, the petrified formulations of an introjected mystery religion that are interposed as a barrier between reader and text. But such "repression" of the text results in a solution that merely replays an element in the text, its most conventional, superficial, or manifest dimension: that of Gothic melodrama. In this intense, simplistically dualistic world of obsessional neurosis, the analyst discovers truth.

One thinks of the novel's melodramatic climax, the Creature's ravishment of the bride on Frankenstein's wedding night: if any literary work can be opened up by a psychoanalytic approach, this incident suggests that *Frankenstein* must be the text. Reflecting "how fearful the combat which I momentarily expected would be to my wife," Frankenstein bids Elizabeth retire to the bridal chamber while he paces restlessly through the house in anticipation of the Creature's advent. Roused by a scream, he rushes in to find her limp body thrown across the bed, when, through the open casement, he beholds his monstrous rival: "he seemed to jeer as with his fiendish finger he pointed towards the corpse. . . . I rushed towards the window and, drawing a pistol from my bosom, fired; but he eluded me . . . and, running with the swiftness of lightning, plunged into the lake." However polymorphously perverse an analytic rendering of the incident, I would not seriously dispute its applicability to Frankenstein, whose evocation the reading is based on, though it could be claimed that an exposition of his sexual trouble merely brings one to the horizon of a larger spiritual problem. But how apposite is such a commentary to Elizabeth? Where the analyst would place sexuality, for her there is a void. As for the Creature, he is not, at this point, sexless, his desire having become eroticized because his hideousness limits him to spying on the women of the De Lacey household and to gazing on the loveliness of Frankenstein's mother and Justine in the aesthetically distanced form of a portrait or a sleeping body. Unless

Elizabeth somehow means these images, it is hard to understand why she should matter to the Creature. Frankenstein does matter to him, however—certainly not because of some repressed homosexual attachment and not because Frankenstein is the Lacanian or Girardian "other" who confers value on the object of (the other's) desire. What, then, does the Creature want from Frankenstein? He seeks reparation for his sorrows, and to this end he attempts to engage Frankenstein in dialogue, again not because Frankenstein is the Lacanian "Other" whose recognition is all he really wants but because Frankenstein alone can provide a suitable mate with whom to share his enforced solitude. After Frankenstein breaks his word, mangling the half-finished monsteress in full view of the Creature, the Creature keeps his. The killing of Elizabeth is at once a way of establishing a relationship with the only human being to whom he can claim kinship and a desperately antierotic act designed to teach his creator what he suffers. The Creature's murderous career, an ingenious counterplot, compels Frankenstein to read what amounts to a Freudian text in reality.

The foregoing may seem not only naively overliteral but sentimental. Am I not resorting to "pernicious casuistry" (Shelley), excusing the Creature because he is an "exception," and how can I justly argue that his truth is intersubjectivity when his only contacts are hypothetical? In dealing with the Creature one needs to exercise the hesitancy such questions induce; that is, the critic should, insofar as possible, respect the text. When J. M. Hill, a psychoanalytic adept, claims that the Creature "cannot fathom the depths of passion which urge vengeance" and when a generally skeptical George Levine remarks that the Creature "doesn't fully understand the power of irrational energies which he himself enacts," they are presumably thinking about the unconscious of the unconscious, whatever that means, but I am fairly sure these are not critical statements. Despite appearances, the Creature remains a scandal for analytic readers because he does not fit Freud's specifications: his unpresentable outside (only apparently idlike) balks (but not purposefully, as in Freudian repression) his unambiguously presentable inside. Of course, given the sophisticated rhetorical techniques of the psychoanalytic arsenal, there is nothing to prevent critics from remaking the Creature in whatever image they wish, from transforming any presence into an absence or any absence into a presence, as they see fit. Critics can thereby preserve the coherence of a reading, but in so doing they sacrifice too much. For the Creature's story is something finer than just another version of, or a sentimental recoil from, Frankenstein's, and the Creature himself is *Frankenstein's* great, original turn on tradition, a disturbingly uncanny literal figuration that ought to rouse the critical faculties to act.

An editor of a recent collection of essays on *Frankenstein* observes, "So pervasive has been the recognition that the Monster and Frankenstein are two aspects of the same being that the writers in this volume assume rather than argue it." Among the powerful forces responsible for collapsing the two into one is the inertial drift of both reading and textuality, fostered here by the mystifying allure of those grand figures of thought, doubling and monsterism. Within us there is also a need, perhaps a compulsion, to return things to an originative, determining source, especially when the human producer of an object or act is involved. This exigency is manifest in forms ranging from the ghoulish rage of Shelley's Count Cenci, who would reappropriate a "particle of my divided being" by raping his daughter, to the comparatively mild critical reduction of the Creature to the dark complement of Frankenstein's light or of creator and created to epiphenomena of some larger whole, be it Blake's inconceivable unfallen Albion, Mary Shelley's psyche, or the Freudian psychic apparatus. At this stage of *Frankenstein* criticism, the motif of the double can be useful only if it sharpens awareness of the irreducibly complex otherness intrinsic to the self or of the Creature as an autonomous "other self" duplicitously representing the traditional alter ego. Even supposing that the Creature owes his engenderment to Frankenstein's oedipal scene, he is no more reducible to it than any of us is to what our parents happened to be thinking when they conceived us. How different from Frankenstein's is the Creature's recurrent catastrophic scene of rejection and exclusion. The Creature's utmost desire is that another reciprocate his need for sympathetic relationship, and even after he becomes searingly conscious of his exclusion from the human community and begins to objectify the negativity he arouses in others, we recognize that his aggression is a by-product of disintegration, not an innate drive that has been cathartically unbound. If, with a reader's ideal blindness, we can hear the bereavement of the Creature's whole self, we recognize too that he looks back at us with "speculative eyes." Freed, by the end, from his creator's self-consuming rage, he makes his destiny his choice, emblazoning himself as a giant form of Solitude, an existence made absolute by its confinement to the hell of being itself.

Still, the Creature's fate is to be misread, and any thematic capture necessarily restricts, however much it restitutes. In a moment of remarkable self-awareness he reflects that if he had been introduced to humanity not by the patriarchal De Laceys but "by a young soldier, burning for glory and slaughter," he would "have been imbued with different sensations." His history, then, is only a possible actualization of his essence, which is to say that the Creature's principal virtue is virtuality. A kind of wandering signifier, the Creature proceeds through the text triggering various signifying effects. As the reader increasingly acknowledges the larger cultural and biographical context that constitutes the penumbra of the fiction, critical representations of what the Creature represents multiply endlessly. If, for the orthodox Freudian, he is a type of the unconscious, for the Jungian he is the shadow, for the Lacanian an *objet a*, for one Romanticist a Blakean "spectre," for another a Blakean "emanation"; he also has been or can be read as Rousseau's natural man, a Wordsworthian child of nature, the isolated Romantic rebel, the misunderstood revolutionary impulse, Mary Shelley's abandoned baby self, her abandoned babe, an aberrant signifier, *différance*, or as a hypostasis of godless presumption, the monstrosity of a godless nature, analytical reasoning, or alienating labor. Like the Creature's own mythic version of himself, a freakish hybrid of Milton's Adam and Satan, all these allegorizations are exploded by the text. The alert reader, at a given moment of interpretive breakdown, will resort to another signifying chain, and thence to another, and will be left wondering whether to receive this overload of signification as a mutually enriching profusion of possibilities or as an unmeaning chaos.

While the most sensible response may be a benign ecumenical acceptance of difference, certain problems remain: for instance, how can the same text sustain divergent critical representations and what authorizes or disqualifies any representation at a particular moment? Moreover, such negative capability is likely to mask mere incapacity or a failure of will and is rarely conducive to interesting readings. Exemplary of a potentially stronger critical position are the psychoanalytic readers who would compound with the world of the text's imaginings by penetrating to its center of mystery. Entering the circle of the text and operating Freud's ingenious meaning-making machine, they will discover that an oedipal focus limits only the range of interpretive options, and if they are open to the possibility that the oedipal material they uncover may defend against other types of psychic conflict, their critical anxieties will mount. To salvage their integrity they must found a reading by arbitrarily limiting it, restricting at the same time their own cognitive, erotic, and imaginative capabilities. To construct a plausible narrative they will resort to such tactics of secondary revision as lacunae, decontextualization, distortion, and rationalized contradiction, and to persuade us that their story is not simply another revocable text they will enlist the aid of some extratextual model to underwrite both the fiction and the critical discourse. Ultimately, however, the authorizing model relies on an interpretation of how things are (or, for the growing number of the novel's psychobiographers, how things were), and whether or not the representation is privileged depends on the particular analyst's rhetorical skill and our willingness to be lied to.

A possible way out of or around this hermeneutic circle is to stop viewing the Creature as a thing apart. We might consider "meaning" as a constantly shifting relational event, asking what the Creature means, at a certain point in the novel, to himself, Frankenstein, Elizabeth, or such and such a reader. The danger here is hazy relativism, an openness akin to the indifferent free trafficking that deconstructionists tend to elevate to a principle of principles. Even misreading has its map. Why one interpretive pathway should be preferred to another may be impossible to determine, but we must not forget that all must pass through the Creature, that something is there to solicit us. That something demands careful scrutiny because of its unsettling effect on our habitual ideas about what signs may be up to. Luckily barred from the overwhelming presence of the Creature, in the face of which interpretation becomes mute, we must dream our dreams of the Creature not only as a signifier in search of its proper signification but as a literal being that means only itself. The literal Creature, in other words, is as much a figuration as the figurative Creature, and in reflecting on what the letter of the text allows us to surmise about the Creature, whose "reality" we know is but a textual effect, we are always in an indeterminate borderline situation. Frankenstein never speaks more truly than when he calls the Creature his "daemon." A marginal or boundary being, the daemon is a powerful representation of our uncertain lot, suspended as we are between knowledge and power, nature and supernature, objectivity and subjectivity. Conceiving the Creature as a genius of liminality, a type of art's duplicitous interplay of revelation and concealment, restores his virtuality, which is betrayed as soon as he comes to signify something determinate. An emphasis on meaning as process also encourages the interpreter to participate in the work of the work, a dreamwork more efficacious than that of the mind abandoned to sleep. The literalizing power of Frankenstein is, of course, only a dream that haunts literature. But "labour is blossoming" (Yeats) within this marginal ontological zone, where letter and spirit forge a meaning that can never be anything more than a dreaming to signify, to become significant, to touch reality. We are touched by the passion of the signifier, a perpetually renewed *dreaming to* that no dream of satisfaction can satisfy.

Who, in our century, understood or exemplified the insistence of the dream of signification better than Freud? Psychoanalysis, for him, was always a stopgap until the real thing (biochemistry) would come along, but his inventive genius transformed the analytic field into an ample domain of spirit, an autonomous power that his system goes on calling by false names. Decentered or detraumatized, the Freudian corpus becomes an indispensable guide to the intentional play of forces that keeps meaning wandering restlessly through the mind. From Freud we can gather many enabling fictions, forms of the spirit's cunning and resourcefulness, and he can instruct us in the virtues of hovering attention, the need to look at something again and again until it begins to declare itself, and of alertness to the heterogeneous. Seeking to mediate the discrepancy between two suggestively dissimilar stories, *Frankenstein* and the orthodox psychoanalytic rendering I venture above, I now want to enter what I understand to be the true Freudian space—a place where Freud joins the company of such alienists as Blake, Milton, and Kierkegaard—as I attempt a sustained reimagining of Frankenstein's scene of creation.

II

Writing on the occasion of *Frankenstein*'s canonization, its inclusion in a "standard novels" series, Mary Shelley begins the Introduction as if discharging a grim obligation to a text that should long ago have been consigned to her buried past. She is roused again, however, when she returns to the moment of the novel's origin, her waking dream of Frankenstein's emergence as a creator. Focusing on the creator's terror, she evokes the disturbing thrill of being there, in the midst of the traumatic scene, her prose mounting in intensity and shifting to the present tense as she recounts the successive stages of her vision: the powerful engine stirring to life the "hideous phantom"; Frankenstein's hysterical flight; the "horrid thing" opening the bed curtains and fixing its eyes on him, an experience of ultimate dread that shatters the vision, leaving her breathless on her "midnight pillow." What does it mean to be there, in the midst? It is to be swept up into a sublime dimension and to be faced by a dizzying void, to be at once an excited witness, the terrified artist, and the aroused form of chaos that gazes back at both creator and dreamer. Invention, Mary Shelley reflects, consists in creating "out of chaos." Once her imagination asserts itself, presenting her with the dream vision, we may associate the engine (*ingenium, genius*) with the usurping imagination, the animated Creature with the scene itself, and the chaotic mass to be set in motion with the writer's own chaos, the panic at the center of her authorial consciousness. Creator, creation, and creative agency are varying manifestations of the same anxiety that elaborates itself to compose the scene of authorship.

The novel's monstrous heart of darkness is the creation, and the creative self that inaugurates the drama resembles the "self-closd, all-repelling...Demon" encountered at the opening of *The Book of Urizen*. Frankenstein's founding gesture, like that of Blake's fearful demiurge, is a stepping aside, but while Urizen secedes from Eternity, Frankenstein absents himself from our world of ordinary awareness and relatedness, which recedes from him in much the manner that a dream fades at the instant of awakening. Severing all contact with his family, other beings, and familiar nature, he is intent on hollowing out a zone in reality where he can be utterly alone. This ingressive movement is attended by self-loss, a radical shrinkage of his empirical self, and self-aggrandizement, a heightening of his isolate selfhood to daemonic status. He becomes a force instead of a person as all the energy of his being concentrates on his grand project: "My mind was filled with one thought, one conception, one purpose"; "a resistless, and almost frantic, impulse urged me forward; I seemed to have lost all soul or sensation but for this one pursuit." The animation project, like the object intended by the Freudian libido, is a secondary affair. What matters is that it enkindles in the projector a lust for self-presence so intense that it drives out of consciousness everything except itself. Reality must yield if the self is to appear, and Frankenstein's primary creative act is to originate his own creative self.

The vertiginous upward fall that founds the creative self coincides with a rupture between daemonic mind and all that is not mind. What may loosely be termed consciousness (of self, an extravagantly augmented self so full of itself as to allow neither time nor space for self-awareness) and unconsciousness (of the normative world from which the self has detached itself) are twin-born, factoring out as discrete loci that mark the decisiveness of Frankenstein's psychic dislocation. Only in the catastrophic nature of this birth is there any significant point of contact with the repressive process that institutes ego and id as opposing agencies in the Freudian economy. Narcissism and, probably closer, psychosis are the appropriate psychoanalytic analogues, though the usefulness of these nosological entities here is questionable. I see no need, for example, to posit a specific libidinal stage or fixation point to which Frankenstein is regressing. But everything would resolve itself into a structural conflict anyway: Frankenstein's oedipal trouble impels his defensive "episode," which signals a victory of the forces of repression; and with the creation he spills back into the domain of assured analytic knowledge, the Creature amounting to a bizarre symptomatic return of the repressed that can be interpreted in the same way as the dream of a neurotic. For the psychoanalyst, then, the Creature is a figure that redoubles Frankenstein's literal unconscious complex, which is already present as an a priori with a determinate constitution; in fact, however, he is an autonomous agent, not a psychic agency, and Frankenstein's supposed unconscious is a figurative device, a critic's overhasty recourse designed to mediate or neutralize a puzzling discontinuity.

By what name shall we invoke discontinuity? For Milton in *Paradise Lost* it is Hell, a space carved out in the universe to receive the daemonic selfhood of Satan, for whom everything is a universe of death. The depth of one's particular hell is an index of how far one has fallen away from what might be perceived or known. The unconscious, in other words, is a modality of subjective experience whose meaning is estrangement. What

Frankenstein creates, in order to create, is distance between his daemonized self and a newly alienated reality, and it scarcely matters whether we conceive this space as interior or exterior since it is a fantastic medial zone where the boundaries between self and world are impossible to distinguish. Within this void, between two created "nothings," self-consciousness appears. It is the place into which the baffled residue of Frankenstein's ordinary self has been cast. From its vantage, somewhere in the corner of Frankenstein's mind, it takes notes, watching with horrified fascination the extravagant career of a stranger that is also an uncanny variation of the self.

Out of this phantom place, in addition, the Creature emerges, as Blake's Enitharmon emanates from Los once Los "closes" with the death image of Urizen, thus embracing the world view of the solipsistically withdrawn creating mind. The ungraspable Enitharmon, Los's loss and shadowed gain, embodies the suddenly exterior, objectified space that has opened up between Los and Eternity, or Los's alienated potential. The Creature is similarly a token of loss, a complex representation of the estranged universe Frankenstein has summoned into being by pushing away reality. Yet does the Creature, strictly speaking, represent Frankenstein's alienated potential? I suppose he can be read as the responsive, sympathetic imagination Frankenstein suppresses in order to create. From the psychoanalytic perspective, such repression would be very odd: imagine the id repressing the sublimated ego. The repression hypothesis must be rejected in any event because the Creature is something radically new and different, no more a double or a part of Frankenstein than Enitharmon is of Los. Instead, these emanative beings "stand for" their creators in the sense that they are interpolations, "transitional objects" (Winnicott) or texts, intended to rectify a catastrophic disalignment of self and world.

The creation is at once a new departure for Frankenstein and the climax of a developmental process that, as Wordsworth says, "hath no beginning." Frankenstein's narrative begins with an idyll of domestic bliss: in the protected enclave of his household all are incomparably virtuous and lovable; affections go deep, and yet everyone lives on the surface. Of course, it is all a lie, but the reader should be troubled by this absurdity no more than by the newborn Creature's walking off with Frankenstein's coat as protection against the cold. Just as anyone who wishes can discover the source of an individual's troubles in the past, since so much happened "there," readers inclined to locate the cause of Frankenstein's aberration in his youth will see what they expect to see in his narrative or will find that what they seek is all the more confirmed by its absence from the account. His fall may have been occasioned by Elizabeth's admission into the family circle, by William's birth, by the sinister "silken cord" of parental constriction, or by a repressed primal-scene trauma. It doesn't matter: any psychotrauma is as true or as false as any other. Like all of us, Frankenstein begins fallen—or, better, falling. The brief idyll of his youth gives him something to fall away from; and the more remotely idealized the starting point, the more absolute or self-defining is his point of departure. Frankenstein simply announces that, as far back as he can remember, "the world was to me a secret which I desired to divine." That is, the fall from the wholeness of origins is rooted in his lust to overtake a hidden, receding presence, or a tantalizing absence, that lies behind appearances and disturbs his contact with things. This dualizing consciousness is a given of his temperament, the destiny-assigned identity theme that he lives out in the sphere of science but that he could have expressed as well in exploration or authorship. Can we improve on Frankenstein's version, or on Coleridge's characterization of Iago as "a motiveless malignity"? The aptly named Iago is the ego principle, the sublimely arbitrary human will that originates everything, including all myths of a catastrophic or transcendental point of spiritual origination, and motive hunting no more explains his willfulness than it does Desdemona's love for Othello.

Motivation, like sequential logic, is a falsification the mind cannot do without. The signal importance Frankenstein ascribes to the death of his mother suggests that the reanimation project is a deferred reaction to this event, which he terms "the first misfortune of my life...an omen...of my future misery." He dwells on the "irreparable evil" brought about by the rending of ties and on the "void" created by death, which he raises to quasi-supernatural status as "the spoiler." Presumably her death reactivates an original anxiety of deprivation associated with the departure of the maternal body, and the irrevocable loss of the mother, the primary focus of the child's reality bondings, could help to explain the intensification of Frankenstein's temperamental dualism. But while psychoanalytic theory is suggestive here, it is too restrictively bound to a particular mythic version of the past, too fetishistically centered on one of many possible mythic representations of loss. Like the oak-shattering bolt, the death of the mother is preeminently a narcissistic insult for Frankenstein. Confronted by the fact of death, he is overtaken by a primordial anxiety, not an anxiety-provoking repressed wish; and although such anxiety is apt to recoil from any number of fancied antagonists, its proper object is the most inclusive and irreducible of forces: life, our human life, in relation to which death is not an external agency but an internal component. Yet, as Kierkegaard knew, consciousness of this radical fault in existence need not, or need not only, paralyze the spirit. Dread, and perhaps even the fear of being delivered over to it, can be a sublime energizer, arousing the infinite spirit that longs for a house as large as itself.

Seeking to undo the consequences of sexuality, the sin of being born of woman, Frankenstein engages in a pursuit at once regressive and projective, mobilizing old energies in an attempt to discover a new meaning for himself. Adrift for a time after his mother's death, he is eager, once he leaves for the university, to cast off his dependence and put his talents to work. All that remains is for Waldman's sermon, perhaps more the sheer power of his voice than his overt message, to render an occasion for Frankenstein's restless drive for autonomy:

> Such were the professor's words—rather let me say such the words of fate. ...As he went on, I felt as if my soul were grappling with a palpable enemy; one by one the various keys were touched which formed the mechanism of my being.... So much has been done, exclaimed the soul of Frankenstein—more, far more, will I achieve...I will pioneer a new way, explore unknown powers, and unfold to the world the deepest mysteries of creation.

This powerfully charged moment of conversion, or reconversion, founds Frankenstein as an artist. From the struggle of his second birth he emerges as a force of destiny, genius in a human form, first pronouncing the fateful name of the modern Prometheus: *franken Stein*, the free rock, the free-unfree man.

After two years of reviewing the current state of scientific knowledge, Frankenstein is abruptly halted by an audacious, yet for him inevitable, question: "Whence...did the principle of life proceed?" The way is opened for his first descent into the world of the tomb: "I beheld the corruption of death succeed to the blooming cheek of life; I saw how the worm inherited the wonders of the eye and brain." At this stage Frankenstein presents himself as a detached observer of death's work, and nature offers little resistance to his inquiries. "A sudden light" breaks "from the midst of this darkness," whereupon he is dazzled to discover himself the first of mortals capable of disentangling life from death. Modern criticism, generally empowered by demystifying reversals, has tended both to devalue Frankenstein's discovery, regarding his life principle as a type of natural energy rather than as a genuine first, and to view his enthusiasm as a mechanical operation of the spirit. Although the great Romantic faith in the omnipotence of thought is unquestionably allied to the scientist's baleful drive for manipulative control, they remain very distinct forms of the Cartesian legacy. To the extent that the artist in Frankenstein collapses into the technician he is a loser. But now, as he stands at the source, Frankenstein is a sublime quester who has found his muse, an answering subject to inspire and direct the quest, and his delight is that of a man who has come to recognize the glory of his own inner source, his originative *I am*.

Once Frankenstein begins to describe the lengthy creation process his hitherto sequential narrative becomes curiously perturbed. The style is spasmodic, juxtapositive, and repetitive, obscuring temporal relations yet underscoring how radically divided the creator is. We hear from a practical Frankenstein, who reasons that even an imperfect effort will lay the ground for future successes; a secretly selfish utopian idealist, who dreams of a new species blessing him "as its creator and source"; and a domestic Frankenstein, who procrastinates "all that related to my feelings of affection until the great object, which swallowed up every habit of my nature, should be completed." Being swallowed up is the principal terror of the narrative consciousness dominating these pages, a depersonalized, though suffering, observer of the wreck Frankenstein is becoming. Little is heard from the daemonized Frankenstein, in part because his experience of sublime uplift is wordless and in part because this "hurricane" has no time for words, though for the troubled eye of the storm time is agonizingly slow. Complicating matters is the superimposition of the narrative present on an episode that the fallen Frankenstein can be relied on to misconstrue, so that the complex web of the account becomes virtually impossible to unweave. Then, we may surmise, a dialectic of the following sort was at work: driving out and driven in, the creative self is agonistic, aggressively excluding otherness, and hence agonized, defensively immuring itself in resistance to any foreign body that would encroach on its sublime solitude; the barrier keeps breaking, however, leading to disabling bouts of self-consciousness, which in turn provoke even more audacious sublime rushes that threaten to overwhelm the ordinary self, that residual underconsciousness which clings ever more desperately to its bewildered identity. How one interprets the meaning of the entire experience—whether from the point of view of the daemonic self or from that of the ordinary self—probably tells more about the interpreter than about the experience itself, just as the Abyssinian maid of "Kubla Khan" emerges as the muse of paradise or the voice of the abyss depending on whether one stands inside or outside the magic circle of the conclusion.

The breathlessly eager self that is in, or is, the enthusiasm soars above the body that is taking shape. Frankenstein's workshop is located "in a solitary chamber, or rather cell, at the top of the house, and separated from all the other apartments." This is a masterful emblem of the mind that is its own place. The windows are barred, at least for the enthusiast, whose eyes remain "insensible to the charms of nature." Those "charms" are an interpolation of Frankenstein the notetaker or narrator; the creator is an innerness—pure, unconditioned spirit—seeking innerness—the life or light in, but not of, things. Things themselves do not exist for him except as "lifeless matter" to be animated, the *fort* to his *da* (*sein*), and the more they are leveled to a deadening continuity the more discontinuous is the fiery spirit that would stamp its image on a world rendered pliable to its projects and projections.

The problem is that if the sublime artist is to "pour a torrent of light into our dark world" of mortal life, he must take a detour through reality. To wrest the spirit from things he must, for a second time, penetrate into the center of the earth, and to prepare a frame for the reception of life he must now not only see and know but also touch the body of death. Undertaking a shamanistic descent into chaos, a place of "filthy creation" where life and death conspire to breed monstrous shapes, Frankenstein is flooded with nausea: "Who shall conceive the horrors of my secret toil, as I dabbled among the unhallowed damps of the grave, or tortured the living animal to animate the lifeless clay?" Is Frankenstein speaking of vivisection, or is the tortured living body his own? His aggression, whether directed outward or against himself, recalls that of Blake's Urizen:

> Times on times he divided, & measur'd
> Space by space in his ninefold darkness
> Unseen, unknown! changes appeard
> In his desolate mountains rifted furious
> By the black winds of perturbation
>
> For he strove in battles dire
> In unseen conflictions with shapes
> Bred from his forsaken wilderness
> (*The Book of Urizen* I.2–3)

Frankenstein too is entrapped by his own phantasmagoria. The oppressively close, enveloping tomb world into which he descends is a self-engendered abyss that discloses what our finite bodily ground looks like from the heights to which the spirit has ascended. Transforming an evacuated reality into a grotesque naturalization and the denied natural passions into a perversely eroticized shadow life, the sublime artist's exaggerated distance from things has also transformed him into a graveyard poet. In short, Frankenstein has discovered, or invented, an inchoate version of the Freudian unconscious.

Frankenstein's aggression and perverse perception are inscribed in the Creature's appearance. The artist envisioned something quite different: "How can I . . . delineate the wretch whom with such infinite pains and care I had endeavoured to form? His limbs were in proportion, and I had selected his features as beautiful." What *did* Frankenstein intend? Treading "heaven in my thoughts . . . exulting in my powers," he conceived the Creature as a representation of the transfigured creative self, a grandiose embodiment of the creator's mind. But it is also a desperate compromise, designed to mend an intolerable dualism. The beautiful Creature of Frankenstein's imaginings is analogous to Sin, the perfect narcissistic image of Satan, the interior paramour who explodes from his brain when heaven rolls away from him and with whom he proceeds to copulate; Frankenstein's dread monster corresponds to Sin's unrecognized "nether shape," but even more closely to Death, that chaotic "darkness visible," who is the ultimate issue of Satan's deranged spirit, his love of his own thought. The moving Creature, like Death, is unrepresentable. However, directly after the infusion of life, while the Creature is still dazed, Frankenstein ventures the novel's only description of this formless form:

> Beautiful!—Great God! His yellow skin scarcely covered the work of muscles and arteries beneath; his hair was of a lustrous black, and flowing; his teeth of a pearly whiteness; but these luxuriances only formed a more horrid contrast with the watery eyes, that seemed almost of the same colour as the dun white sockets in which they were set, his shrivelled complexion and straight black lips.

An "unearthly" figure, the Creature bodies forth the horrid contrast between heaven and hell that Frankenstein experiences as a dizzying, instantaneous descent.

How is one to explain this catastrophic turn? The only way to fathom the Creature's appearance, which is more a rhetorical effect than a natural fact, is to comprehend how it was made. For Frankenstein, putting together and dismembering are one. The parts he chooses are beautiful, but they are monstrous in conjunction—or, rather, since the Creature lacks a phenomenological center, in their absolute disjunction. Frankenstein is similarly unbalanced, a confused collectivity. The daemonized self that initiates the project is a force inimical to form, and it cannot see or guide properly from the heights. The normative self, desperately in need of bridging back to reality, patches over the rift in the fabric of Frankenstein's existence as best it can. But although its eyeballs start "from their sockets in attending to the details," it cannot recollect the original inspiration. The result of all this frantic alienated labor is a being geared to self-torment. As such, the Creature is also a figure that reveals, with more startling accuracy and profundity than discursive reason can command, the existential condition of its progenitor: his relation-disrelation to his world, his thoughts, and himself. The incomplete Creature, unmated and unmatable, an inconceivably lonely free-standing unit whose inside is hopelessly divided from its outside, is indeed a "filthy type" of the modern Prometheus.

Any representation of the creative process, whether the novel's narrative or my analytic account, is bound to distort the experience of the whole self. Suspended between heaven and hell, those absolutely disjoined fictive polarities that are in fact mutually sustaining correlates, the creator is at once ravished and ravaged by sublimity. He is filled and swallowed up, but not entirely full or emptied out; for to be wholly abandoned to the sublime would amount to autism, and there would no longer be a self to experience the uplift or downfall. It is always, to modify Emerson slightly, a case of I *and* the abyss. Since he cannot be the thing itself and cannot be nothing, Frankenstein is a spirit destined to "exult in the agony of the torturing flames." Another name for this giant agony is despair. "Despair," writes Kierkegaard, cannot

> consume the eternal thing, the self, which is the ground of despair, whose worm dieth not, and whose fire is not quenched. Yet despair is precisely *self*-consuming, but it is an impotent self-consumption. . . . This is the hot incitement, or the cold fire in despair, the gnawing canker whose movement is constantly inward, deeper and deeper. . . . This precisely is the reason why he despairs . . . because he cannot consume himself, cannot get rid of himself, cannot become nothing. This is the potentiated formula for despair, the rising of the fever in the sickness of the self.

Kierkegaard, dangerously on the verge of becoming the dread itself, is a better guide here than Freud, the great analyst of the concept of dread. As Kierkegaard would have it, Frankenstein is a prisoner of despair because his volatile spirit desires only to augment itself, because the self is not "grounded transparently in the Power which posited it." That Power, which may simply be a potentiated form of the despairing spirit, exists beyond the purview of Mary Shelley's fiction. But *Frankenstein* is empowered, and at times disabled, by a despair over the human condition, whose limits condemn the creator's sublime quest to the status of an extravagant, desperate wish. The novel's wisdom, not only imperfectly expressed by an advocacy of domestic bliss but in fact undercut by overt moralizing, is that we need "keeping," that we must be concrete in the same measure as we are abstract and that we must abide with the antinomies (life and death, ideality and actuality, will and fate) that constitute our ground. Frankenstein may be said to err in misreading both his own reality and the larger reality that circumscribes his existence. No matter how great the spirit within him, the universal life principle he thinks he has captured, although it is not merely a trick of spirit, can never become his instrument for correcting existence. It "was now within my grasp," he says; he adds, however, that "the information I had obtained was of a nature rather to direct my endeavours so soon as I should point them towards the object of my search. . . . I was like the Arabian who had been buried with the dead, and found a passage to life, aided only by one glimmering, and seemingly ineffectual, light." Dazzled by an obscure revelation, he can only move toward the light, for the power source he taps is a constituent element in an ongoing process, a continuum of animation and deanimation according to whose subtle rhythm of recurrence we live and die every moment. Frankenstein is a thief of fire, and the utmost he can do is to transmit the power to a body capable of sustaining life.

His nervous symptoms become increasingly pathological as the time for the Creature's inspiration nears, and once he is about to perform the deed, finding himself in a recognizably realistic setting, Frankenstein is less anxious than melancholic, as though calamity has already struck. What possible act or object could satisfy the aspirations of the uncreated soul? The dream of the sublime artist's overflowing fullness is grotesquely parodied as Frankenstein sickens into creation: "the rain pattered dismally against the panes, and my candle was nearly burnt out, when, by the glimmer of the half-extinguished light, I saw the dull yellow eye of the creature open." What is bracketed here, at the decisive moment of Frankenstein's reentry into reality, is the infusion of the spark of life. The creative act is a mindless reflex, an indication that the creator has fallen away from his desire into a void that nothing can fill but that somehow must be limited, as in *The Book of Urizen*, by a barrier of "solid obstruction." The Creature, though not quite setting a limit to Frankenstein's nightmare, is hell's bottom. Landing there, Frankenstein sees his Creature for the first time when its eyes open, a negative epiphany revealing to him that he is not alone, that he too is now visible. The nightmare follows, with its horrific climactic emblem of the condition of corporeality, and he wakens to confront the self-impelled Creature, the living image of death this new Orpheus has brought back from the house of the dead. The creator's terror attests to his lack of mastery, the grim fact of his own creatureliness, which is what set the creative process in motion. Beholding the Creature, Frankenstein is back at his original impasse, uncannily subject to the recurrence of his dread of time, space, and the body of death.

It is impossible to know what Frankenstein apprehends at the pivotal instant when his half-extinguished candle is eclipsed by the Creature's dull yellow eye, but the former seeker of the inner light almost immediately fixates on appearances. The overwhelming irony is that Frankenstein has opened up a space in reality for the emergence of something radically new, realizing the power to make literally present what the poets have always dreamed of. A presence so full that it is as unapproachable as light or an absence so great that it confounds the representational faculties, the Creature is the sublime or grotesque thing itself. Frankenstein's all too human failure of response is to petrify his living artifact into an otherness that cannot be restituted by mind. The Creature becomes a blocking agent, standing between Frankenstein and the normative world he longs to rejoin, and an uncanny reminder of the creator's alienated majesty, the sublime experience from which he is henceforth irremediably estranged. This unproductive misreading, though saving him from an encounter with Dread itself, condemns both Creature and creator to anguished incompleteness. Locked into an interminable pursuit of the shadow he has become, Frankenstein emerges as the man who cannot emerge, a prisoner of the passage arrested at the moment of his falling away from his own possible sublimity. The final irony is that his solitude is confirmed. Frankenstein achieves his own separate consciousness of himself as the most wretched of mortals. But even if his egotism is such that he glories in this doom as the token of a special destiny, he has become just another Gothic hero-villain, a tiresome neurotic whose presence impoverishes the larger portion of the novel that bears his name.

III

There is an intriguing relation between Frankenstein's history and the account of the novel's genesis in the Introduction. Although the vocation of protagonist and novelist is in a sense chosen by their temperaments and circumstances, the origin of the creative enterprise is supremely arbitrary: a spell of bad weather. Confined indoors, Frankenstein is set on the path toward creation after he "chanced to find a volume of the works of Cornelius Agrippa," and Mary Shelley is bestirred after "some volumes of ghost stories"—less threatening models for a literary aspirant than are her companions, Shelley and Byron—"fell into our hands." This archaic matter requires supplementation, and the means of carrying out the project is offered by Waldman's lecture on modern science and by Shelley and Byron's conversation about galvanism. At this juncture, however, two defensive reversals aim to differentiate the careers of active author and passive subject. The sudden light that breaks in upon Frankenstein impels him toward his catastrophic creation scene, but it is only after her waking dream that Mary Shelley experiences her vocational moment: "Swift as light and as cheering was the idea that broke in upon me. 'I have found it!' . . . On the morrow I announced that I had *thought of a story.*" The vision of the would-be master's victimization is her means of mastery, as though the scene of authorship were already behind her. "And now, once again, I bid my hideous progeny go forth and prosper," she writes, as though the novel were the Creature and she had put on its power to overwhelm others. In the Introduction she passes over the actual writing of *Frankenstein,* and while her creative labor was doubtless less calamitous than Frankenstein's, the novel is necessarily another "imperfect animation." How much, one wonders, was lost in "translation" when the airy book imagination wrote in the mind became the novel we read? But the likelihood is that the ecstatic dream of the book, as represented in the Introduction, is an afterbirth, that now, once again, Mary Shelley is begetting it by replaying both Frankenstein's and *Franken-stein*'s catastrophe of origination. Her mind, too, was the haunt of a terrible idea, which became her means of mastery insofar as it inspired the novel's transcendent or paradigmatic vision of the genesis of any sublime artwork, any uncanny reanimation project.

According to the novel's representation of the creative process, the work emanates from an authorial self whose decisive break with normative experience clears a space for the work to appear. The emergence of this authorizing agency necessitates such a massive withdrawal or sacrifice of the writer's identity that the work is likely to be more estranged from writer than reader. To argue thus is not to deny that Mary Shelley, as mother and mourning mother, was ideally suited to preside over the account of Franken-stein's fearful literal creation. But even if we agree that the novel is informed by her personal experience and that the novel, had it been anonymously published, would be recognizably a woman's book, we cannot necessarily trace its creation back to her empirical self or conclude that its meaning is coextensive with its point of departure in personal experience. The role of the writer's biography and psychobiography in the work is analogous to that of what Freud calls the "day's residue" in the dreamwork. Once the author crosses from the empirical sphere to the transcendent dimension of art, the stuff of ordinary experience is reconstituted as an element in the work's fantastic scenario, and the empirical self, transformed for good or ill by the author's rite of passage, is simply along for the ride. Still, if it is the Real Man or Woman, the Blakean Imagination, that solicits our response in a literary text, we must be careful not to be carried away by Blake's sublime idealizations or capital letters. The authorial self must not be vaporized into an impersonal transcendental consciousness. The writer may be powerfully tempted to become a force refusing all form, but the constitutive subject I am positing has its own complex psychology, determined by its relations to the forms, images, and desires that compose the field of literature. That is to say, the authorial self, like the empirical self, is a living consciousness, not so much disembodied as differently embodied.

What does it mean for the Word to be incarnated, for the work to be written? "When composition begins," writes Shelley, "inspiration is already on the decline, and the most glorious poetry that has ever been communicated to the world is probably a feeble shadow of the original conception of the poet." We recall that when Frankenstein infuses the spark of being into the lifeless thing before him, his candle is "nearly burnt out." Shelley's version is that "the mind in creation is as a fading coal." Composition is at once the shattering of mind and the scattering of dead or dying thoughts, mere leavings, ashes and sparks that are the casual by-products of the "unextinguished hearth" of original inspiration. Art is a betrayal of its source. Lapsing into discourse, the artist utters a dismembered Word. Alienated by the words intended to mediate it, the Word assumes the opacity of what stands for it and is evacuated by what stands in its place. To be represented by the text is thus to experience a bewildering effacement or defacement of the self; the authorial self, in other words, is as much estranged from the work as the empirical self. Of course, it can be argued that the authorial self is merely an effect of textuality, not an originative presence: "Always already"—one hears the insistent murmur of Derrida, echoing Heidegger—textualized. That may be so. But I find it impossible to think about literature without retaining the notion of the creative imagination, if for no other reason than that some such mythic agency is needed to link the completed text to the self that paces about the room and chews pencils. Dr. Johnson, who greatly respected literary power, shows himself to be at least as advanced as the most modern demystifier when he terms imagination a "hunger... which preys incessantly upon life" (*Rasselas*, Ch. 32). Perhaps, then, it would be more accurate to say that the artist, instead of falling into textuality, falls back on the text to avoid becoming lost in his or her own void. Composing the work, the writer touches ground. Inasmuch as writing is always a reworking of the already written, of literary tradition, it is not the writer's own ground, but it is just as surely the true ground of his or her being, inasmuch as reanimating the dead is the self-alienating labor that constitutes authorship.

However universal Frankenstein's experience may be, his failure as an artist is also particular, a merely personal torment. He counsels Walton not to aspire to be greater than human nature will allow. How great is that? In flight from his catastrophic scene of authorship, Frankenstein seeks consolation in the Alps, declaring that the Power is there, elsewhere, invested in Mont Blanc. Here the human being is a dwarfed latecomer, the sole unquiet thing, and Frankenstein, with dubious ecstasy, yields up his spirit to the "solitary grandeur" presiding over this ancient desolation. But although vowing not "to bend before any being less almighty than that which had created and ruled the elements," he is surprised by his massive and all but omnipotent Creature, the only presence amid this blankness and a fit emblem of his god of Power. Ultimately, the terrific god means "I am terrified"—whether by chaos or the space of absolute freedom remains for the interpreter to decide. Like the speaker of Blake's "Tyger," whose own estranged genius can be read in his distorted visions of a beast and of a beastly creator so fearsome he can be represented only by piecemeal images, Frankenstein is absurdly frightened out of his creative potential by his own creations.

Is it possible to put on power and yet avoid crippling anxiety? Shelley believed so, and his "Mont Blanc" is a serious parody of the "ceaseless ravings" of Coleridge's "Hymn before Sun-Rise," a poem Frankenstein might have written. Shelley himself is nearly overwhelmed by nature's power display and the spectral deity it represents. However, "one legion of wild thoughts," a saving remnant, wanders to "the still cave of the witch Poesy," and from within this zone of calm, carved out of the rock of nature, he recalls the power of his own adverting mind to image and give voice to "the secret Strength of things." In *Prometheus Unbound*, among other things a reply to *Frankenstein*, Shelley exemplifies his hope that an impotently self-consuming despairing man can be therapeutically re-membered as an artistic self whose strength derives from the embrace it gives. Bending reality to the shape of his desire, Shelley does not overlook that aspect of the self which cannot participate in a radiant world new-made by mind. Rather, he enjoins a heroic labor of self-creation, an unceasing struggle to redeem "from decay the visitations of the divinity in man" (III, 139) by converting man's spectral component into the medium through which imagination discovers and presents itself. I know that many nowadays regard the Shelleyan creative eros as a phantom. But this supreme fiction, barred from the power that would express it and perhaps coming to be recognized as imagination by virtue of its very inexpressibility, is no lie. The imagination is a real ghost haunting the ceaselessly active mind, and if it can rightly be called a "linguistic fiction," the reason is that this efficacious spirit is the voice that powers the shuttle of representative language. Representation is not only hounded by the curse of mediacy; it can better an original "presence," subliming instead of merely sublimating it, even as Franken-stein engenders a being superior to, or at any rate sublimely other than, his creator.

It is at once peculiar and apt that when we begin reading *Frankenstein* the authoritative voice that addresses us in the Preface is not the author's but her husband's. That the author herself experienced some confusion between mine and thine seems likely. According to James Rieger, Shelley's "assistance at every point in the book's manufacture was so extensive that one hardly knows whether to regard him as editor or minor collaborator." Is it coincidental that Frankenstein, discovering that Walton "made notes concerning his history... asked to see them, and then himself corrected and augmented them"? The Shelley–Frankenstein connection has been a frequent source of speculation among the novel's critics, and there is general agreement that Mary Shelley is either deeply divided in her response to Shelley and the entire Romantic enterprise or else downright hostile, using the novel as an instrument of revenge against her (supposedly over-idealistic, uncourageous, and insensitive) husband. But in the Introduction, as elsewhere, she deifies Shelley and Shelleyan poetry, writing of his "far more cultivated mind" and ascribing his failure to pursue the ghost-story competition to his annoyance with "the platitude of prose." In part, I suspect, she aggrandizes Shelley here because she wants him out of reach. When she says that "he was for ever inciting me to obtain literary reputation," it sounds like a complaint; and when she maintains that she was indebted to him only for his encouragement, she ignores the challenge that Shelley's literary efforts represented to her and their critical role in the genesis of her novel.

Although the banal note Mary Shelley was to append to *Alastor* belies the extraordinary generative power of that work, Shelley's first major poem, published a year before *Frankenstein*'s conception, exerted a more decisive influence than any of the traditional analogues the novel engages. I think it is safe to say that the focal enigma of *Alastor*, a poem that becomes more difficult to read the better one knows it, is the visionary maid who inspires the Poet's quest. Most obviously, she is an autoerotic projection of the Poet, himself an autoerotic projection of Shelley's authorial self. Both narcissistic double and incestuous twin, she figures forth not only the imaginary other, text or muse, that is the Poet's perfect complement but whatever he lacks. Whether or not there is indeed an answering subject for the Poet to quest after is left unresolved. What is clear, however, is that so long as he remains mortal he can no more capture or merge with her than he can embrace the wind. Hopelessly divided between a historical narrative of disenchantment and a hysterical rage to cast out all that stands between the Poet and his desire, the poem is a kind of moving fixation. Bursting every natural limit that impedes his quest, the Poet keeps encountering new abysses, dangerous centers of power or vacancy that he is daemonically driven toward yet that his daemonic drive to be always ahead of himself keeps impelling him beyond, and in this perpetual self-rending movement the poem profoundly realizes the essence of the quest tradition.

It might seem that, although *Frankenstein* aspires to be a paradigmatic text of texts, *Alastor* is the paradigm defining the novel's vision and scope. Anticipating Frankenstein's career, the Poet renounces home and hearth to pursue "Nature's most secret steps" (1. 81); in the midst of the ruins of the past, he is startled by a sudden light, as meaning flashes "on his vacant mind/ . . . like strong inspiration" (11. 126–27); he is now ready to envision the form of his desire, whereupon his lust to body it forth precipitates him "beyond all human speed" (1. 361) while at the same time wasting his "frail . . . human form" (1. 350); finally his spirit is wasted too: pursuing the path of a departure to its inevitable terminus, this frightful solitary has become a hollow voice, "Ruin call[ing]/His brother Death" (11. 618–19). In one respect Mary Shelley exceeds the literalizing ferocity of her husband's poem. While the visionary maid is a teasingly elusive or illusive literalization of

Wordsworth's visionary gleam and Coleridge's Abyssinian maid, the Creature is a figuration that is at once richer and more sublimely literal than its original. This transformation, moreover, suggests that *Frankenstein* may be viewed as a deidealizing critique or misreading of *Alastor*. Retaining the poem's fundamental desire, the novel subverts it by altering the context in which it is lodged. The idealized quest for the epipsyche, or soul out of my soul, engenders the Creature, who is not only a "horrid thing" from which Frankenstein recoils in disgust but a voice of protest against his creator's lack of responsiveness. *Frankenstein*, then, would seem to oppose *Alastor*'s desperate sublime yearnings with a countermyth of continuity and reciprocity.

The main trouble with this reading is that it underestimates the strength, complexity, and sophistication of Shelley's poem, which subverts *Frankenstein* far more powerfully than the novel subverts the poem. What is most remarkable about *Alastor* is that the force of the Shelleyan sublime is great enough to withstand the rugged doubt to which it is always in danger of succumbing. Thomas Weiskel, a superb interpreter of the poem and of the Romantic sublime in general, argues that the energy of Shelley's high style "results almost entirely from what is being denied or suppressed." But I think Shelley neither ignores nor represses what Weiskel terms the "fictionality of desire"; he simply outstrips his own self-consciousness. If the light of sense were to go out in Shelley's moments of glory, he could not gauge how high he had risen or how fast he was going and he would have no limits to mock. Such mockery, which is the utmost the sublime mode can achieve for both writer and reader, applies to the Poet insofar as he affixes his desire to a single image and is in turn mocked, though not canceled, by all that checks the spirit's flight. As the Poet, an "elemental god" (1. 351), surges across the ocean in his rifted boat and the tormented element rages below, the self-division that characterizes the scene of writing is rendered more vividly and subtly than in *Frankenstein*. The continually felt presence of the Narrator, at once deeply attracted to and repelled by the Poet's solipsistic quest, is an additional enrichment. Like Mary Shelley's novel, *Alastor* can be reduced to a moral fable advocating human sympathy, but the poem embodies this theme in the Narrator's response and expresses it overtly only in the Preface.

While Shelley gives the overwhelming impression of being the voice of "Kubla Khan"'s chasm world and at the same time a consummately ironic outsider, Mary Shelley is neither inside nor outside enough. Ultimately, *Frankenstein* is not a masterful representation of Frankenstein's failure, because the author is more bewildered by than secure in her liminal status. She is akin to the Narrator of *Alastor*, who knows the sublime only through the more relentlessly driven Poet, or her Walton, a failed poet who remains susceptible to the allure of the daemonic yet preserves his contacts with home and hopes to regulate his frightening desires. There is, however, no true domestication of desire in *Frankenstein*, and certainly the novel's praise of domestic affection opens no liberating verbal space. Perhaps Walton will be a wiser man when he returns home, but he will be embittered by all he has failed to achieve. The terrible truth haunting *Frankenstein* is that, despite its redundant melodramatic excess, "a voice/is wanting" (*Prometheus Unbound* II.iv.115–16). According to Walton, Frankenstein is a type of Milton's Raphael: "he possesses ... an intuitive discernment ... unequalled for clearness and precision; add to this a facility of expression, and a voice whose varied intonations are soul-subduing music." But we never hear this music, and only the Creature's poignant farewell, a passage that Shelley seems to have been largely responsible for, exemplifies the effortless control or grace that is the supreme mark of power. Except for the *idea* of the Creature, an instance of the critic's sublime rather than of the reader's, the novel does not achieve sublimity, which remains an alienated episode of Frankenstein's recollected history. Free to fall, the modern Prometheus discovers that on his tongue there is a stone.

JAY MACPHERSON

"Mathilda" and "Frankenstein"

PART ONE

The involuntary Siren is the heroine of Mary Shelley's prose idyll, *Mathilda*, 1819. This maiden's mother dies at her birth, and the father, leaving his child to be brought up by a relative among the romantic solitudes of the Scottish Highlands, flees to the Continent to forget his loss. When he returns, Mathilda is sixteen, and in her the beauty of her mother lives again. Her father falls in love with her; she forces him to confess the trouble that is preying on him; he leaves suddenly and hastens "towards the sea," pursued through night and storm by Mathilda, who has no clear intention but finds him, as she expected, drowned. She then departs to a cottage on a lonely heath, where she pines until she dies. The pastoral framework is built largely on allusions to Dante's Matilda and to Wordsworth's Lucy, both maidens whom we know less in themselves than as their presence or absence affects their poets. Though the narration is in the first person, Mathilda still manages to give us descriptions of herself as from outside, like her father's first sight of her on Loch Lomond:

> As I came, dressed in white, covered only by my tartan *rachan*, my hair streaming on my shoulders, and shooting across with greater speed than it could be supposed I could give to my boat, my father has often told me that I looked more like a spirit than a human maid.

On the journey towards the sea, her hair again streams wildly as she dashes through the night, this time soaked with rain and shaking with fever. In her most Siren-like mood after the catastrophe, she sets two cups of laudanum for her sympathizing friend Woodville and herself and invites him to drink:

> What fool on a bleak shore, seeing a flowery isle on the other side with his lost love beckoning to him from it would pause because the wave is dark and turbid?
>
> > What if some little payne the passage have
> > That makes frayle flesh to fear the bitter wave?
> > Is not short payne well borne that brings long ease,
> > And lays the soul to sleep in quiet grave?
>
> ...I am Despair; and a strange being am I, joyous, triumphant Despair. ...Behold the pleasant potion! Look, I am a spirit of good, and not a human maid that invites thee, and with winning accents (oh, that they would win thee!) says, Come and drink.

Incest in *Mathilda* is by no means a mere device of plot to make impossible the marriage of lovers; it suggests what should be an ideal relation. The father does not love in his daughter merely the image of his lost Diana, for an old servant, speaking of his master's mysterious grief, tells Mathilda,

> ... when I heard that he was coming down here with you, my young lady, I thought we should have the happy days over again that we enjoyed during the short life of my lady your mother—But that would be too much happiness for us poor creatures born to tears.... You are like her although there is more of my lord in you....

Mathilda never confesses to a guilty passion—the action that has set the mark of Cain on her brow is extracting her father's secret—but there has never been nor can be another love for her, and she sets out after him with no thought but to force him to live. The only happiness afterwards remaining for her is the thought of meeting him in heaven; she expects that her own guilt will be eradicated then, but speaks as if he had never incurred any.

The book is full of images of pursuit and elusive objects. The ride towards the sea is prefigured by a dream in which Mathilda follows her fleeing father and sees him plunge over a precipice into the sea. During his wanderings after Diana's death,

> At first... I could not bear to think of my poor little girl; but afterwards as grief wore off and hope again revisited me I could only turn to her, and amidst cities and deserts her little fairy form, such as I imagined it, for ever flitted before me.

After her father's death, Mathilda seeks solitude in which to indulge the "shadowy happiness" of communing with her father's spirit; for

> ...never again could I make one of the smiling hunters that go coursing after bubbles that break to nothing when caught, and then after a new one with brighter colours; my hope also had proved a bubble, but it had been so lovely, so adorned that I saw none that could attract me after it; besides I was wearied with the pursuit, nearly dead with weariness.

Happiness a number of times is imaged as a fleeting ray, like the smiles of Woodville's lost beloved:

> ...not like a human loveliness...but as a sunbeam on a lake, now light and now obscure, flitting before as you strove to catch them, and fold them for ever to your heart.

Mathilda in her father's eyes, before jealousy provokes him to carnal passion, is a spiritual being from higher realms and also something of a nature spirit—"a nymph of the woods," as he calls her. The two realms are not in opposition, as Nature in these early days of their relationship has still something of a transcendent light. To quote her father's last letter:

> All delightful things, sublime scenery, soft breezes, exquisite music seemed to me associated with you and only through you to be pleasant to me.... You appeared as the deity of a lovely region, the ministering Angel of a Paradise to which of all human kind you admitted only me. I dared hardly consider you as my daughter; your beauty, artlessness and untaught wisdom seemed to belong to a higher order of beings; your voice breathed forth only words of love: if there was aught of earthly in you it was only what you derived from the beauty of the world; you seemed to have gained a grace from the mountain breezes—the waterfalls and the lake....

References to Beatrice and to the world of Spenser add suggestively to her Matilda-aspects, while the ambiguous Lucy side—or rôle of Nature with regard to Lucy—is borne out perhaps by the allusions to Proserpina, betrayed by her father and by Earth, and to Psyche, who lost an enchanted palace and discovered the two-sided nature of Love.

Mathilda's father figures too somewhat as an elegiac subject. His idyllic marriage to a childhood sweetheart, whose name Diana suggests a moony chastity, is broken by her death, and the loss drives him out to wander the world. Returning to enjoy the promise of restored happiness in his daughter, he discovers the promise is delusive; he cannot enjoy without possession, because in adult life that is the way things are. His paradise is altogether lost in the past—he is by now the inhabitant of another region— and any attempt to continue living in it is mistaken and harmful.

A rather wandering path brought us from *Alastor* to *Mathilda*; now we have her, can we relate her more directly to the subject of Narcissus?

"Narcissus" is the name we are giving to the subjective figure who is to Romantic elegy what Adonis or Orpheus is to earlier pastoral elegy. If we place *Alastor* among such poems as "Ode: Intimations," "Dejection," "Kubla Khan," and Goethe's "Elegie," it fits naturally in with them but at the same time is the most mythological, presenting a "genius" figure who resembles Adonis and Orpheus only less than he does Narcissus. This group of poems we can call male-centered elegy. Poems of the corresponding female-centered group are apt to be less subjectively lyrical, more mythological-narrative like *Alastor*: they include Blake's *Book of Thel*, Wordsworth's Lucy poems, perhaps "Christabel," certainly Shelley's "Sensitive Plant." The archetypes here are Persephone- and Eurydice-figures, and not least Echo. It is with these that Mathilda belongs: her idyll is a kind of prose equivalent, if we consider the numerous nature-spirit suggestions attached to her. However, she is less passive than the maidens of the poems; she brings on her own fall through her (in effect) fatal curiosity, breaking a taboo just as Eve and Psyche do. The event is of the same kind as the trespass of Mary's father William Godwin's Caleb Williams, who is more or less a male Psyche. There is an element of broken taboo in the story of the original spring-and-fall maiden, Persephone: not only does she pledge herself to the underworld by eating the pomegranate seeds, but as she is flower-gathering on the field of Enna Earth sends forth to beguile her "for a trick" a wonder never seen before, the bright narcissus, and as she leans to pick it Hades seizes her. "Narcissus," like "narcotic," implies a numbing power, hence the flower's sinister associations. The story of Persephone and the narcissus will be found in the "Homeric Hymn to Demeter."

Besides "pastoral" and "fall" connections, we can note two kinds of "narcissism" in *Mathilda*, the heroine's and her father's. Let us say at once that we do not get far in mapping the associations of the Romantic Narcissus without stumbling into an analogy with what Freud meant by "narcissism" as a psychological term. The narcissism of the young child is natural, innocent, and even charming, a necessary self-centeredness before in adolescence he begins to develop an interest in other people for themselves and a sense of his place among mankind, the latter process being very gradual and never total in its transference of "psychic energy," and its central event being the birth of love. The ego-centered universe is the paradise into which the child is born, and growing up requires learning to move out of it. In literature the positive aspects of this state are often represented by absorption in vision, dream, and noble fancy, or by communion with nature or idyllic human companionship of a virginal or suprasensual kind. Its symbols, regularly ambiguous, tend to suggest a watery or mirror world, with overtones not only of self-love but also of fleetingness, instability. Allusion to Ovid's myth of Narcissus allows Milton to present with great delicacy the state of mind of the newly created Eve:

> I thither went
> With unexperienc't thought, and laid me downe
> On the green bank, to look into the cleer
> Smooth Lake, that to me seemd another skie.
> As I bent down to look, just opposite,
> A Shape within the watry gleam appeerd
> Bending to look on me. I started back,
> It started back; but pleas'd I soon returnd,
> Pleas'd it returnd as soon with answering looks
> Of sympathie and love; there I had fixt
> Mine eyes till now, and pin'd with vain desire,
> Had not a voice thus warnd me, What thou seest,
> What there thou seest fair Creature is thy self....
> (PL IV. 456–68)

When she is led to Adam, she finds him

> ... less faire,
> Less winning soft, less amiablie milde,
> Then that smooth watry image.

In the manner of a Renaissance emblem this does indeed point the reader forward to the self-love that leads Eve to her fall; but within its immediate context it also leaves with us a persuasive impression of the untouched grace of body and mind in this new being. A quality of "watry gleam" appears again in Blake's introduction of Thel:

> Down by the river of Adona her soft voice is heard,
> And thus her gentle lamentation falls like morning dew:
>
> "O life of this our spring! why fades the lotus of the water,
> Why fade these children of the spring, born but to smile & fall?
> Ah! Thel is like a wat'ry bow, and like a parting cloud;
> Like a reflection in a glass; like shadows in the water...."

In both cases the message that comes to the pining maiden directs her to sympathy with other beings as a release from a world of shadows.

However, besides a natural and inevitable narcissism of inexperience, Freud recognizes also a morbid narcissism in the person who has failed to move out of immaturity. The usual indications of such a state, in literature as well as in life, include incestuous, homosexual, impossible, and vampiric loves: all are disguises of self-love, and, unlike the imperfect loves of Eve and Psyche, usually there is no cure for them.

Mathilda's father, like the hero of *Alastor*, is subject to a morbid narcissism which he fails to outgrow. However, both are more victims than persecutors, and evoke pathos rather than horror. Pathetic too is the Eve- or Psyche-maiden, like Viola or Mathilda, who readily becomes the involuntary siren. Less involuntary and more sinister, because nothing will ever really change her, is Rosamond Vincy: Henry James, describing her with relish as "this veritably mulish domestic flower," is outdone by her husband, who likes to call her "his basil plant,... a plant which had flourished wonderfully on a murdered man's brains." Since at present we are dealing with youthful and only passively harmful figures, let us leave demonic narcissists of both sexes for later treatment. They are usually much older, sometimes by centuries, and very well able to wait.

PART TWO

The most famous, and still the most powerful, of alchemical fables is Mary Shelley's *Frankenstein, or the Modern Prometheus*, 1818, whose pivot is that favorite device of Mary's father Godwin, the ironic recognition. The frame of *Frankenstein* is a long letter written by one Captain Walton on the northern seas to his sister Margaret in England. Walton, young and enthusiastic, has embarked on a polar expedition for the sake of scientific discovery. He confides to his sister his longing for a friend, and shortly afterwards rescues from a sledge on the frozen sea the exhausted Frankenstein, in whom he finds just such a one as he would have chosen. Thunder-scarred and dying, Frankenstein still possesses the charm, eloquence, and sensitivity of idealized genius, and he devotes them during his last hours to a recital of his history intended to deter Walton from throwing himself into the fatal pursuit of knowledge.

Frankenstein's own researches have led him to "pursue nature to her hiding-places" and "spend days and nights in vaults and charnel-houses" (iv), following which he is able to create a living man. But beyond its creation he has had no future intention regarding his creature; already as it struggles into life Frankenstein is horrified and flees in terror, abdicating all further responsibility. He never even gives his creature a name, calling him usually "the Being" or "the daemon." Wandering out into the world in vague search of an identity and an education, the Being is everywhere rejected as a monster. His original benevolence turns under this treatment to rancor, and he avenges his wrongs by destroying members of Frankenstein's family. The smiling Swiss valleys of Frankenstein's youth are now exchanged for horrific Swiss icefields, where Frankenstein encounters the Being and hears his bitter reproaches. Hated and feared by man, he has found himself doomed to solitude. This self-revelation induces remorse and compassion in Frankenstein, who agrees to make him a female counterpart on the understanding that both will leave the haunts of man forever. Frankenstein retires to a remote spot in the Orkney Islands to carry out this project; but having nearly finished, he changes his mind and undoes his work. The Being in a renewed outburst of vengeance then strangles, first Frankenstein's bosom friend Henry Clerval, then Elizabeth, his adoptive sister and his bride. From now on Frankenstein has but one object in life, his creature's destruction, and from now on the author handles him ironically: following Elizabeth's death he undergoes a long illness, and he arises from it as the original demon scientist. He pursues the Being over the face of the earth, and always when his strength is giving out he finds indications of direction and fresh supplies of food left mysteriously in his path. He assumes these are sent by his murdered loved ones to help him in his task of vengeance; but in fact, and more appropriately, they are left by the Being, who watches over him with almost motherly care. The chase continues into the dreary North, where Frankenstein is picked up by Walton. Having concluded his story, he dies; whereupon the Being comes and laments over him, "the select specimen of all that is worthy of love and admiration among men," before departing to put a fiery end to his miserable existence.

We briefly noted the shift of locale in Frankenstein's story, from idyllic scenes to horrific ones; we shall say more later about the place of scenes watery or wintry. While the third edition's frontispiece shows the creation of the Being, a title page vignette shows Frankenstein parting from a dirndl-clad Elizabeth at a flower-surrounded rural door, with the world very evidently all before him.

A single phrase will start us on a brief detour through magicians' houses. Like il Penseroso in his "high lonely tower," Frankenstein carries on his researches "in a solitary chamber... at the top of the house" (iv). In the 1931 movie *Frankenstein* this has become a stone tower; the special fittings of the laboratory at its top include a roof hinged to open so that the swathed figure on the operating table can be raised into the heart of an electrical storm, since animation by fire is the filmmakers' not unreasonable understanding of "The Modern Prometheus." Originally in mythology, Prometheus's creation of man and his theft of fire are quite separate stories. They come together in late classical traditions used in turn by Shakespeare and Byron, and presumably supplying the English phrase "spark of life" (cf. *Frankenstein*, opening of iv in 1st ed., v in 3d). However, for Mary Shelley, Victor Frankenstein's Prometheanism consists, first, in his playing the creator-god and, second, in his realization of both sin and punishment. If it was an electrical phenomenon that first led him in the direction of scientific enquiry, that is entirely in line with the contemporary speculations mentioned in the 1831 preface.

In later films, in a way that chronologically telescopes other developments we have mentioned, the attic and what is above it lose prominence to cellar and downward stair. *Frankenstein*'s successor *The Bride of Frankenstein*, 1935, begins with the monster emerging from the cellar; the tower has been burned down, but he has been preserved by a pool of water underneath. Later versions continue to make play with the cellars of the building: they contain pits of sulphur or blocks of ice, or they are connected with caverns running in from the sea (a detail likely borrowed from George Reynolds's *Varney the Vampire*, 1849). The house reappears in the (otherwise dismal) last of the Universal series, *Abbott and Costello Meet Frankenstein*, 1948, with a scene which shows how thoroughly accustomed its public has become to Castle Frankenstein's leading down to a watery underworld. The two comics are searching the house for their friend Count Dracula. The fat one (Costello) opens a door: one horrified glance shows him a dank downward stairway leading to a stone jetty where a boat sits on dark waters: hastily closing the door, he replies to his thin colleague's query, "Broom closet." Other horror movies—*Murders in the Rue Morgue*, 1932; *White Zombie*, 1932; *Evil of Frankenstein*, Hammer, 1964—show cellars with trapdoors over surging waters where the demon experimenter, more hardened than the young idealist in the attic, can dispose of failed experiments. Older moviegoers will remember (who could forget?) the place of underworld waters in *The Phantom of the Opera*, 1925, or *Metropolis*, 1926. Just as with the Romantic Venice that links fire and water, with these structures raised or inhabited by evil magicians we are once more in the presence of a version of the house of life, embodying the order of the elements.

   Frankenstein can, undoubtedly, be read as a parable about the fatality of impious aspirations, and *St. Leon* along with it. Alchemical fiction is after all an offshoot of the line that runs from the Faust legend down through *Vathek*, *The Monk*, *Zofloya*, *Melmoth the Wanderer*, and *Confessions of a Justified Sinner*, where extraordinary powers come explicitly from the devil and at the price of one's soul; and the alchemist-hero's decision to receive or use his secret can in itself constitute a temptation and fall. This becomes clearer in his modern embodiments, where the hero is less the adept and occultist student and more the doctor or scientist.

   Usually the discoverer of the alchemical secret thinks he is conferring the greatest possible benefit on those close to him and mankind at large, only to find that he has brought down on them a scourge. The ironic fulfillment of his hopes is consistent all the way down the tradition through Hawthorne's "The Birthmark" and Stevenson's *Dr. Jekyll and Mr. Hyde* to Huxley's *After Many a Summer*, 1939, and Siodmak's *Donovan's Brain*, 1942. This last, a straightforward and very standard piece of science fiction, recounts the history of a monomaniac doctor in a superlaboratory in the Mexican desert who manages to keep alive a particularly powerful brain after its owner's decease, and through telepathy to follow its processes. He supposes that with enriched feeding and unlimited time for meditation, it will devote itself to all the great questions of life and perhaps find the answers. Instead, it is completely bound up in the sordid details of its earthly career, and succeeds in forcing the doctor out of his role of Olympian spectator; he becomes its agent in all manner of messy errands, climaxing in murder. He is saved only when his laboratory is wrecked and the brain destroyed.

Though something of an idealist in his belief in science, in everything else the doctor of *Donovan's Brain* is a cynic and skeptic, like the rationalistic young doctor of Bulwer Lytton's *Strange Story*. They both learn that there is such a thing as impiety. The alchemist figure usually either denies God or arrogates to himself powers that are God's alone; where he is not presented as directly in rivalry with God, he may aim at a knowledge of and manipulating control over other lives that is felt to be indecent and unforgivable. Further, the alchemist once he has acquired special powers is in bondage to them, like any old-fashioned magician, and usually can free himself only by a renunciation like Prospero's, burning his books or smashing his instruments. Where the alchemist is a doctor or scientist, he may be enslaved to an elixir that has unpredictable or undesirable side effects, or to the repeated necessity of murder.

More prominent still in *Frankenstein* than the theme of impious desires is that of solitude and the search for love and friendship. Several apparently digressive incidents are brought in to emphasize it, but the narrative structure of tale within tale, more complex than that of *Alastor*, is surely sufficient: to put it briefly, Walton, who seeks a friend and has a sister, finds Frankenstein, who had a friend and a sister-bride but has lost both through the Being, who in turn longs for a friend and demands a sister-bride. Moreover, this theme is brought out early in Walton's references to "The Ancient Mariner"—it is the latter's solitude, not his guilt, that is stressed. Nor is it exactly guilt from which Frankenstein suffers: "I felt as if I had committed some great crime, the consciousness of which haunted me. I was guiltless, but I had indeed drawn down a horrible curse on my head, as mortal as that of crime" (III.ii; xix). The theme of solitude is prominent in alchemical fiction; it is felt at its most acute by the possessor of endless life. St. Leon, Melmoth, and Zanoni all descant on the hopelessness of human love, attaching you to the frail flower, if you happen to be the eternal rock.

Walton, seeking a friend, finds Frankenstein, who appears to him a god among men—and yet Frankenstein has the rôle of the old adept in *St. Leon*, the old gambler in Hoffmann's "Spielerglück," the old dandy in *Death in Venice*. He is the prophetic double, the Satan to Walton's Adam: this is what Walton may become if he pursues his passion for discovery to the bitter end. This framing theme is not developed, as circumstances in the end force Walton to give up his mission and return home; perhaps vicariously his experience is complete.

Frankenstein has grown up with two inseparable companions, his friend Henry Clerval and Elizabeth, the cousin or adoptive "more than sister" (first and third editions respectively) brought up with him. He allows his researches to keep him away from these and from his family, and when he returns to them he is divided from them by his horrible knowledge. Both then fall victim to the rancor of the Being. A perfect harmony formerly existed among the interests and temperaments of the three. Elizabeth, besides being the ideally sympathetic companion, shares with Frankenstein the same filial ties and affections. Clerval's name has the "happy valley" associations appropriate to a romance hero's youth; and in his ardor and eagerness the altered Frankenstein recognizes "the image of my former self" (III.ii; xix). Elizabeth and Clerval appear to him later, with the Being's other victims, in dreams that strengthen his desire for vengeance.

The Being too finds his greatest calamity in being alone. He considers his creator as his natural protector:

> I am thy creature, and I will be even mild and docile to my natural lord and king, if thou wilt also perform thy part, the which thou owest me. Oh, Frankenstein, be not equitable to every other, and trample upon me alone, to whom thy justice, and even thy clemency and affection, is most due. Remember that I am thy creature. I ought to be thy Adam, but I am rather the fallen angel whom thou drivest from joy for no misdeed. Everywhere I see bliss, from which I alone am irrevocably excluded. I was benevolent and good; misery made me a fiend. Make me happy and I shall again be virtuous.
>
> (II.ii; x)

His appeal is that Frankenstein should at least imitate the creator-God and make him a companion: "My evil passions will have fled, for I shall meet with sympathy!" (II.ix; xvii). It is when Frankenstein finally refuses that the Being destroys Clerval and Elizabeth, the latter on her wedding night.

Behind the action of *Frankenstein* loom the outlines of *Paradise Lost*, far from indistinct. Both Frankenstein and the Being continually compare themselves in its phrases to Adam and to Satan, in respect of infinite happiness lost and endless misery gained. On the sea of ice, Frankenstein is reproached by the Being somewhat in the terms in which Milton's Adam accuses his creator (X.743–45), as quoted on *Frankenstein*'s title page:

> Did I request thee, Maker, from my clay
> To mould me man? Did I solicit thee
> From darkness to promote me?—

The alternation of settings suggests the same model: from enclosing pastoral scenes to tremendous perspectives of icefields, North Sea, and the desolate regions approaching the Pole. Storms mark points of crisis, and calamity is imaged consistently as storm, torrent, flood. Two Romantic versions of the Fall also play their part—besides "The Ancient Mariner," there is *Werther*, to whose attentive readers the Being belongs. The world of *Werther* is suggested in the alteration of the Being's character and outlook from benevolence to savagery, and more particularly in the scenes near the end where Frankenstein pursuing through the desert peoples it in his dreams with phantoms of memory and desire.

The use of water is consistent with what we have seen elsewhere. Following an idyllic boat ride down the Rhine, Clerval is murdered on or beside the northern sea, close to the bleak spot in the Orkneys where Frankenstein has been working, and it is after being almost swallowed down by the sea himself that Frankenstein is led to his body. After his wedding, Frankenstein spends his last happy hours with Elizabeth being rowed along on the Lake of Geneva to Evian, which is to be their first stopping place. As they arrive a storm arises, and during the night the monster appears, strangles Elizabeth, and swims away in the lake.

The original tragic separation of the book is that between the Being and his creator. Frankenstein has in fact produced a creature as humane and idealistic as himself. Each is embittered by his experience and becomes a lonely destroyer, but the monster both suffers more and seems to retain more real magnanimity, so that by the end of the book he has almost become the hero, with the author's permission though not her full cooperation. Frankenstein and the Being should have been friends, like the unfallen Adam and his creator in *Paradise Lost*; they are inseparably connected, for better or for worse. In the words of Shelley's poem recalled in the monster's speech above:

> Thine own soul still is true to thee,
> But changed to a foul fiend through misery.

In the encounter on the sea of ice, the Being declares to Frankenstein that they are bound together "by ties only dissoluble by the annihilation of one of us"; and it becomes clearer as the action proceeds that the plot will require the practically simultaneous annihilation of both.

Together they constitute one of those Gothic fatal pairs between whom the potentiality of love has turned to mutual hate and who can no more pursue separate and independent destinies than Siamese twins—who necessarily suggest a man and his own darker side, shadow or Specter. The relations of such a pair are not always fully worked out in the plots where they appear, but still we know them by their desperate utterances or reflections; Maturin gives a fair specimen of the rhetoric:

> Our situation has happened to unite very opposite characters in the same adventure, but it is an union inevitable and *inseparable*. Your destiny is now bound to mine by a tie which no human force can break,—we part no more for ever. . . . We must pass life in each watching every breath the other draws, every glance the other gives,—in dreading sleep as an involuntary betrayer, and watching the broken murmurs of each other's restless dreams. We may hate each other, torment each other,—worst of all, we may be weary of each other, (for hatred itself would be a relief, compared to the tedium of our inseparability), but separate we must never.

That is the parricide monk's address to Monçada in *Melmoth the Wanderer* (viii), and immediately thereafter follows the account of lovers imprisoned together whose relations deteriorate to the point of cannibalism. We shall encounter other such fatal relations with shadow-selves in dealing with the Avenger. For *Frankenstein*, the point is that the hero fails to recognize in his creation, because of its outward ugliness, his own image, with his best potentialities as well as his worst, and that the consequences of his failure develop until the Being has become a fiend and his creator if anything a worse one, whatever outward charm he may retain. If this is not completely explicit in the book, it is the feature seized on and developed all the way down the line of its progeny.

Frankenstein's equivocal creation, combining fearsomeness and pathos, belongs to a type we may call, borrowing a phrase from Archibald Lampman, "the animal man." Its historical connections are with the homunculus, or artificial man, of alchemy and the Golem of Jewish legend. A scholar of great sanctity could animate a man made of clay by placing in its mouth an amulet bearing the Name of God; it would then obey its master's orders until the Sabbath, when the amulet would be taken from its mouth and it would rest according to the commandment like any other servant. Once the Great Rabbi Loew of Prague, who had made a Golem, forgot to release it on the Sabbath, whereupon it went berserk and tore up everything it could reach.

GIOVANNA FRANCI

A Mirror of the Future: Vision and Apocalypse in Mary Shelley's "The Last Man"

If I am to be judge of the future by the past and the present, I shall have small delight in looking forward.

—MARY SHELLEY

The Gothic or horror novel is one of the most representative models of fantastic literature, even if this particular type of narrative production does not reveal structural characteristics which are so very distinctive as to make it a self-contained literary *genre*, separate from the novel. The "modern romance" follows on from the bourgeois novel at a distance of about fifty years—if we take Walpole's *The Castle of Otranto* (written 1764) as the first and characteristic work of this type—and accompanies its development with varying fortunes until the present time, passing through moments of total coincidence and fusion. What is important is not so much whether we are dealing with a "romance" or a "novel" but rather, since both are "fictions," what rôle their fiction-reality relationship plays with respect to the thorny problem of "verisimilitude." If we accept the assumption that all literature, as such, is "fantastic" (we could, of course, invert this proposition, following Borges, by asserting that literature, the verbal universe, is the *only* reality), the Gothic novel is even more certainly so, since it opens "the doors of the unconscious." It is, as Bachelard says, *true* poetry, that which comes from the depths of the being. "Literature is a dream, a controlled and deliberate dream, but fundamentally a dream," as J.L. Borges says and like all "true" literature, the Gothic novel and/or Romance, from Walpole onwards, begins with a dream.

In Mary Shelley's works, nightmare is superimposed on the dream, the supernatural fuses with the natural in the form of science, and the "demon," expressed as both symbol and symptom, the great metaphor of the problem of evil, becomes internalised to the point that the self-destruction of humanity itself becomes necessary to vanquish this evil.

The spectre of the *doppelgänger*, or the *divided self*, is foreshadowed clearly at the height of the Romantic period but Mary Shelley goes well beyond the first implications present in the classical Gothic novel, and not merely from the point of view of technique. Whereas the gothic novel remains fundamentally a "ghost-story," Mary Shelley is not content to remain at this level of phenomenology as a means of conveying or promoting the uncanny, and for her the ghost-story remains merely an intellectual drawing-room entertainment or an élite literary game. This may be clearly revealed by the evenings spent at Villa Diodati which produced two monsters from the collective imagination, *The Vampyre* and *Frankenstein*.

In the brief tale, "The Dream," Mary Shelley manipulates the classic Gothic romance in the style of Lewis and Radcliffe (which had made a deep impression on her during her childhood) skillfully but with an evident detachment and irony. *Frankenstein* is not at all "a mere tale of spectres and enchantment": here the horror resides elsewhere and the metaphorical projection is no longer fixed on the ghost, but on the *monster* in an identification of creator and creature.

In *Frankenstein*, the "vision" comes to the writer in a state of drowsiness or even trance, "with shut eyes, but acute mental vision." In *The Last Man*, the device becomes yet more refined and the search for the deep mechanisms of literary production and for the very reasons for life itself is fused and confused: literature and autobiography are united in the purest sense of the term. Here too the horror is not produced by the supernatural but, instead, by the sense of death and ending: the monster now is "the last man," the horror and solitude caused by the confrontation of an "empty world."

In this work, Mary Shelley comes extremely close to the grotesque, absurd and nightmare imagination of modern writers such as Kafka and Beckett. What we are here confronted with is a product of the Romantic imagination all the more powerful for its solitary desperation. The "theme of the self" which Todorov describes as "the structuring of the relation between man and the world" is here experienced as a tragic conflict. As Harold

Bloom has written about *Frankenstein*, "The profound dejection endemic in Mary Shelley's novel is fundamental to the Romantic mythology of the self, for all Romantic horrors are diseases of excessive consciousness, of the self unable to bear the self."

PRE/TEXT

The Last Man, the work which Mary Shelley wrote after the death of her husband, Percy Bysshe Shelley, and of close friends, such as Byron, is a book which is fairly complex in form and far from simple in interpretation. On one level it may be read as an autobiographical work, fruit of a desperate solitude, yet at the same time it reveals a far more insistent and intricate message which may be read as a lucid *dystopia*, an apocalyptic prophecy of the end of the world.

In *Frankenstein*, and even more so in *The Last Man*, Mary Shelley reveals herself as an "unwilling prophetess" of a human destiny of death and self-destruction. In this way she takes her place among the ranks of numerous other authors of "tales of the future" written in the first decades of the nineteenth century, a symptom of a profound uneasiness which followed the failure of great revolutions and the crisis of radical and liberal ideology which expressed a negative response to the effects of the industrial revolution.

Frankenstein and *The Last Man* may be placed between the Gothic or the literature of terror, which represents the "dark" side, the "unsaid" of bourgeois literature, even its guilty conscience, and science fiction conceived as prophetic writing or anticipation of catastrophe, as *Apocalypse* or *Revelation*. However, in the case of Mary Shelley definitions in terms of "genre" are not possible. Past and future, Gothic and science fiction are unified in the dream-nightmare, and the bourgeois world is presented as both self-creation and self-destruction. Reason produces monsters; the true "robot" is Man who creates a pale caricature of himself, a double, a *doppelgänger* which proves worse than the original, a monster. It is the failure of Modern Prometheus: Man is condemned to solitude, able only to create a desert around himself. It is also the negation of the doctrine of evolution and of progress.

The Introduction to *The Last Man* takes up again the technique which was partially used in *Frankenstein*, that of simulating the authenticity of the "unnatural" by means of natural opening, of inserting the fantastic, understood not in Todorov's terms of *"merveilleux,"* but rather as the symbolic or visionary, in the "familiar." Muriel Spark has defined this novel as "a domestic romance": perhaps we should add that it is indeed a perfect example of *Unheimliche*.

A tour of the archaeological sites around Naples, which Mary Shelley visited with her husband in 1818, provides the motivation for an unusual narrative fiction which also becomes an apology on the myth of Writing. Following the visit to the "so-called Elysian Fields and Avernus," through dark tunnels and dismal caves we finally reach the "gloomy cavern" of the Cumaean Sibyl, where piles of leaves represent the scattered fragments of her answers. The story begins from this point and thus lies between a "re-discovered manuscript," a voyage to the underworld and a plunge into the darkness of the psyche, where the use of this device renders the formulation of the tale possible. The work of the writer therefore takes on another form: by assuming the task of re-ordering and deciphering the leaves, of giving them a "consistent form" so that they may be intelligible to the reader, the writer places herself as not merely the mouthpiece of her individual imagination, of her own "wild dreams," but also as the interpreter of the "collective unconscious."

Writing, in the form of the tale, is simultaneously pure narration and prophetic apology, and literature, written on the leaves which scatter in the wind like the message of the Sibyl, is a trail to be followed, a hieroglyphic which must be interpreted. It is these concepts which we find in the work of Mary Shelley who consciously makes her point of departure the depths of the Sibyl's den.

HISTORY AND TIME

The events of the novel take place in the twenty-first century and are narrated in the first person by Lionel Verney, an alter-ego of Mary Shelley herself and the sole survivor of a terrible plague which has exterminated the whole of humanity. The circular structure of the story, which is entirely told in the past as a single flash-back, is enclosed in the mind of the author-narrator-protagonist, and the story unfolds slowly following the threads of his memory.

In the first part of the work the reader is witness to the birth of the individual and the development of his relationship with the world, in a type of *bildungsroman* which recounts the process of the production of a self. 'I' stands as the first word and into this are threaded the individual biography and the history of the world, all filtered through a single point of view "according to the subject." Here we have the *origins*, the first moment when the human mind believes itself to be "The creator of all that was good or great to man," when "Nature itself was only his first minister," when all was harmony and England was the universe and the centre of the world. This is the period of nostalgia—personal affections (friendship, love)—then the political illusions of a young Republic are the dominant themes. However, the romance, the utopia of a "new paradise" as conceived by Percy Bysshe Shelley, remains still-born because "the earth is not and cannot be a paradise." The tone, therefore, rather than elegiac is on the contrary tragically ironic. The crisis of the relationship between the individual and the world is immediately thrown into relief by a constant awareness of an *after*, an ending. As Lionel says: "My fortunes have been, from the beginning, an exemplification of the power that mutability may possess over the varied tenor of man's life." Time advances, then, ever more quickly as the action becomes intense and dramatic, encompassing political clashes, revolutions, wars and finally, plague.

At this point the motivating structure of the plot is that of the journey. The epidemic journey of the plague as it spreads across every part of the globe is matched by the desperate journey of the characters as they attempt to save themselves from the plague by fleeing. From Constantinople, recently fallen to liberating troops, the epidemic spreads through Europe and through the whole world. At first England seems to be immune to the contagion while "the vast cities of America, the fertile plains of Hindostan, the crowded abodes of the Chinese, are menaced with utter ruin." Then the plague strikes even there; "Death, cruel and relentless, had entered those beloved walls." The epidemic has become pandemic.

Day by day, hour by hour the end grows ever nearer; the end of the novel and the end of the world. In the final part of the novel, a group of survivors are moving down towards the south of Europe, passing through desolated landscapes and images of destruction. From Venice, now an utterly dead city, they attempt to reach Greece by sea in a desperate hope to return to their origins, but a terrible storm shipwrecks them in the middle of the Adriatic Sea (we may mark here an evident doubling of the archetype, life and death in water). Lionel is the only one left alive; "A solitary being is by instinct a wanderer, and that I shall become." As he wanders through Italy, now nothing but a huge grave-yard, he reaches Rome, the "Eternal City." Here, he climbs St. Peter's and ironically marks, as did the Popes of old, the beginning of the era 2100, the last year of the world, that is, the end of the Western Church, the *Ecclesia*, and thus of Western civilisation and of History. It is at this point that he decides to write *the book* and he invites the shadows to rise again to read the history of their fall by listening to the story of the Last Man still alive in the total death of the world, the Last Man now beyond death.

Left alone on the earth the Last Man now finds himself surrounded by an absence of time; where there are no social relationships time is nullified. Having closed the era 2100 on the last year of the world, Lionel

Verney moves outside of the circle of both his story and history to take his chance in the unknown, on the sea.

If *Frankenstein* is considered to be one of the first examples of science fiction and the most important link between the Gothic and science fiction, *The Last Man* must be considered in turn a perfect realisation of early science fiction, set as it is in a future which is very distant from both its author and the public to whom it is addressed. The use of verb tenses also follows, for the most part, one of the most widely used models in science fiction; the use of the past in the narration to describe things which are supposedly to happen in the future, what J. Favier calls "le Passé du futur." This playing with time is fairly complex in Mary Shelley's works and goes beyond simply the technical implications of a literary *genre*. Whereas the projection into the future of present conditions, along with an apocalyptic conclusion, may mark a prophetic intonation assumed by the work in question (approaching in this sense a negative utopia), the use of the past represents the time of remembering, of regretting and yet at the same time a wish for detachment and distancing. The autobiographical element is more clearly revealed when, as occasionally happens, the verb tenses move into the present. "Oh my pen! haste thou to write what *was*, before the thought of what *is* arrests the hand that guides thee." But past and future are nullified in a single time in writing, a time which goes beyond chronology, which surpasses even the present because the present is suffering. Faced with a blank page, Mary Shelley writes: "Again I feel that *I am* alone," falling "ten thousand fathom deep, into the *abyss of the present*—into self-knowledge—into tenfold sadness."

There is very little "futurology" present in this world of the twenty-first century, except perhaps the "sailing balloons," a sort of passenger airship. The setting, the events, the problems described are entirely those of the author's contemporary reality, transferred to the written page to form a framework for the plot.

As with every story of the end, this novel may be inserted in the apocalyptic line of works which traces back to the Biblical model which, as Frank Kermode writes, "begins at the beginning (In the Beginning...) and ends with a vision of the end (Even so, come, Lord Jesus); the first book is Genesis, the last Apocalypse." However, the "concordant structure" of the Bible sees a harmony of all in the identification—surpassing the beginning and the ending, while in *The Last Man* the ending remains unended in that all remains yet to be told; the real story has yet to begin.

MYTH AND MESSAGE: THE INDIVIDUAL AND NATURE

Among the *Romanes* a Poet was called *Vates*, which is as much as a diviner, foreseer, or Prophet.

(Sir Philip Sidney)

(The Poet) not only beholds intensely the present as it is, and discovers those laws according to which present things ought to be ordered, but he beholds the future in the present, and his thoughts are the germs of the flower and the fruit of latest time.

(Percy Bysshe Shelley)

Frankenstein and *The Last Man* both form part of a single imaginative trend; both represent symptoms of a critique and are cryptic carriers of a common message. The contradictory tragedy and modernness of *Franken-stein* lies in the placing of the classical hubris myth within a situation of conflictual division of Man and Nature; almost all modern art springs from and expresses such a division. It is precisely the situation of the Modern Prometheus who must move from the foolish exaltation of the individual capacities of Man in the rôle of a creator of a *new nature* (and of new life) to reach an awareness of the futility of his own exertions. Even Rome, symbol of civilisation and history, "eternal" through the reproduction of her culture, comes to an end. All that remains are the ruins, the stones, it is Nature who achieves vengeance, asserting a final victory by continuing her cycle now without Man. "We have lost the cosmos. The sun strengthens us no more, neither does the moon. In mystic language, the moon is black to us and the sun is as sackcloth," as D.H. Lawrence writes in his *Apocalypse*.

The "artificial" nature of eighteenth century figurative and literary landscapes is present in the reassuring guise of a "tamed" nature in Italianate gardens, or a "picturesquely" wild nature in English-style gardens. Yet in the fierce, threatening backgrounds lurking behind them we may see the sign of a kind of promised vengeance on the part of distorted Nature.

The figures and natural metaphors in Lionel Verney's "Apocalypse" lie within this same tradition: sinister portents in the sky, wolves and lions howling in the desert, spectral figures wandering restlessly, manifestations of panic and collective madness, riots, invasions, storms, conflagrations, floods and plague.

Nature has turned to the demonic and to be in 'correspondence' with it is to be destroyed.

The solitary Romantic individual stands stark against a "wild and sublime" Nature and draws definition and relief from this background. In Mary Shelley's works he is still the *in-dividuum*, the un-divisible, yet he is already casting the shadow of his own *doppelgänger* onto the *fin de siècle*.

The encounter is heightened as a titanic clash of primordial forces, and the tone becomes heroic and thus tragic. For the individual (represented through culture or science) can achieve nothing against Nature. He succumbs and is overpowered precisely at the moment of supposed triumph: in destroying Nature he destroys also himself. As D.H. Lawrence puts it, "Our science is the science of a dead world."

In *The Last Man*, the destruction of the world implies the end of the heroic affirmation of the individual, and is in fact its direct consequence. This may indeed be taken prophetically as a parable of the history of the "modern."

In *Dialectics of Enlightenment*, Adorno and Horkheimer put forward the thesis that a self-sufficient individual will produce self-destruction as an inevitable consequence of self-affirmation since his entire development, as indeed the genesis of civilisation and of the bourgeois world, is based on the *sacrifice of the self*. In *The Last Man*, Lionel-Mary is the 'I' who tells the story, the sole survivor of a total catastrophe, who, in identifying himself once more with God, (as in *Frankenstein*), creates history but contemporaneously narrates the ending of story/history and thus implies the crisis of the self-world relationship.

The problem is, fundamentally, the problem of *identity* which will form the dominant theme of almost all modern bourgeois literature, "the great puzzle," as Lewis Carroll will later define it. Mary Shelley is fully aware of this. The endless questions about his origins which the monster, creature and alter-ego of Frankenstein asks, "Who was I? What was I? Whence did I come?," are only answered when his reflected image—his specular *cogito*— brings him to the recognition that "I was in reality the monster that I am." The terrifying spectre which the mirror casts up before Lionel towards the end of his wanderings is a further manifest sign of the identity dichotomy. The reflected image in this instance is the last tattered shred of *individuality*, "the miserable object there portrayed," its final identification. Mary Shelley created an impressive myth of the present time in *The Last Man*.

> What are we, the inhabitants of this globe, least among the many that people infinite space? Our minds embrace infinity; the visible mechanism of our being is subject to merest accident...In the face of all this we call ourselves lords of the creation, wielders of the elements, masters of life and death, and we allege in excuse of this arrogance, that though the *individual* is destroyed, man continues forever.
>
> Thus, losing our *identity*, that of which we are chiefly conscious, we glory in the continuity of our species, and learn to regard death without terror. But when any nation becomes the victim of the destructive powers of exterior agents, then indeed man shrinks into *insignificance*, he feels his tenure of life insecure, his inheritance on earth cut off.

The audacious construction which humanity had created "on the eighth day," resting on the individual poised at the centre of the world, collapses wretchedly.

THE END OF REVOLUTIONS

The crisis of the Individual gives way to the crisis of society and the crisis of liberal ideology gives way to the crisis of both democratic and socialist ideologies. It marks the end of the bourgeois principles of Enlightenment, of the ideas of democracy, liberty, equality, of progressive reforms, of violent uprisings, of all such ideals which by now had been reduced to faded ruins or sepulchral monuments.

Mary Shelley experienced in her life and recounts in her works the end of illusions and of revolutionary zeal; one of her characters in fact says: "I know now that I am not a man fitted to govern nations; sufficient to me, if I keep in wholesome rule the little kingdom of my own mortality."

To those who accuse her of being conventional, of not 'rebelling,' she replies that as far as the *good cause* went (i.e. the attainment of liberty, the rights of women, liberal ideas), she did not hold opinions: "When I feel that I can say what will benefit my fellow-creatures, I will speak; not before...I believe we are sent here to educate ourselves, and self-denial, and disappointment, and self-control, are a part of our education."

For Mary Shelley the "individual" themes of an isolated sensitivity are always irrevocably intertwined with the "universal" themes of the death of a civilisation. In public affairs she criticised what we would today call political "alliances" and her writings draw attention to the lack of any real, positive link between theory and practice. She moved away from the views of her father, William Godwin, on account of his excessive faith in human nature, from Percy Bysshe Shelley because he was too idealistic, from Byron because he was too impulsive and finally even from the radical William Cobbett, that stalwart protector of the working class who was also the proposer of a utopia which she maliciously defined as "domestic." Even if she took Cobbett's side against the Conservative Edmund Burke, she accredited certain of the latter's criticisms and reflections on the French Revolution, and it is perhaps significant that she refers to Burke twice in *The Last Man*.

All these figures may be traced in characters of the novel and discussion of the political situation becomes particularly heated when the news of the plague arrives.

In his *La fine del mondo*, (*The End of the World*), Ernesto De Martino uses the plague metaphor to analyse the contemporary interpretation of "ending": "Il mondo occidentale va denunciando la propria malattia, che assume le forme di una rischiosa apocalisse senza escaton...Bisogna ricercare quindi il significato dei diversi sintomi del male, l'estensione del contagio e il suo condizionamento" (The western world is becoming aware of its own malaise, which is taking on the form of a perilous apocalypse which has no eschaton... We must therefore look for the meaning of the various symptoms of the illness, the spread of the contagion and its origins).

One question remains unanswered: what *is* the plague, this invincible monster, this grotesque enigma for which we know neither the causes nor the means of transmission? Dr. Rieux, in Camus' *La Peste*, when asked "Qu'est-ce que ça veut dire, la peste?," replies simply, "C'est la vie, et voilà tout." Lionel Verney, the last man, defines life as "this evil labyrinth, this wretched scheme of mutual torture."

FIN DE PARTIE

And the seven Angels which had the seven trumpets prepared themselves to sound.

(The Apocalypse of St. John)

The end of the world (and of the story of the Last Man) is also the end of a social relationship which could not break out of the servant-master dialectic and which plainly reflects the crisis of interpersonal relationships. Frankenstein may be interpreted as the other, darker side of Robinson Crusoe in his relationship with Man Friday and Lionel Verney, too, may be seen as a "monster" in his solitude, "a monstrous excrescence of nature." The last man, the sole survivor bears witness to all that this implies, leaving in both the book and in his story a document of the end, but at the same time liberating himself of the burden of memory.

A story of the end (of the world) is often a vehicle for fear of the end which thus succeeds in distancing death and asserting identity: *I* write about *me*. In this sense "the end is the metalinguistic utterance which appears to be capable of generating all possible texts." However, in Mary Shelley's novel the book in which Lionel Verney narrates his own story and the history of the end of the world is dedicated to the dead, to the past, and is not projected into the future. In contrast to messages which are intended to be discovered or received, cast in a bottle on the sea or hidden in some secret hiding place, this message has no intended end. It is rather a way of settling accounts with himself, of having nothing further to do with history. Here writing and myth are seen as a hieroglyphic which must be deciphered, but it is also the end of all myth because myth forms part of history. At the end of Lionel Verney's story there is only a final glance back to the "original opening scene" before the curtain drops for ever: "He is solitary; like our first parents expelled from Paradise." Separating the end from the beginning there stands "the flaming sword of plague."

It is at this point that the book moves from a negation of utopia into its own utopic dimension, from being an apocalypse with no eschaton or definitive ending it takes on more precisely eschatological forms. Lionel now becomes the artist who, recognising the failure and nullity of both preceding historical experience and of its recording, projects himself instead into the future of imagination and prophetic vision.

"I sought to escape from my miserable self": thus he rids himself finally of regrets and illusion and dissociates himself from the guilt and errors attached to the past. In order to begin again a radical change is required: "neither hope nor joy are my pilots—restless despair and fierce desire of change lead me on."

Thus the shadow of the New Man is cast into the future on the screen of the imagination, having passed through experience, as Blake recounts, announced by prophets, artists and madmen. The New Man we can only attempt to "imagine."

As he sets off once more in his boat with only a few books as companions, though with all the books in the world at his disposal, and the very world itself lying open to his perusal like a book, Lionel Verney is no longer the Last Man, last heir to the past. Already we can see forming around him the "new dawn" which Nietzsche predicts:

> At long last the horizon appears free to us again, even if it should not be bright; at long last our ships may venture out again, venture out to face any danger; all the daring of the lover of knowledge is permitted again; the sea, *our* sea, lies open again; perhaps there has never yet been such an "open sea."
>
> (*The Gay Science*, V)

Chronology

1797   Mary Wollstonecraft Godwin Shelley born August 30 at Somers Town, daughter of the radical philosopher William Godwin, and the even more radical writer and feminist, Mary Wollstonecraft, who dies ten days later.

1801   William Godwin is remarried to a widow, Mary Jane Clairmont, mother of two children, Charles and Jane, later known as Claire Clairmont.

1812   First meeting with Shelley, November 11.

1814   Meets Shelley again in London. Elopes with him to France and Switzerland, accompanied by Claire Clairmont. Returns with him to England.

1815   In February, Mary gives birth to a premature girl child, who dies two weeks later.

1816   Birth of son, William, in January. In May the Shelleys and Claire depart from England to Geneva, where Byron awaits Claire. In July, they visit Mont Blanc. *Frankenstein* begun. September sees return to England. In October, Fanny Imlay, daughter of Mary Wollstonecraft, kills herself. This is followed in December by the suicide of Harriet Shelley, the poet's first wife. Mary is married to Shelley in London on December 30.

1817   The Shelleys move to Marlow. *Frankenstein* finished in May. Birth of daughter, Clara. *History of a Six-Weeks' Tour* published.

1818   Departure of Shelley household to Italy in March. Publication of *Frankenstein*. Clara dies in Venice, in September, during a visit of the Shelleys to Byron. They go south, first to Rome, and then to Naples for the winter.

1819   Death of her son, William, in Rome in March. In November, her son, Percy Florence, is born. He is to be the Shelleys' only survivor.

1820   Residence in Leghorn and Pisa.

1821   The Shelleys join with Edward and Jane Williams, at Pisa, with Byron close by. Love affair of Shelley and Jane Williams.

1822　Move to Casa Magni, near Lerici. Death of Percy Bysshe Shelley and Edward Williams in July, when the poet's sailboat, *The Ariel*, is lost at sea. In September, the widowed Mary joins Byron and Leigh Hunt at Genoa.

1823　*Valperga* published. Return to London in August.

1824　Publication of Mary's edition of Shelley's *Posthumous Poems*. The volume withdrawn when Sir Timothy Shelley, the poet's father, raises objections.

1826　*The Last Man* published.

1830　*Perkin Warbeck* published.

1835　*Lodore* published.

1836　Death of her father, William Godwin.

1837　*Falkner* published.

1844　*Rambles in Germany and Italy* published.

1851　Dies on February 1 in London.

Contributors

HAROLD BLOOM, Sterling Professor of the Humanities at Yale University, is the author of *The Anxiety of Influence, Poetry and Repression* and many other volumes of literary criticism. His forthcoming study, *Freud: Transference and Authority*, attempts a full-scale reading of all of Freud's major writings. He is the general editor of *The Chelsea House Library of Literary Criticism*.

MURIEL SPARK, the celebrated English novelist, is the author of *The Prime of Miss Jean Brodie* and *The Mandelbaum Gate*, among many other works.

LOWRY NELSON, JR. is Professor of Comparative Literature at Yale, and has written extensively on European Renaissance and Baroque literature.

JAMES RIEGER, Professor of English at the University of Rochester, wrote *The Mutiny Within*, a study of Shelley's poetry.

WILLIAM A. WALLING, Professor of English at Rutgers University, writes on literature and film, as well as on the Romantics.

PETER BROOKS is Professor of French and Comparative Literature at Yale. His books include *The Novel of Worldliness*, *The Melodramatic Imagination* and *Reading for the Plot*.

SANDRA M. GILBERT and SUSAN GUBAR are co-authors of *The Madwoman in the Attic* and many other studies in Women's Literature. Ms. Gilbert is Professor of English at Princeton University. Ms. Gubar is Professor of English at the University of Indiana.

PAUL SHERWIN is Dean of Humanities and Professor of English at the City College of the City University of New York. He is the author of *Precious Bane*, a study of the poetry of William Collins.

JAY MACPHERSON, Canadian poet and critic, is Professor of English at Victoria College of the University of Toronto. Her books of poems include *The Boatman* and *Welcoming Disaster*. Her principal work of criticism is *The Spirit of Solitude*.

GIOVANNA FRANCI is Professor of English at the University of Bologna. She has written extensively on nineteenth century English literature and on modern critical theory.

Bibliography

Brooks, Peter. " 'Godlike Science/Unhallowed Arts': Language and Monstrosity in *Frankenstein.*" *New Literary History* 9: 591–605.

Church, Richard. *Mary Shelley.* London: Gerald Howe, Ltd., 1928.

Cude, Wilfred. "Mary Shelley's Modern Prometheus: A Study in the Ethics of Scientific Creativity." *Dalhousie Review* 52:212–25.

Dunn, Jane. *Moon in Eclipse: A Life of Mary Shelley.* New York: St. Martin's Press, 1978.

Gilbert, Sandra. "Horror's Twin: Mary Shelley's Monstrous Eve." *Feminist Studies* 4(2):48–73.

Grylls, Rosalie. *Mary Shelley: A Biography.* London: Oxford University Press, 1938.

Hill, J. M. "Frankenstein and the Physiognomy of Desire." *American Imago* 32(1975):332–58.

Johnson, Barbara. "My Monster/My Self." *Diacritics* 12(2):2–10.

Jones, Frederick L., ed. *The Letters of Mary W. Shelley.* 2 vols. Norman: University of Oklahoma Press, 1946.

Levine, George, and Knoepflmacher, U. C., eds. *The Endurance of Frankenstein.* Berkeley: University of California Press, 1979.

Marshall, Julian (Mrs). *The Life and Letters of Mary Wollstonecraft Shelley.* 2 vols. London: Richard Bentley and Son, 1889.

McInerney, Peter. "Frankenstein and the Godlike Science of Letters." *Genre* 13(4):455–75.

Nitchie, Elizabeth. *Mary Shelley: Author of Frankenstein.* New Brunswick: Rutgers University Press, 1953.

Norman, Sylvia. "Mary Wollstonecraft Shelley." In *Shelley and His Circle,* edited by Kenneth Neill Cameron, vol. 3. Cambridge: Harvard University Press, 1961, 1970.

Pollin, Burton R. "Philosophical and Literary Sources of *Frankenstein.*" *Comparative Literature* 17:87–108.

Poovey, Mary. "My Hideous Progeny: Mary Shelley and the Feminization of Romanticism." *PMLA* 95:332–47.

Seed, David. "Frankenstein: Parable or Spectacle?" *Criticism* 24(4):327–40.

Shelley, Mary. *Falkner.* 3 vols. London: Saunders and Otley, 1837.

————. *Frankenstein; or, the Modern Prometheus.* Edited by Harold Bloom. New York: The New American Library, 1965.

————. *Lodore.* New York: Wallis and Newell, 1835.

————. *Mathilda*. In *Studies in Philology, Extra Series* 3, edited by Elizabeth Nitchie. Chapel Hill: University of North Carolina Press, 1959.

————. *Proserpine and Midas: Two Unpublished Mythological Dramas*. Edited by A. Koszul. London: Humphrey Milford, 1922.

————. *Tales and Stories*. Edited by Richard Garnett. London: William Paterson and Co., 1891.

————. "The Choice." In *Mary Shelley*, edited by R. Glynn Grylls. London: Oxford University Press, 1938.

————. *The Fortunes of Perkin Warbeck*. 3 vols. London: Henry Colburn and Richard Bentley, 1830.

————. "The Heir of Mondolfo." In *Seven Masterpieces of Gothic Horror*, edited by Robert and Donald Spector. New York: Bantam Books, 1963.

————. *The Last Man*. Edited by Hugh J. Luke, Jr. Lincoln: University of Nebraska Press, 1965.

————. *Valperga: or, the Life and Adventures of Castruccio, Prince of Lucca*. 3 vols. London: G and W. B. Whittaker, 1823.

Sherwin, Paul. "*Frankenstein*: Creation as Catastrophe." *PMLA* 96(5):883–903.

Spark, Muriel. *Child of Light: A Reassessment of Mary Wollstonecraft Shelley*. Essex, England: Tower Bridge Publications, 1951.

Tillotson, Marcia. "A Forced Solitude: Mary Shelley and the Creation of Frankenstein's Monster." In *The Female Gothic*, edited by Julian E. Fleenor. Montreal: Eden, 1983.

Todd, Janet M., ed. *A Wollstonecraft Anthology*. Bloomington: Indiana University Press, 1977.

Wade, Philip. "Shelley and the Miltonic Element in Mary Shelley's *Frankenstein*." *Milton and the Romantics* 2(1976):23–35.

Walling, William A. *Mary Shelley*. New York: Twayne, 1972.

Acknowledgments

"Introduction" by Harold Bloom from *The Ringers in the Tower* by Harold Bloom, copyright © 1971 by The University of Chicago Press. Reprinted by permission.

"*Frankenstein*" by Muriel Spark from *Child of Light* by Muriel Spark, © 1951, renewed 1979 by Muriel Spark. Reprinted by permission of Harold Ober Associates, Inc.

"Night Thoughts on the Gothic Novel" by Lowry Nelson, Jr. from *The Yale Review* 52, no. 2 (Winter 1963), copyright © 1963 by *The Yale Review*. Reprinted by permission.

"*Frankenstein; or, the Modern Prometheus*" by James Rieger from *The Mutiny Within* by James Rieger, copyright © 1967 by James Rieger. Reprinted by permission of George Braziller, Inc.

"Victor Frankenstein's Dual Role" by William A. Walling from *Mary Shelley* by William A. Walling, copyright © 1972 by Twayne Publishers, Inc. Reprinted by permission of Twayne Publishers, a division of G. K. Hall & Co., Boston.

"*Frankenstein*" by Robert Kiely from *The Romantic Novel in England* by Robert Kiely, copyright © 1972 by the President and Fellows of Harvard College. Reprinted by permission of Harvard University Press.

"*Frankenstein* and the Tradition of Realism" by George Levine from *Novel* 7, no. 1 (Fall 1973), copyright © 1973 by Novel Corporation. Reprinted by permission.

" 'Godlike Science/Unhallowed Arts': Language, Nature, and Monstrosity" by Peter Brooks from *The Endurance of Frankenstein*, edited by George Levine and U. C. Knoepflmacher, copyright © 1979 by the Regents of the University of California. Reprinted by permission of the University of California Press.

"Horror's Twin: Mary Shelley's Monstrous Eve" by Sandra M. Gilbert and Susan Gubar from *The Madwoman in the Attic* by Sandra M. Gilbert and Susan Gubar, copyright © 1979 by Yale University Press. Reprinted by permission.

"*Frankenstein*: Creation as Catastrophe" by Paul Sherwin from *PMLA* 96, 5 (October 1981), copyright © 1981 by the Modern Language Association of America. Reprinted by permission of the Modern Language Association of America.

"*Mathilda* and *Frankenstein*" by Jay Macpherson from *The Spirit of Solitude* by Jay Macpherson, copyright © 1982 by Yale University Press. Reprinted by permission.

"A Mirror of the Future: Vision and Apocalypse in Mary Shelley's *The Last Man*" by Giovanna Franci, copyright © 1984 by Giovanna Franci. Reprinted by permission.

Index

J
James, Henry, 174
Jane Eyre, 30
Jekyll-and-Hyde theme, 19, 20
Johnson, Samuel, 33, 42, 163
Joseph, M. K., 66, 89
Jude the Obscure, 97
Jung, Carl, 147

K
Kafka, Franz, 182
Keats, John, 116
Kermode, Frank, 186
Kierkegaard, Søren, 8, 151, 154, 159
Klein, Melanie, 143
"Kubla Khan," 172

L
Lacan, Jacques, 103, 106, 107, 147, 149
Lampman, Archibald, 180
language, 101–09, 113–14
Lara, 65
Last Man, The, 66, 136, 181–91
Lautrémont, 47
Lawrence, D. H., 71, 187, 188
Levine, George, 81–99, 147
Lewis, Matthew Gregory, 32, 34–36, 41, 47, 67, 80, 83, 182
love, 72
"Loves Alchymie," 134, 135
Lowell, Robert, 49
Lycidas, 117
Lyrical Ballads, 84

M
Macaulay, Thomas B., 67
MacPherson, Jay, 169–80
Manfred, 4, 116, 121
Maria, or the Wrongs of Woman, 135
Mathilda, 169–74
Maturin, Charles, 32, 33, 180
Melmoth the Wanderer, 32, 82, 91, 176, 177, 180
Melville, Herman, 45, 46, 47, 49, 56
Metropolis, 176
Milton, John, 2–3, 7, 8, 47, 51, 53, 65, 82, 107, 115, 118, 119, 120, 122, 123, 125, 129, 130, 131, 133, 134, 136, 149, 152, 167, 172, 178
Moby Dick, 43, 44–46, 47, 49
Moers, Ellen, 116, 121, 124

Monk, The, 34–36, 40, 41, 42, 65, 80, 83, 176
Mont Blanc, 4–5, 50, 111, 164
Mostellaria, 31
"Murders in the Rue Morgue," 176
Mysteries of Udolpho, The, 11, 33, 65
mythology, 2, 6, 32, 175

N
narcissism, 40, 129, 152, 172–73
nature, 101, 102, 109–12, 187–88
Nelson, Lowry, Jr., 31–48, 86
Nietzsche, F. W., 191
Nitchie, Elizabeth, 68
Northanger Abbey, 30, 33, 129
Nouvelle Héloïse, La, 65

O
"Ode: Intimations," 172
Oedipal conflict, 106, 139–40, 141, 149
Ovid, 172

P
Paradise Lost, 2, 3, 6, 7, 17, 29, 39, 58, 59, 60, 79, 91, 103, 105, 115, 117, 118, 119, 122, 123, 125, 126, 129, 131, 134, 135, 152, 178, 179
Paradise Regained, 117
Peacock, T. L., 72
penis-envy, 126
Peste, La, 190
Persephone, 172
Phantom of the Opera, 176
Platonism, 72
Plautus, 31
Pliny the Younger, 31
Plutarch's *Lives*, 29, 39, 103, 105, 129
Poe, Edgar Allan, 15, 16, 77
Polidori, 65
Political Justice, 50, 78
Pope, Alexander, 57, 58
pornography, 83
potentiality, 67
Pottle, Frederick A., 5
pride, 69
Prometheus, 2–3, 5, 17, 44, 49, 66, 122, 175
Prometheus Unbound, 4, 5, 17, 49, 61, 62, 63, 66, 116, 164, 167
"Prophet, The," 36
psychoanalysis, 139–51

Modern Critical Views

Continued from front of book

Gabriel García Márquez
Andrew Marvell
Carson McCullers
Herman Melville
George Meredith
James Merrill
John Stuart Mill
Arthur Miller
Henry Miller
John Milton
Yukio Mishima
Molière
Michel de Montaigne
Eugenio Montale
Marianne Moore
Alberto Moravia
Toni Morrison
Alice Munro
Iris Murdoch
Robert Musil
Vladimir Nabokov
V. S. Naipaul
R. K. Narayan
Pablo Neruda
John Henry, Cardinal
  Newman
Friedrich Nietzsche
Frank Norris
Joyce Carol Oates
Sean O'Casey
Flannery O'Connor
Christopher Okigbo
Charles Olson
Eugene O'Neill
José Ortega y Gasset
Joe Orton
George Orwell
Ovid
Wilfred Owen
Amos Oz
Cynthia Ozick
Grace Paley
Blaise Pascal
Walter Pater
Octavio Paz
Walker Percy
Petrarch
Pindar
Harold Pinter
Luigi Pirandello
Sylvia Plath
Plato

Plautus
Edgar Allan Poe
Poets of Sensibility & the
  Sublime
Poets of the Nineties
Alexander Pope
Katherine Anne Porter
Ezra Pound
Anthony Powell
Pre-Raphaelite Poets
Marcel Proust
Manuel Puig
Alexander Pushkin
Thomas Pynchon
Francisco de Quevedo
François Rabelais
Jean Racine
Ishmael Reed
Adrienne Rich
Samuel Richardson
Mordecai Richler
Rainer Maria Rilke
Arthur Rimbaud
Edwin Arlington Robinson
Theodore Roethke
Philip Roth
Jean-Jacques Rousseau
John Ruskin
J. D. Salinger
Jean-Paul Sartre
Gershom Scholem
Sir Walter Scott
William Shakespeare
  (3 vols.)
  Histories & Poems
  Comedies & Romances
  Tragedies
George Bernard Shaw
Mary Wollstonecraft
  Shelley
Percy Bysshe Shelley
Sam Shepard
Richard Brinsley Sheridan
Sir Philip Sidney
Isaac Bashevis Singer
Tobias Smollett
Alexander Solzhenitsyn
Sophocles
Wole Soyinka
Edmund Spenser
Gertrude Stein
John Steinbeck

Stendhal
Laurence Sterne
Wallace Stevens
Robert Louis Stevenson
Tom Stoppard
August Strindberg
Jonathan Swift
John Millington Synge
Alfred, Lord Tennyson
William Makepeace
  Thackeray
Dylan Thomas
Henry David Thoreau
James Thurber and S. J.
  Perelman
J. R. R. Tolkien
Leo Tolstoy
Jean Toomer
Lionel Trilling
Anthony Trollope
Ivan Turgenev
Mark Twain
Miguel de Unamuno
John Updike
Paul Valéry
Cesar Vallejo
Lope de Vega
Gore Vidal
Virgil
Voltaire
Kurt Vonnegut
Derek Walcott
Alice Walker
Robert Penn Warren
Evelyn Waugh
H. G. Wells
Eudora Welty
Nathanael West
Edith Wharton
Patrick White
Walt Whitman
Oscar Wilde
Tennessee Williams
William Carlos Williams
Thomas Wolfe
Virginia Woolf
William Wordsworth
Jay Wright
Richard Wright
William Butler Yeats
A. B. Yehoshua
Emile Zola